KINDERGARTEN PANIC

Kindergarten Panic

PARENTAL ANXIETY
AND SCHOOL CHOICE INEQUALITY

BAILEY A. BROWN

PRINCETON UNIVERSITY PRESS
PRINCETON & OXFORD

Published by Princeton University Press
41 William Street, Princeton, New Jersey 08540
99 Banbury Road, Oxford OX2 6JX

press.princeton.edu

GPSR Authorized Representative: Easy Access System Europe - Mustamäe tee 50, 10621 Tallinn, Estonia, gpsr.requests@easproject.com

All Rights Reserved

ISBN 978-0-691-26978-8
ISBN (pbk.) 978-0-691-26979-5
ISBN (e-book) 978-0-691-26980-1

British Library Cataloging-in-Publication Data is available

Editorial: Rachael Levay, Erik Beranek and, Tara Dugan
Production Editorial: Jenny Wolkowicki
Cover design: Karl Spurzem
Production: Lauren Reese
Publicity: William Pagdatoon
Copyeditor: Joseph Dahm

Cover image: underworld / Shutterstock

This book has been composed in Arno Pro

10 9 8 7 6 5 4 3 2 1

For my children, who remind me every day
why we must continue the fight for educational equity.

CONTENTS

ILLUSTRATIONS

Figures

Tables

ACKNOWLEDGMENTS

MY JOURNEY in writing this book has been shaped by the collective contributions of the generations before me and those who raised me. This project would not have been possible without my parents and grandparents, who took so much care to craft my own educational journey in and outside of school. To my extended family, I thank you for your constant love and support.

So many life changes also happen through a multiyear commitment such as this. To my spouse Emile, thank you for listening to presentations about this book, discussing my ideas for the book, and always encouraging me. To my children Luno and Nova, thank you for showing me just how important this research is for the future of all children. Becoming a mother during this journey has deepened my sense of purpose and intention in writing this book.

I am also tremendously grateful to my extended community of scholars who have supported my work in graduate school and beyond. I thank my advisors, mentors, and dissertation committee members: Thomas DiPrete, Alondra Nelson, Van Tran, Jeffrey Henig, Linn Posey-Maddox, Jennifer Jennings, and Joanne Golann. Thank you for reading my work, always providing helpful feedback, and inspiring my research journey.

My deepest gratitude also extends to my fellow writers and accountability partners through this process. This book would not have been possible without our organized commitment to write together and read each other's work. Thank you, Kathleen Griesbach, Dialika Sall, Brittany Fox-Williams, Kelley Fong, Anthony Urena, Nicol Valdez, and Anna Hidalgo; I am so grateful for the opportunity to write with you all in a supportive and uplifting space.

I am indebted to an even larger community of scholars through my many sociology graduate student friends from Columbia University's Sociology Department who listened to presentations and encouraged my work. My gratitude also extends to the late Devon Tyrone Wade, whose intellectual drive and commitment to social equity has been a source of inspiration as I crafted this book. Thank you also to all the workers, students, and mentors who played even a small role in my life as an undergraduate and graduate student, I thank you. I cannot emphasize enough how important the work of others has been to my growth and development as a scholar.

I am also indebted to the many organizations that have fostered community and professional development and supported the development of my research. Thank you to the National Center for Faculty Development and Diversity for introducing me to wonderful accountability partners who motivated me throughout the writing process. Thank you to Dara Delgado, Mari Christmas, and Brittany Taylor for discussing, planning, and writing with me. I also extend my gratitude to the Ronald E. McNair Postbaccalaureate Achievement Program, the Leadership Alliance, the Ford Foundation Fellowship program, MDRC, and the Princeton Presidential Postdoctoral Fellowship program. The relationships and research development facilitated through these organizations have been instrumental in bringing this book to life.

I also extend my gratitude to my editor Rachael Levay and my anonymous reviewers, whose keen insights and constructive feedback improved the clarity and impact of the book. Your collective contributions strengthened the book, and I appreciate your time, effort, and dedication.

Most importantly, I want to extend a special thank-you to all the participants who made this study possible. To all the parents who took time to speak with me and share your words with me, I truly appreciate you. My goal in writing this book has been to share your perspectives and experiences. It is my hope that your stories shine through to all the readers of this work.

KINDERGARTEN PANIC

The new labor of school decision-making in an era of school choice

ETCHED VIVIDLY in my memory is a day when I was four years old. I sat in a dimly lit room playing with blocks of different shapes and answered a stranger's questions. As we sat together at a long rectangular table, the stranger showed almost no emotion. He nodded after I answered questions and jotted down notes in a medium-sized notebook. At the time, I had only a vague idea what the test was for or why the questions I was answering were important. When I left, I didn't know how to explain the test to my parents. I learned years later that I had taken New York City's Gifted & Talented (G&T) test with a testing administrator. My parents raised me in Brooklyn, New York, in the mid-1990s. When my mom learned about the city's coveted G&T program, she signed me up to be tested as quickly as she could. My parents waited anxiously for my results, wondering what would happen if my score was not above the 90th percentile.

Several months later, my parents received notice that I could attend one of the G&T schools in my borough. From there, I was tracked into a G&T class at PS3, a public school just outside the boundaries of my neighborhood. I stayed in my G&T class for only a few years before my parents decided a move to the suburbs was in my best interest. They worried about how tracked classes would shape my experiences in the school. They also wondered what would happen in fifth grade, when I would attend a middle school, and in eighth grade, when I would need to find a high school. If the pressure was so overwhelming in kindergarten, wouldn't it be even tougher later? The heightened urgency around competing for admission to schools in New York was different from their experiences walking to the neighborhood school some decades earlier, and they hoped for a simpler school enrollment process outside the city.

My parents' reflections on navigating New York City's school system over the years piqued my interest in how parents are faring more recently, as school

TABLE 1. Kindergarten choice rates New York Citywide (2007–8 to 2016–17)

Kindergarten students in all NYC public schools with valid zone assignment	School year				Percentage change over 10 years
	2007–8		2016–17		
Total	**64,304**		**75,634**		**18%**
Enrolled in their zoned school	46,075	72%	45,130	60%	−2%
Opted out of their zoned school	17,458	27%	27,116	36%	55%
Living in a "choice district"	771	1%	3,388	4%	339%
Exercised school choice	**18,229**	**28%**	**30,504**	**40%**	**67%**

Source: Data retrieved from Mader, Hemphill, and Abbas, "Paradox of Choice."

choices beyond G&T programs have proliferated in urban areas across the country, particularly in New York City.[1] Across the nation, nearly 20 percent of families send their children to a school other than their regularly assigned public school, and enrollment in traditionally assigned public schools has decreased.[2] Parents may consider district transfers, magnet schools, and charter schools as alternatives to their assigned public school. Since the early 1990s, the sheer number and availability of school options in New York City have increased dramatically.[3]

The number of kindergarteners in New York City attending their zoned schools is a shrinking, narrow majority, as shown in table 1 and figure 1. Instead, many kindergarteners are traveling outside of their catchment zones to charter schools, schools with G&T classes and dual language programs, and traditional public schools.[4] As figures 2 and 3 demonstrate, this is especially true for Black kindergartners in New York City. In alignment with a national policy agenda centered on school choice, options in New York City have expanded rapidly. This growth has been fueled by the New York authorization of charter schools in 1998, the development of magnet programming in school districts across the city, and the elimination of school attendance zones for schools in District 1 on the Lower East Side, District 7 in the South Bronx, and District 23 in Brownsville, Brooklyn.[5]

By vastly expanding the range of school choices, school districts also create new tasks for parents. Now that the sheer number of options has increased, making a school decision has become complex, requiring an investment of time, energy, and—for many parents—worry and anxiety. Parents now engage in time-consuming work to sift through more and more school options. They face a historically unparalleled demand to *make school choices*. The choices parents make during their children's elementary school years can significantly influence the educational paths their children follow in middle school, high school, and

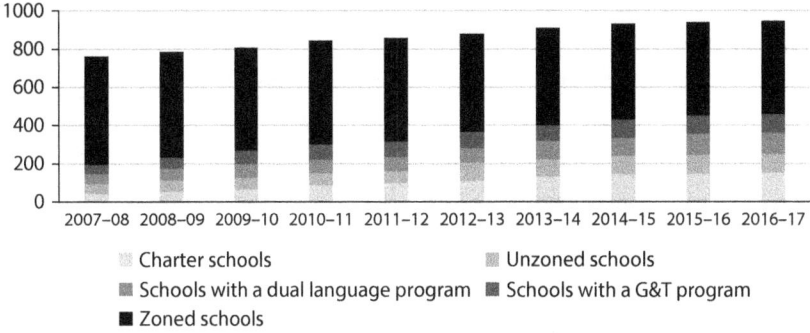

FIGURE 1. Number of elementary schools by admissions method, 2007–16.
Source: Adapted from Mader, Hemphill, and Abbas, "Paradox of Choice."

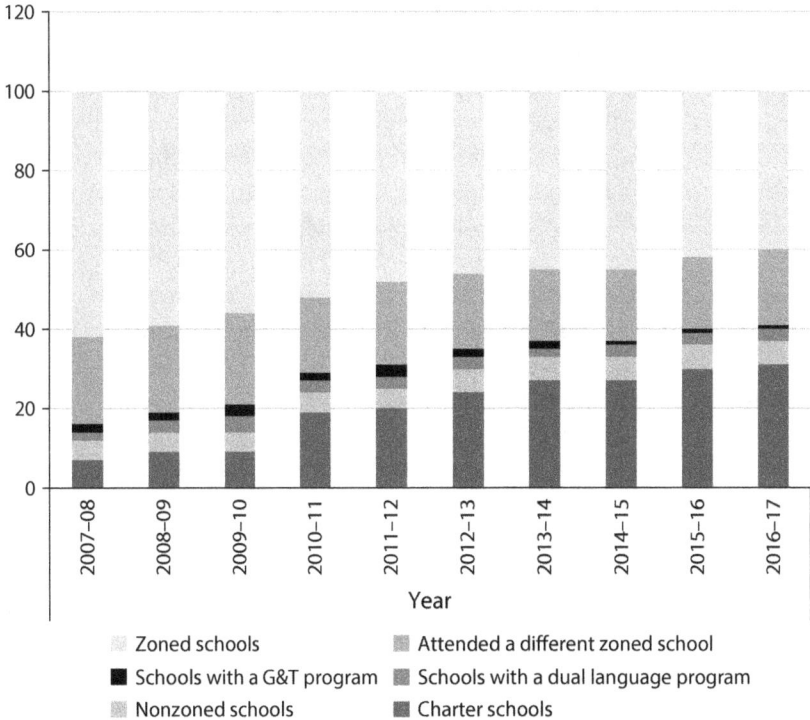

FIGURE 2. Black kindergarten enrollment by admission method.
Source: Adapted from Mader, Hemphill, and Abbas, "Paradox of Choice."

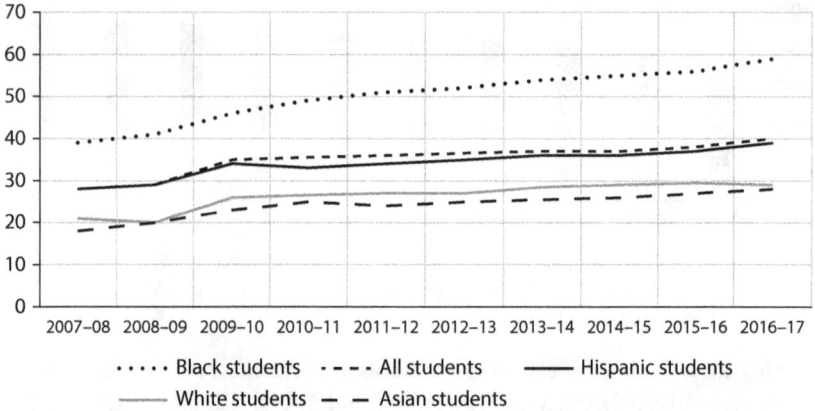

FIGURE 3. Rates of kindergarten school choice by race/ethnicity, 2007–16.
Source: Adapted from Mader, Hemphill, and Abbas, "Paradox of Choice."

college. In this book, I illustrate how decision-making is a significant area of inequality. The concept of school decision-making labor illustrates how inequality manifests in the routine school decisions families face in their daily lives. Persistent inequalities create broad variation in how families develop and manage their labor strategies. These vast differences in turn reproduce inequities within New York City's high-stakes school choice environment.

When the Department of Education (DOE) in New York City hosts enrollment informational sessions, the rooms overflow with parents. Websites, blogs, and books provide "how-to" guides for the enrollment process. During one fall, District 3, which encompasses Harlem and parts of the Upper West Side in Manhattan, held an informational elementary admissions event. It was a dreary October evening, but I managed to arrive at the meeting early. Twenty minutes before the start of the meeting, the seats were all filled. Mothers and fathers lined the walls and stood behind the last row of auditorium seats, anxiously waiting to hear more about admissions to pre-K, kindergarten, and G&T programs across the city. A slideshow illustrated that the process for getting into kindergarten would be a complicated one. Parents learned that applying to each of these programs would require separate application procedures and that they would have to keep track of a host of different dates. I watched as parents fumbled through their papers, took pictures of slides, and anxiously jotted down notes. A feeling of dread permeated the large auditorium as parents quickly realized the application process would be more complicated than they had anticipated.

The proliferation of school options in New York City has meant that school selection and enrollment for kindergarten is a multistep process beginning months and years before the start of the school year. Parents are expected to attend informational sessions just like the one held for District 3, rank twelve schools in order of preference, and tour the schools they are considering for enrollment. As elementary school options increase, parents must make sense of a highly complex school choice system and manage the uncertainties of school decision-making. During our interview, Louise, a white, middle-class independent filmmaker referred to the rush to find schools as "kinder panic." Louise explained that finding a school required an intensive investment of time and energy. She and other mothers she had come to know through various babysitting groups and park associations felt this idea of kinder panic depicted the great uncertainty they experienced and the fear they had as they navigated the application process.

A Tug of Wills

Nearly all the parents I interviewed expressed similar anxiety about the school enrollment process. The multitude of options can be overwhelming. In this book, I demonstrate how parents take on additional labor as they search for schools, form preferences for schools, and monitor their child's experience in schools. The literature on school choice has extensively documented the rising expectations placed on parents to find the best educational options for their children. This shift reflects a more consumer-oriented approach to education, in which parents are seen as consumers who must navigate a marketplace of educational options.

I conceptualize parents' increased expectations to make school decisions as a new form of labor parents must manage. Labor, in this context, refers to the time, effort, and resources parents invest in the process of choosing a school. Previous scholarship has identified forms of labor parents take on to raise children. For instance, mothers manage intensive care work responsibilities,[6] working-class families work to evaluate neighborhood safety amid impoverished conditions,[7] and families of color take on additional labor to evaluate racial inclusion in schools.[8] While the school choice literature has identified the increasing expectations parents take on to search for schools, scholars have not conceptualized new school decision-making as a form of labor. I argue that parents' labor requirements to search for schools are unevenly distributed. As I demonstrate, how parents engage in labor is shaped by gender and socioeconomic background and parents' neighborhood contexts.

Over time, school choice systems have created more educational opportunities for families; however, parents are expected to engage in increased labor to make school decisions. By conceptualizing school decision-making as labor, I make visible the often-unseen work that goes into making educational decisions for children. Recognizing the school search process as a labor process deepens our theoretical understanding of the challenges families experience, the inequities within school choice systems, and the need for better school support systems to help all families navigate school choice. Viewing school choice decision-making as labor also identifies vast disparities in parents' labor across socioeconomic background and gender. I argue that disparities in parents' decision-making labor reproduce inequalities within New York City's school choice system. To illustrate this clearly, consider the experiences of two mothers: Catherine, a middle-class Latina mother who lives on the Upper West Side, and Kelly, a working-class Black mother who lives in the Bronx.

Catherine was somewhat familiar with schools in New York City; she grew up in Queens during the 1970s and spent time working for the DOE. Catherine explained that she lived in a zone that was on the "edge." District 3 has a mix of well-performing schools and schools struggling to meet academic goals. Catherine, who is clearly aware of the options, explained, "I don't like that my apartment sits on the northern boundary of our zone. There are schools that are really great and then there are schools that are very terrible in the neighborhood. So, you know it depends, it's very hit or miss and sadly as you move south, they get better and as you move north, they get worse. So, it's just the reality."

Catherine started her school search when her daughter was in prekindergarten by reviewing school websites, visiting schools, and examining the curricula. She explained, "I invested a lot of time and money, taking off work, visiting schools, touring and speaking to administrators and teachers and figuring out my ideal setting." Catherine's research was extensive. She began the search for schools well before the start of the school year and completed her applications by the deadline. Catherine sifted through these options to determine which twelve pre-K schools to include on her list.

While her research was extensive, Catherine believed that the entire process was a waste of time. With lingering agitation, she explained, "Out of the twelve choices we got none of them. We're in District 3 and we were assigned to a school in District 5. A horrible school in District 5. When we visited, I wanted to cry."

Catherine went back to all the pre-K schools that had not accepted her daughter but soon learned that her daughter's chances were slim: "I was so far down, that dozens of children would have to leave the city in masses at each school for my daughter to even make it off of the waiting list." Catherine was desperate, but school officials explained that there was little they could do. Catherine tried her nearby pre-K, but staff there explained that they could not give her daughter a spot. Unlike in kindergarten, when all students are guaranteed a seat in their zoned neighborhood school, pre-K children do not have this guarantee.[9]

Catherine persisted. She walked into every school she applied for in her district. She was in disbelief: none of the schools had an opening, and she had no idea what to do. She recounted, "I was told by the people at all these schools: don't even bother, try somewhere else, we can't do anything for you."

At that point, Catherine took her chances calling and writing to the DOE directly:

> I blew a fit. I wrote to the chancellor, and I called the office, and I just went crazy and complained and complained and complained. And I guess to get rid of me, they assigned me a person to call me back and work on my case. So, he was able to get me on waiting lists for different schools that I wasn't on waiting lists for. These were places where I probably had a better chance of getting called.

Catherine noted that the back and forth between the DOE and the school they asked to wait-list her daughter continued through the summer. According to Catherine the ordeal turned into a "tug of wills," and she, her husband, and daughter left for vacation with little idea of where their daughter would be attending pre-K that fall. "We spent the entire time in Europe freaking out that our child wouldn't have a spot. When we came back, I had all these phone calls on my voicemail saying 'your daughter has a spot at our school. Come tomorrow to claim it.' But I was in Europe for two months, so I lost all those spots."

Just days before the start of the school year and with some additional "finagling and begging," Catherine was able to get her daughter a spot at a pre-K that she noted is "not perfect, but okay for the year." Based on her experience for pre-K, Catherine was not looking forward to the kindergarten process. In New York City, after applying for pre-K, parents must apply again for kindergarten. Catherine described with dismay her recent experience with the application system:

> The kindergarten applications opened up, and the whole nightmare begins again. The first day I opened up my application, I filled out my twelve schools, I clicked continue, and it erased all my schools and kicked me out of the website. So, I tried it again, and it did again. So, I just gave up. I'm waiting until later tonight maybe tomorrow. I'm figuring a lot of people were on it and that's what happened but I'm going to wait and try it again, but I don't have a good feeling about it and going into kindergarten it's more serious because you're trying to get a school where she can stay.

At the close of our interview that December afternoon, Catherine's feelings of worry and desperation persisted. She was unsure of what the next school year would hold for her daughter. Would she be admitted into any of the twelve schools on her list? Would her daughter be put on a waiting list for all of the schools? Would she have to scramble once again to find a school?

Kelly's experience searching for schools in the Bronx was just as complicated and chaotic. I met with Kelly, who also grew up in New York City, in a local library just down the street from her daughter's school. I learned that, unlike Catherine, Kelly had a previous experience with the school enrollment process a decade earlier, when her now twenty-year-old daughter was a fourth grader. When Kelly's older daughter was in elementary school, a teacher recommended a local charter school. That teacher had noticed that Kelly's daughter scored lower in reading and had some trouble recognizing words. The teacher said, "I think she'll have a better way if she goes to a school named SUN." Kelly recalled that at the time she had not heard of the school, but following the teacher's recommendation, she took her daughter out of the local zoned school in fourth grade and enrolled her in SUN. Reflecting on her older daughter's progress since then, Kelly explained with pride, "That was the best thing I could do for her. She's twenty now and in college."

About ten years later, when her younger daughter was ready to attend elementary school, Kelly hoped that daughter would also be able to attend the SUN school. Her older daughter enjoyed the SUN school so much that Kelly felt it would also be a great fit for her younger daughter. Realizing that charter school admission is by lottery, Kelly also applied to several other charter schools in Manhattan.

Charter schools have their own procedures for admission, with preference given to families who live in the district, siblings, and English language learners. Kelly believed that because her older daughter attended the SUN school, her younger daughter would receive sibling preference. "When my youngest one was on the lottery, I just assumed that because my older daughter went to SUN that the little one would go right in because they were siblings. But they said it was only for one of the schools."

After finding out her daughter would not receive an admission preference, Kelly had no idea what to expect. She knew that in the past several years charter schools had become popular, and more families apply than the schools can accommodate. Shaking her head with dismay, as if reliving the experience, Kelly explained that she lost hope and the whole ordeal became "really depressing."

Kelly, like Catherine, persistently reached out to the SUN school about an open spot. "Every day, and I mean every day, I was calling asking what number is she? What number is she? I did that every day till they knew who I was." Kelly called the other charter schools as well, only to find that her daughter was even farther down the waiting list elsewhere.

Even though Kelly called all of the schools repeatedly, by the start of the school year none of the charter schools had any open spots. Left without any other options, Kelly enrolled her daughter in the local zoned school. Shaking her head sadly, Kelly explained how she felt like she had failed: "I did not want her to go there because that's where my daughter used to go, and it's now a failing school. I was depressed about the whole situation." Kelly was so disappointed in the outcome that she thought about sending her daughter to one of the Catholic schools in the area. Although private school was virtually unaffordable for Kelly, she knew the zoned school had lower rankings and did not know what else she could do.

She recalled how her daughter's first few days at the school were tough. Each afternoon her daughter would tell her how she was the only Black student in the class and the class was entirely Hispanic.[10] Kelly worried about how her daughter would fare in a class without any other Black students.

Fortunately, the SUN school called a few days later to see if Kelly was still interested in the school. Her face beamed thinking back to the moment she received the phone call. "I was at work when they called to ask if I was still interested. Before they could even finish, I said 'Yes! Yes!' I was in tears." The moment was so special for Kelly that she captured it in a picture she showed me that day. She explained how she put the photo on her Facebook page. She was so excited that a spot had opened for her daughter.

Kelly later learned that a spot had opened only because a family moved out of the city. She was grateful but noted that the process was not easy. Kelly recognized that only a stroke of luck allowed her daughter to attend the charter school. She keeps this in mind during her grueling early morning travel routine. She and her daughter wake up at five forty-five in the morning and later take naps on the train to make it to her school by seven twenty-five. The commute is tough on them both, but "as long as it's a good school, where I know she's getting her education, I'll do it. I hate the travel, but I'll do it because I want the best."

Her daughter has been at SUN since pre-K, and Kelly plans for her to stay at the school: "She's not going anywhere. I won't even move because I want her in that school." Kelly loves that SUN charter school is hands-on, that school officials know all the students by name, and that they frequently call to check up on the families.

Even as Kelly spoke with joy about her daughter's experience at the school, she remained aware of the rarity of such opportunities and how stressful the school search can be. Her daughter shared with her that students in the traditional public school—in the same building as SUN charter school—express resentment at the better services and resources the charter school students receive. Kelly explained with exasperation, "It's really not right to me. It shouldn't be a lottery." Kelly was happy that the SUN school worked out for her daughter, but her own daunting and turbulent experience pointed to a glaring and hard-to-forget reality: all school choices are not equal, and a parent's persistence, effort, and investment do not guarantee admission.

School Decision-Making Labor

Throughout this book, I examine the experiences of parents, like Catherine and Kelly, who are trying to make sense of the New York City elementary school choice process for their young children. Parents are variously frenzied as they sift through hundreds of school options across the city, bewildered by complex school quality measures, unsure of how to rank twelve schools in order of preference, or filled with unbearable anxiety as they wait months to hear back from schools. The process of making school decisions is fraught with uncertainty—an uncertainty that has increased with the proliferation of school choice options. During the past few decades families with young children have faced an ever-changing school choice landscape that is both liberating and debilitating. Choice-based educational policies have increased the school options available at the elementary level—significantly amplifying the uncertainty and complexity of school decision-making. I use the term "decision-making labor" to conceptualize how parents work to make school decisions and form school preferences. This book illustrates the different ways parents take on additional labor through the school search and how the system reproduces the very inequalities school choice policies were meant to reduce.

Researchers writing about school choice have examined how parents form preferences for schools;[11] others have considered the range of social and institutional advantages and disadvantages parents face.[12] Their findings suggest that how parents make school decisions is shaped by their relative social positions and access to resources. As demonstrated by Kelly and Catherine's stories, engaging in the school search process has also become time-consuming, painstaking work. Parents spend more time than ever before navigating school options outside of their neighborhoods and discerning which school would be a good fit for each child. Parents increasingly perceive of school decision-making as an uncertain and risky endeavor, yet parents' tactics for minimizing the potential risks and unpredictability of school decision-making are shaped by their relative social positions. As parents make school decisions, they are evaluating a variety of costs and benefits associated with different schools and hoping to minimize enrollment uncertainty.

These uncertainties are also amplified because of the neoliberal assertion that people operate as rational actors and the belief that public education should be distributed in markets.[13] My argument offers new pathways for understanding how advantage and disadvantage operate as parents make school decisions. I examine how parents cope with the uncertainty of school enrollment. To navigate this uncertainty, parents engage in decision-making labor. I argue that school choice inequality is driven by parents' unequal decision-making labor as they search for schools.

Similar to the managing of uncertainty that families take on in times of economic precarity or in times of danger and global calamity,[14] parents perceive of school decision-making as an uncertain and risky endeavor. Psychologist Barry Schwartz notes that increasing the number of choices can be powerfully liberating and equally debilitating.[15] Having a multitude of school options can have negative consequences for parents who thereby face increased expectations to select "excellent" schools.

As sociologist Marianne Cooper has shown, in an era of great insecurity families engage in "security projects"—various strategies to get by during economically risky times.[16] I focus here on how security projects can be understood through the lens of urban school choice policy. Due to legislation stemming from the No Child Left Behind Act (NCLB) of 2001, an increasing number of charter schools and out-of-zone options offer families more autonomy in selecting schools.[17] Parents gain more flexibility but also shoulder greater responsibility to make school decisions. Just as Cooper notes, the risks that Americans must individually manage have steadily increased. In the case of school choice, government responsibility has retracted while parents have taken on the high stakes of school decision-making.[18]

The expansion of school choice options limits the government's authority in assigning children to schools and shifts school decision-making authority to parents.[19] While families have always had to engage in work to raise their children, the task of deciding on a school is challenging and increasingly unpredictable. School choice policies focus on individual decision-making and require parents to engage in intense relational work to gather and evaluate information.[20] Parents must take on additional labor to handle their new decision-making expectations. When mothers like Catherine write letters to school administration to access schools, and when mothers like Kelly tirelessly call schools to see if enrollment slots have opened, they take on additional labor in hopes of minimizing the potential risks and uncertainty of school decision-making.

Vast economic and social differences also shape how parents engage in decision-making labor and experience the risk of school decision-making. All the parents I interviewed believed that the quality of the school would influence their child's ability to get ahead in life. Parents managed the uncertainties of school decision-making sensitive to what their school decision would mean for their child's future. Yet parents' feelings of uncertainty are framed by their relative social positions and access to resources. I argue that school choice produces additional labor that is racialized, classed, gendered, and more challenging depending on home residence. Throughout this book, I argue that if parents are increasingly charged with searching for schools, we must take seriously how school choice policies reproduce inequality. We must also invest in providing broad access to high-quality public schooling for all families.

Past scholarship has evaluated the effectiveness of school choice as a reform mechanism.[21] Often missing from this discussion is the standpoint of parents. How we study educational policies also matters for parents' experiences.[22] Parents' ability to feel more secure about their school decisions is constrained by their social position and access to resources. There are many potential school opportunities, and the possibilities seem open, available, and limitless. In reality, all options are not created equally, and parents worry about the risk of making a wrong decision. School choice should provide opportunity, but schools are nested in segregated neighborhoods and not all parents have equal access to all school choice choices or have equal opportunity to get into each available school.

How Did We Get Here?

Catherine's frenzied and chaotic search for schools, Kelly's tumultuous journey to enter a charter school, and even my own parents' anxiety about school enrollment are linked to broad increases in public school options in New York City in recent decades.[23] Three decades ago, complex school decision-making may have been a New York story, but increased school options have become common in urban and suburban areas across the United States—significantly amplifying the uncertainty and complexity of school decision-making for all families of young children.[24]

Federal and state legislation since the mid-1990s has ensured the growth of school choice and altered the accountability systems surrounding public education in New York City. The NCLB of 2001 and the Race to the Top Act (RTT) of 2011 fueled the growth of school choice options across the United States.[25] In addition to expanding school choice, legislation has also given families in New York City greater access to school performance data. NCLB required school performance data be made available to families.[26] Several years later, the RTT grants encouraged performance-based evaluations for teachers. Parents now have far greater access to school performance data, grade-specific academic standards information, and a host of new school options.

School choice legislation at the federal level significantly broadened options at the local level, particularly in New York City. Under former school chancellor Joseph Fernandez, the city expanded the availability of school choice options through a citywide school choice plan in 1992.[27] Over the next few years, school choice continued to expand, and in 1998 New York signed into law charter school legislation. School choice increased dramatically at the high school level throughout the 1990s and reformed dramatically following 2002, when Mayor Michael Bloomberg assumed control of New York City's public schools. These reform efforts, known as Children First, led to significant changes in the K–12 public school landscape.[28] In 2004, New York City introduced a universal high school system in which all incoming freshmen were required to rank up to twelve high schools for enrollment. Several years later, school choice expanded to the younger years, and in 2009 parents were first able to apply to any elementary school through a standardized admission process. During the 2013–14 academic year, New York City broadened enrollment and adopted a comprehensive on-line open enrollment system for elementary school.[29]

The introduction of open enrollment policies in New York City over the past thirty years has allowed students to attend public school within or outside of their district across K–12 levels. Open enrollment policies seek to expand the number of public school options by dissolving geographic attendance zone boundaries.[30] Following national trends, several New York City school districts have also introduced experimental magnet programs, most notably the Central Park East Elementary School in East Harlem's District 4.[31] At the elementary level, school choice continues through a variety of schools and programs including charter, magnet, dual language, and nonzoned schools.

Today, more and more elementary students in New York City have enrollment opportunities outside of their neighborhood public schools. Compared to the early 1990s, when there were fewer than forty elementary schools with Gifted & Talented programs in New York City, there are now more than ninety. In addition, there are nearly one hundred nonzoned schools, more than one hundred dual language schools, and over one hundred fifty charter schools serving elementary students.[32] Urban areas across the country have also experienced an unprecedented shift in demographics, so parents across socioeconomic backgrounds traverse cities to enroll their children in schools.[33] Given these changes, how are parents coping? How are parents handling the new expectations to choose schools in New York City, and what can we learn from them that can help us make sense of school choice across the United States?

The New York school choice process is unique due to the high levels of competition to enroll in the highest performing preschools early in a child's education and reliance on testing and applications for enrollment into top high schools. Across the United States the evolution of school choice reflects the greater complexity of enrollment. Federal legislation and the continued expansion of options now place the burdens of research, assessment, selection, and sacrifice on parents, whose anxiety levels are rising.

The Limits of Markets-Driven School Choice Theories

The expansion of school choice policy at the national and state levels has been fueled by dominant ideologies around school choice that posit that schools will function most efficiently as education marketplaces.[34] Under the free market ideology, the education marketplace is meant to provide effective levels of choice and competition.[35] A central motivation behind the market orientation is that increased school options will promote equity in education, providing greater access to high-quality schools for low-income families in underperforming school districts. Under this premise, parents should experience more opportunity to exercise choice and more families will have access to high-quality schools. Early market theorists also argued that detaching school assignment from a family's place of residence had the potential to decrease the consequences of residential segregation by reducing inequality across schools, drawing middle-class families to cities, and giving working-class parents greater access to higher-performing schools.[36]

In practice, school choice policies can also reinforce segregated school environments—as they did following desegregation in 1954. Even with the introduction of greater school choice options in urban and low-income areas, the most disadvantaged parents do not always reap the full benefits of school choice.[37] Patterns of school segregation persist,[38] and charter school studies reveal that higher educated parents are more likely to participate in choice programs.[39] Schools can also play an active role in shaping their student body through marketing, location, and recruitment methods. These strategies can effectively "skim" students by limiting access for those with disabilities, English language learners, or those who do not perform well on standardized tests.[40]

Consumer behavior theories undergird school choice policies, suggesting that, as rational consumers, parents will make logical school choice decisions and leave low-performing schools in favor of higher-performing schools. Instead, scholars of school choice explain that parental choice is constrained by access to information, social networks, and resources.[41] Substantial barriers, such as having time to gather information and geographic proximity to highly rated schools, further curtail the decisions disadvantaged parents can make. Parents with greater access to cultural and social capital and advice from informed networks benefit more from the multichoice system. The most disadvantaged families and students with the greatest needs are often disproportionately excluded. Existing inequalities constrain a family's capacity to choose between schools. As a result, the practice of increasing school choice has not empowered most families as market theories predicted; instead, disadvantaged families are now responsible for choices they often cannot fulfill. The economic model does not account for the gendered, classed, and racialized disadvantages parents experience when making school decisions.

Integrating a Labor Framework into School Choice Theory

While the market framework has dominated policy conversations about school choice for decades, recent research has made it clear that parents' actual experiences are inconsistent with theories of rational consumer behavior.

Rational choice theory presumes that parents will make decisions that accurately weigh the costs and benefits. However, the various costs and benefits that parents evaluate are shaped by their relative social positions and access to resources.[42] I argue that we need to think about school choice within a new framework centered on parents' decision-making labor as they take on the responsibility of searching for schools.

The decades-long shift in legislation and recent open enrollment policies place the onus on parents to navigate all available options. This legislative turn to expand school choice has happened in conjunction with states' retreat from responsibility for citizens. Through a labor framework, I illustrate how parents navigate their new decision-making responsibilities. I argue that educational inequality is increasingly driven by parents' uneven decision-making labor during the school choice process.

School Decision-Making Labor across Gender, Social Class, Race, and Neighborhood

Important structural factors shape how parents take on additional labor during the school search. Sociologist Shelley McDonough Kimelberg introduced the term "privilege of risk" to describe how advantaged families can accept and manage certain risks, aware that they have the financial resources and a network of support to shift their set of risks if necessary.[43] I describe how similar perceptions of risk shape how working-class and middle-class parents make school decisions. The concerns parents downplay and their worries inform their education preferences and strategies for gaining access to certain schools. Parents' labor strategies lead to disparate outcomes in decision-making, reproducing the very inequalities school choice policies were meant to reduce.

A school decision-making labor framework can help us make sense of the *within-family* dynamics of the choice process across class and racial and ethnic backgrounds. Between parents, school decision-making labor is shared unevenly. Gendered expectations for child-rearing require mothers to assess and manage the labor of the school search with great urgency relative to fathers. Parents' access to resources, experiences as children, and class identity shape how parents perceive of the uncertainty of school decision-making and the logics they use to make school decisions. School decision-making labor is also shaped by parents' racial and ethnic backgrounds. Persistent racism and discrimination require Black, Latina/o, and immigrant families to routinely monitor educational spaces that are known for inequitable practices. Parents from racialized groups navigate threats of marginalization as they search for schools and as they monitor their children's experiences in schools. Variations in school quality throughout New York City neighborhoods shape how families evaluate their options and decide how far they will travel to enroll their child in a school. When parents exit their home neighborhoods for schools elsewhere, community life becomes destabilized. Parents experience this as they lament the loss of community for their children who traverse the city throughout the day, sharing few connections with children in their neighborhoods.[44]

The labor framework helps us make sense of parents' experiences when choosing schools. The framework considers the work parents do on behalf of their children's education. As Lois André-Bechely notes, parents engage in *work* when choosing schools.[45] This "choice work" and the resulting labor strategies parents forge are shaped by the intersection of race, class, and gender. The additional labor parents take on during the school search is also entangled in existing inequalities in schools and further perpetuated through school choice policies. Examining school choice from the parent perspective makes clear that school districts must invest in providing high-quality school options for all families.

The Elementary School Choice Process in New York City

New York City has the largest school district in the United States.[46] The city has a long history of offering public school options and provides an ideal setting for making sense of how parents take on additional labor through the school search. While some especially middle-class parents considered private schools, the book is centered around families who were primarily considering public schools for enrollment and who ultimately enrolled their children in public schools. I center the book on public school because public school options have rapidly increased in recent decades and reflect the shifting school choice landscape for families. Nationally, families are more likely to enroll their children in public relative to private school.[47]

I also focus exclusively on the elementary school enrollment process in New York City. I center the project on parents of elementary-aged children because these families often limit the distance their young children travel to school.[48] Parents also make most of the decisions for elementary students, while high school students are more independent. At the high school level, school choices are less constrained by neighborhood in New York City.[49] More broadly, early school choices affect later enrollment patterns. By studying elementary school enrollment, I can better depict parental decision-making and the impact of new enrollment procedures.[50]

I began this study just a year after New York City significantly broadened elementary enrollment and expanded school choices for kindergarteners.[51] Although not all five-year-olds end up attending public school in New York City, as parents can homeschool their children or opt for private schools, the

rule means that all New York City children are entitled to an education beginning in kindergarten. If parents wish to send their child to kindergarten, school
officials must find a placement for the child. While each child is guaranteed a
spot, in many cases it does not have to be at the local zoned school.

New York City's public elementary schools are organized into thirty-two
individual districts and regulated by the DOE. These districts roughly include
about two dozen elementary schools and are governed by a Community Education Council (CEC) and a superintendent. Each elementary-aged child has
an assigned school that is based on the child's home address. These schools
are generally referred to as zoned schools.[52]

In 2014, New York City introduced a citywide application process for kindergarten, called Kindergarten Connect.[53] Under the comprehensive open
enrollment plan, there are additional public school options available for kindergarten and elementary school. Nearly 50 percent of elementary schools in
New York City are nonzoned, meaning they do not have a geographic zone for
enrollment and are open to all students.[54] Nonzoned schools generally admit
students based on a lottery. These schools are often highly desired because
they typically offer a specialized or enriched curriculum. For instance, nonzoned schools offer dual language programs, G&T accelerated curriculum,
and STEM or arts-related learning opportunities.

Parents can also enroll their elementary-aged children in a zoned school that
is not their assigned zoned school. These schools do have a zone for enrollment
but may have open seats for a given year. Parents, for instance, can select a zoned
school a few blocks away within their district or a zoned school several miles
away in a different district. Across New York City there are a broad array of
public schools technically available to families. At the same time, zoned schools
still exist, and schools are still situated in segregated neighborhoods. Generally,
children have the greatest chance of being accepted to schools within their
district. However, parents can list any school—within or outside the district—
on the application. If parents do not complete the online application, they can
apply to schools over the phone or in person at a Family Welcome Center.

In New York City, the application for public elementary school is open from
November to January for the next academic year. Parents rank, list, and apply
to up to twelve schools. Families hear back from schools in March. A child's
chances of being accepted vary based on the admissions policies of each
school. Each district in New York City provides an elementary school directory and a map search tool, which can help parents determine their child's
chances of being accepted at a school based on past enrollment data.

In March, if a child is not admitted to any of the twelve schools the parents
chose, the child is guaranteed a spot at the neighborhood school—usually the
school in closest proximity to the child's home address. Parents are also

notified if they are wait-listed at any of their twelve preferred schools. Parents can then decide to either preregister their children at the school that has offered an enrollment option or wait to hear back from their chosen schools that may have openings for wait-listed students.

New York City also offers G&T options for students who perform at a certain level on the G&T exam. Parents can elect to have their children tested for the G&T program between kindergarten and fourth grade. The advanced curriculum is offered in two ways: a few schools offer only G&T classes, and some zoned elementary schools provide G&T curriculum as a single class.[55]

Operating outside of the DOE are charter schools—publicly funded independent schools. Charter schools are nonzoned and generally admit students based on a lottery. The admissions process for charter schools is conducted on a rolling basis, but the timeline overlaps with the public school application period so parents can concurrently apply to charter schools that have application deadlines in the spring. Parents can apply to individual charter schools or use the Common Online Charter School Application. Charter schools send admission and waiting list information on a rolling basis after April. Parents' decision-making process is thus very complex and must accommodate long waiting periods, the uncertainty of waiting lists, and separate application procedures for G&T programs and charter schools.

School choice in New York City is further complicated because the rules and requirements for applications constantly change. Over the course of my time interviewing parents and observing meetings and admissions events, the DOE made several changes to the policies and procedures guiding the admission process. For instance, during the 2014–15 academic year, the DOE changed the requirements for applying to the dual language program and then reversed those same changes the following year. Over time other large changes occurred: the number of schools parents could apply to, the application deadline, and the notification dates all shifted. During the study, 3K and pre-K options expanded, providing parents with options for schooling for children at three years old.

An Unequal Landscape: Study Participants and Elementary School Choice in New York City

Relative to other metropolitan areas, New York City offers a moderate level of school choice. According to the Education Choice and Competition Index, of the 112 largest school districts across the nation, New York City ranks 65th in terms of availability of alternatives to traditional public schools.[56] Because New York City adopted a centralized enrollment system, most parents are immersed in the same sort of search processes at around the same time, even if they experience the enrollment period differently.

Over time the rates of kindergarten school choice have increased, as shown in figure 1. In 2007 only 28 percent of New York City kindergarteners attended a school other than the one they were geographically assigned. During the 2016–17 school year, this figure jumped to 40 percent. There is also substantial racial and ethnic variation in who attends school outside of their zone. As figures 2 and 3 show, nearly 60 percent of Black kindergarten students opt out of their zoned school or live in a choice district, relative to 30 percent of Hispanic students, 29 percent of white students, and 28 percent of Asian students. Although school options for kindergarteners in New York City have substantially increased since the early 2000s, these options vary in quality and exist within segregated neighborhoods. Low-income families are less likely to engage in school choice, and advantaged families are more likely to benefit from school choice plans.[57] During the 2016–17 school year in New York City, kindergarteners who were free-lunch-eligible and English language learners were 70 to 80 percent less likely than other students to opt out of their zoned school even when controlling for race, ethnicity, and other demographic characteristics.[58]

Access to options outside of the zoned school also vary across New York City neighborhood. In higher-income and predominately white and Asian neighborhoods (Upper East Side, Midtown, and Lower Manhattan; District 2), families enroll in zoned neighborhood schools. In contrast, families living in neighborhoods that have been historically Black and are gentrifying (Bedford-Stuyvesant, Crown Heights, and Central Harlem; Districts 5, 16, 17) rarely send their children to the zoned neighborhood school. Extensive variation in school quality across districts also drives parents' decisions to exit the neighborhood school.

School choice options in New York City also deepen between-school segregation. In fact, schools in New York City would experience less economic and racial/ethnic segregation if all students in public schools attended their zoned schools. Students across all racial and ethnic groups who opt out of the zoned school and attend a nonzoned school enter an environment with fewer proportions of Black and Hispanic students and fewer proportions of students eligible for free lunch.[59] White families in particular tend to select schools with higher numbers of white students.

With these disparities in school access in mind, I sampled parents to participate in the study with the intention of capturing New York City's diversity and illustrating different experiences with New York City's school search process. I interviewed 102 parents of elementary-aged children in New York City. The study mainly included mothers, with twelve fathers participating. This reflects prevailing norms about child-rearing and existing research that mothers are primary caregivers. To assess parents' social class and disadvantage, each

TABLE 2. Demographic characteristics ($N = 102$)

	Middle class ($n = 48$)	Working class ($n = 54$)
Household income		
≤50,000	6	54
≥50,000	42	0
Race/ethnicity		
Asian	11	1
Black	13	28
Latina/o	11	21
White	13	4
Partnership status		
Married	29	16
Separated or divorced	5	3
Single	11	33
Single with live-in partner	3	3
Education		
No high school degree	0	6
High school degree or GED	1	17
Trade school or some college	4	21
College degree or higher	43	10
Age of parent		
≤40 years old	20	30
≥40 years old	28	24
Gender of parent		
Female	44	46
Male	4	8
Type of school		
Not zoned by address	35	28
Zoned by address	13	26
School academic rating		
ELA rating (>City average—41%)	35	22
Math rating (>City average—38%)	34	20
Distance traveled to school[a]		
≤0.5 miles	12	19
≥0.5 miles	36	35
Age of child		
≤6	22	24
≥6	26	30

TABLE 2. (*continued*)

	Middle class ($n=48$)	Working class ($n=54$)
Number of children		
One child	16	16
Multiple children	32	38
Residential status		
Homeowner	20	0
Renter	28	27
Low-income housing	0	27
Time in neighborhood		
≥10 years	21	30
≤10 years	27	24
Neighborhood poverty[b]		
Low poverty (≤20%)	14	6
Above average poverty (21–30%)	33	38
High poverty (30–40%)	1	10
Residential borough		
Bronx	4	16
Brooklyn	9	4
Manhattan	28	33
Queens	6	1
Staten Island	1	0

a. Distance categories selected based on New York City transportation eligibility parameters (NYC Public Schools, "Transportation Eligibility").

b. Poverty levels retrieved from the American Community Survey and augmented by NYC Opportunity ("Poverty Measure").

interviewee responded to a demographic survey that captured their education, income, job type, access to government assistance, and experiences with economic challenges.

Across the sample, 12 participants were Asian, 41 were Black, 32 were Latina/o, and 17 were white. In terms of income, 41 percent earned above $50,000, and 52 percent had a college degree or higher. Parents were classified as middle-class if they or their partners had managerial jobs, college degrees, and household incomes over $50,000. Those earning less than $50,000, without managerial roles or college degrees, were classified as working class. For more information on the demographic characteristics of the parents I interviewed, see table 2 and the Methodological Appendix.

Interviews with a diverse sample of New York City public school parents revealed that while school choice policy is intended to broaden opportunity and promote equity, school choice in New York City deepens inequality by further segregating students by socioeconomic status, race, and student ability and limiting opportunities for students who remain in zoned schools. Parents' process for making school decisions and sorting school options to access higher-performing schools also perpetuates inequality.[60] Families who opted out of their zoned schools often enrolled in schools with higher test scores, leaving behind concentrations of low-performing and more disadvantaged students in zoned schools.

This deepened inequality is also a consequence of unequal engagement with school choice options. School choice policies place the onus on individual parents to find high-quality schools for their children. As a result, parents expend a significant amount of effort during the school search process, which takes an emotional toll. For families facing barriers, the search requires even greater time investment. I argue that unequal participation in school choice is a result of the additional labor required to search for schools in New York City. Educational inequality is fueled by parents' uneven decision-making labor through the school search process.

Plan of the Book

Each chapter in this book builds an argument for how parents manage the uncertainties of school decision-making by taking on additional labor through the school search. Chapter 1, "A Mother's Duty: Gendered Work and the School Search Process," illustrates how gendered expectations of caregiving influence how families manage school decision-making in the home. In this chapter, I discuss intensive mothering ideologies, which conceptualize the long-standing belief that mothers must invest time and energy in raising children. Throughout this chapter, I highlight mothers' and fathers' accounts of the school choice process. I identify important differences in the school search process for single fathers and married fathers and for low-income and middle-income mothers. I conclude that while social class differences shape mothers' experiences through the school search, mothers absorb more of the labor of school decision-making than do fathers, regardless of class. Comparing the experiences of mothers and fathers through the school search, I also find that regardless of partnership status or socioeconomic background, mothers take on the labor of researching school options and evaluating school preferences. This chapter identifies important household-level inequalities in how school decision-making labor is experienced.

Chapter 2, "'What I Want for My Kids': Classed Work and Parenting Search Logics," describes how parents take on additional labor through the school search by crafting class-based search logics. I profile the working-class parents who invest in the familiar, traditional neighborhood school. I also identify the working-class and immigrant parents who forge search logics in vastly different ways by searching for schools that counter the schools they attended as children. Last, I profile middle-class parents who resist standardization and encouraged individuality through nurturing-oriented search logics. All the parents, regardless of class, strongly believed that education was key to future success, yet they approached school decision-making differently because of variation in their perceived uncertainties about schools. Tracing parents' sociohistorical biographies, constructions of their childhoods, and educational philosophies, the chapter provides a framework for how parents engage in school decision-making. I argue that class inequality substantially shapes the decision-making logics parents use to search for schools, creating uneven labor through the school search process.

Chapter 3, "You Don't Really *Feel* the Diversity: Racialized Work and the Search for a Racially Inclusive School," examines the education work Black, Latina/o, and immigrant parents take on to identify safe and inclusive spaces for their children. Issues of race, ethnicity, and culture shape how these parents engage in school decision-making. This chapter identifies how racialized families across class backgrounds monitor the racial climate within schools to protect their children from marginalization. I discuss the various ways Black, Latina/o, and immigrant families navigate the school search to create security for their children. I find that the additional diversity work they take on requires them to manage marginalizing experiences from school staff and administrators and to monitor their children's experiences in schools following their enrollment decisions. This chapter also highlights parents' feelings of insecurity when they are unable to find racially inclusive spaces for their children or when the schools they believe will support their children do not. I argue that race-based discrimination in schools and continued residential segregation shape how marginalized parents are able to approach their school decisions and which schools feel accessible and safe for their children.

Chapter 4, "Dealing with the World Outside the Door: Community Work and Cultivating Neighborhood Engagement," considers the broader neighborhood context that shapes parents' school decisions and neighborhood engagement. Here, I evaluate how parents forge neighborhood interaction strategies as their neighborhoods undergo demographic shifts and as school choice expands traditional neighborhood boundaries. This chapter examines how school choice availability complicates how parents make school decisions and challenges parents' ability to build community ties for their children. Parents contend with the loss of community they experience when their children attend schools outside their home neighborhoods. I argue that parents' neighborhood interaction strategies vary according to their residential context and social class background. Some parents draw closer to neighbors to build community, and others distance themselves from neighborhood life to protect their children. This chapter helps us understand how parents make sense of their school decision-making in the context of their children's neighborhood experiences. Because schools are nested in segregated neighborhoods, not all parents have equal access to school choices or equal opportunity to enroll in each available school. The uneven labor required to find and access schools based on home neighborhood drives parents' uneven experiences interacting in their neighborhoods.

The final chapter synthesizes all the previous arguments to explore the future implications of school choice expansion. I revisit the broader labor framework for the study and describe parents' ongoing uncertainties for the years to come. This chapter also synthesizes the inequities across social class, gender, race and ethnicity, and place of residence in the context of school choice. I demonstrate that educational inequality is increasingly driven by uneven decision-making labor during the school search process. If parents are expected to engage in increased decision-making labor, we must take seriously the persistent constraints families experience and parents' needs for greater support. I argue that rather than broadening opportunity, school choice policy places the burden on parents to find ways to equalize school opportunities. My conclusion is twofold: I offer suggestions for how districts can invest in improving the choice experience for parents and propose alternatives to current models of school choice that would ensure greater equity.

1

A Mother's Duty

GENDERED WORK
AND THE SCHOOL SEARCH PROCESS

ON A BUSY AFTERNOON at a local public library in Harlem, I met with Ann, a Black working-class mother of three children ranging in age from five to twelve. As we sat together, Ann at first seemed unphased by the busyness of the library. She paused from time to time to speak with her children, who had accompanied her for the interview. Ann's calm demeanor shifted, however, when I asked her about her experiences deciding on schools for her children. Ann's anguish was palpable. She believed the level of competition for quality schools in New York City required her to research different schools for each of her three children. In the process, she had attended four orientations and spoken to teachers in a variety of schools across the city. Ann juggled this research between her work obligations and childcare responsibilities.

Ann grew up in the Bronx, but she lamented that the school environment had changed in recent years. The very school she had attended as a child had become a charter school. She believed her mother's generation had not experienced such urgency in finding the right schools for their children. Instead of simply sending her children to a neighborhood school, Ann felt pressure to spend countless hours researching and touring schools to ensure that each of her children had a customized experience. She sifted through school performance data and compared school rankings. Ann quickly learned that the schools in the catchment area of her home ranked poorly. It was with a sense of disappointment that she explained, "I've lived in my home for about ten years now. But the schools there are not an option for me. It just wasn't an option. I would not send my kids there." After months of scouting, her children ended up at two nonzoned elementary schools and a magnet middle school across Manhattan. Now Ann traverses several neighborhoods each day, riding the subway and bus, to bring each of her children to their respective schools.

Ann's feelings of increased anxiety mirrored the sentiments of other middle-class and working-class mothers I interviewed. Ann, like other mothers, expressed feelings of being overwhelmed when confronting new expectations to search and find schools for her young children.

William, a Black, married, working-class sanitation worker, is also a parent to an elementary school student. While Ann's story reflects her investment in the school search, William described how his wife took primary responsibility of school decision-making for his six-year-old daughter. When asked how he came to a school decision for his daughter, he explained, "I'm not sure. My wife was the one who was on the websites. She wanted to make sure that when she was at work, she didn't have to worry. She was the one who was looking." William continued,

> Mothers are very protective. Women think on the left side of the brain, and we think on the right. We look at things in different ways. When I look at this, what I see is not what she sees. So, she wanted to make sure that when she was at work, she didn't have to worry, and that's why it was difficult finding the right place. She wanted to be able to work and not be concerned about anything.

William connected his wife's primary leadership over the school search to her role as a mother. Although he assisted in the school search process and was also concerned about his daughter's experience at school, he explained that his wife managed tasks like anticipating what his daughter would need in school and identifying school options. He noted that the process worked similarly when he was growing up in the Caribbean: his mother selected the schools he attended in Grenada and decided when he and his brother would move from Grenada to the United States after she settled in Queens.

In his description of the school search process, William frequently mentioned his wife, often on topics not directly related to school search. For instance, when I asked William when he first began thinking about schools for his daughter, he began describing how he first met his wife and how part of what solidified their relationship was their agreement about how to raise their future children: "We wanted to raise our daughter to give her a strong educational foundation." William went on to explain the steps his wife took to find a school for their daughter, including asking for suggestions from an older woman in the neighborhood.

William was unable to share many of the specifics of the school search process. He could not recall the websites his wife used to search for schools or the names of the various schools they toured and considered for enrollment. Although William was unable to recount how he and his wife searched online, he shared his satisfaction with the school his daughter attends. He drops her off each morning and appreciates the safety and security of the school. He also attends parent-teacher conferences. William's secondary and "helper" role through the school search process extended to his connections with other parents. William noted his wife's involvement in school fundraising and her position on the parent board. While William had few connections to other parents at the school, he explained that his wife was very familiar with several other mothers: "All the mothers, they have each other's phone numbers so that they can text. They have a group text that they communicate on."

William shed light on the difference between his own and his wife's roles in school decision-making for their daughter. While William cared deeply about his daughter's experience in school, he relied on his wife to oversee the logistics of school decision-making. As William's words demonstrate, the meanings and expectations of parental involvement vary for mothers and fathers.[1] Compared to fathers, mothers engage in intensified labor to search for schools for their children amid an unpredictable, uncertain, and risky school context.

Intensive Mothering and the Unequal School Search Burden

Parents' new decision-making responsibilities under school choice systems are embedded within a broader context of gendered expectations for raising young children.[2] Across socioeconomic backgrounds, mothers face deeply embedded norms around parenting that adhere to the ideology of "intensive mothering."[3] Intensive mothering ideologies compel mothers to take total responsibility for household planning, decision-making, and child-rearing.[4] Intensive mothering also frames expectations for mothers' involvement in school decision-making, so much so that a "good" school assignment is implicitly a reflection of good mothering.[5] Educational policies that increase labor for families disproportionality fall on mothers. These gendered expectations mean the risks and uncertainties of school enrollment also fall on mothers.

Relative to fathers, mothers absorb the labor of school decision-making. I trace the ways mothers take on this labor as they anticipate their children's needs, prioritize tasks during the search, investigate available options, and evaluate the viability of potential schools. Comparing the experiences of mothers and fathers like Ann and William, I argue that regardless of partnership status or socioeconomic background, primarily mothers engage in extensive labor as they evaluate school options. I identify important household-level inequalities in how mothers and fathers experience school decision-making labor.

School decision-making labor is tied to mothers' conceptions of "good parenting" and is salient to their sense of identity. Across class and racial backgrounds, mothers adhere to the tenets of intensive mothering by engaging in time-consuming and self-sacrificing work to search for schools and evaluate school options. In the following sections, I first demonstrate how middle-class and working-class mothers take primary responsibility for the school search. Regardless of class background or marital status, all the mothers I interviewed described engaging in school decision-making labor on their own and sacrificing time to search for schools and complete enrollment expectations.[6] After identifying similarities across class background, I explore how working-class mothers engaged in additional labor to evaluate school and neighborhood safety and to ensure their children's schools felt secure. Despite these distinctions driven by neighborhood structural inequalities, mothers across class backgrounds engaged in similarly extensive school decision-making labor relative to fathers. As William's words suggest, fathers across social class backgrounds and marital status invest considerably less time and energy to identify sources of support and search for school information. Instead, partnered fathers shift labor expectations to their spouses and single primary caregiver fathers minimize the labor required to search for schools. The intensive mothering ideologies that encourage mothers to invest in time-consuming efforts to search for schools do not similarly shape how fathers approach school decision-making. The development of new school choice systems has forever altered the work of mothering.

Mothers' Self-Directed School Decision-Making Labor

Yolanda, a Black, middle-class single mother and a full-time nurse, explained that her five-year-old daughter's father was not in her life, so she researched schools on her own. In anticipation of her daughter's enrollment, Yolanda gathered a "whole notebook full" of school information: "I looked up all these schools early for my daughter. I've been thinking about it for a long time. It really got tough when she was getting out of preschool. And so, I looked at different kinds of schools. It was hard for me. I was very anxious. I was very scared and had all these expectations and all these fears. It can be overwhelming." Intensively searching for schools and developing a complex plan of action only intensified middle-class mothers' fears and anxiety about where their children would attend school. In addition to searching for online information, Yolanda visited open houses. In her opinion, she got the most honest assessments from talking to parents at her neighborhood playground. Yolanda was strategic about whom she spoke with and her methods of contacting different parents to get advice about schools:

TABLE 3. Sample characteristics across gender ($N = 102$)

	Mothers (90)		Fathers (12)	
	Middle class (44)	Working class (46)	Middle class (4)	Working class (8)
Race/ethnicity				
Asian	10	1	1	0
Black	10	22	3	6
Latina/o	11	19	0	2
White	13	4	0	0
Partnership Status				
Married	27	12	2	4
Separated or divorced	5	3	0	0
Single	9	29	2	4
Single with live-in partner	3	2	0	0
Education				
No high school degree	0	5	0	1
High school degree or GED	1	14	0	3
Trade school or some college	4	19	0	2
College degree or higher	39	8	4	2
Age of child				
6 and under	19	19	3	5
Over 6	25	27	1	3
Household income				
> $50,000	38	0	4	0
< $50,000	6	46	0	8
Employment status				
Employed	35	25	3	6
Unemployed	9	21	1	2
Neighborhood poverty level[a]				
>21% poverty	18	38	1	7
<20% poverty	26	8	3	1
Type of school				
Not zoned by address	33	25	2	3
Zoned by address	11	21	2	5

a. Poverty levels retrieved from the American Community Survey and augmented by NYC Opportunity ("Poverty Measure").

I went to open houses. I used the website that's actually made by parents that go to the schools and visit it. It was a really good resource for me because it had reviews from people who just went to visit these schools. . . . They talk about the pros and cons. . . . I did so much googling. And then I asked people on the street. I would see kids with a uniform on and I would ask them, "Hey how do you like that school?" And they would say they like it, or "the people are mean." And then sometimes if I would see a parent with their kid I would go over and say, "Hey, how do you like the school?" And they might say, "I don't really like it, I'm thinking of taking my kid out of there because of A, B, C, or D." People were happy to share their experience.

Yolanda recognized that looking for the perfect school might require leaving her neighborhood. She believed that sacrificing her time through extended travel would be a necessary step if the school was one of the only top options her daughter received: "I mean if she got into a great school in Brooklyn, any-where within the boroughs or even in Westchester, I would make it happen. If she had gotten into an absolutely amazing school then I would sacrifice whatever I needed to, if it was something I wanted for her. I didn't want to go far but I would if the school was that great." Yolanda's mention of Westchester, a suburb forty-five minutes outside of the city by rail, is notable. Ultimately, Yolanda enrolled her daughter in a nonzoned school a short, five-minute walk from her home. Even so, the school search process carried an emotional toll for Yolanda. Finding a school required an intensive investment.

Other married middle-class mothers also described extensively seeking out information to search for schools on their own. Janet, a white, married, middle-class mother and a web designer with an infant and a three-year-old, started a Google group to connect with other mothers when her child was a toddler. Many of the discussions inevitably focused on schools. While Janet recognized the benefit of having access to this information, hearing from other moms made her feel like she was always one step behind in the school search process. Janet believed that she had started her research for schools too late, and so she anxiously sacrificed her time and energy to look up information in the bit of spare time she had while caring for her new baby. With exasperation and a look of guilt, she explained, "I have these two kids under four. I'm like, wait, I was supposed to think about life before kindergarten? And suddenly I'm thinking about this like at the last minute? So, this has been a major research journey."

Though Janet's husband was also concerned about their school options, Janet took charge of the school search on her own. Janet's anxiety and the emotional toll of the school search were palpable as she described how she weighed the pros and cons of distance during her school search:

But then there's this other private school that I'm considering that I would need to drive my child to. I'm not hiring like a chauffeur [laughter], like I know other families do that. So, I would have to drive my kid every day to Long Island, and that would be like anywhere from thirty minutes to an hour. There and back, every day. But I love this program so much . . . my husband and I were thinking, if I was really serious about this program out on Long Island, renting a house out there and then renting our house out here. That would mean making a big sacrifice for school, because you're like, these are the most important formative years of their life.

As Janet's laughter suggests, she could hardly believe she was considering renting a home outside of the city or driving her child nearly two hours each day to school. Yet Janet's thought process for searching for schools is reflective of middle-class mothers' strategies for engaging in additional labor through the school search. Janet's connections to other middle-class mothers encouraged her to think about schools early while at the same time made her anxious about whether she was investing enough in the school search process for her child. While not all middle-class mothers suggested they would make such a move, they were similarly anxious about the scarcity of high-quality, available schools. Middle-class mothers described their single-handed efforts and a sacrificial investment of time and energy to search for schools.

Similarly, Sally, a married, middle-class Latina mother and a remote IT specialist, took the lead in trying to get her twin seven-year-old sons removed from a waiting list and considered for enrollment at her preferred school: "We had to list the schools in the application by order, but we still ended up on the wait list. So, I just became very persistent with the school. I kept going to the school and inquiring to see what number we were on the wait list. And so, I was just very persistent until my persistence paid off. So that's how we got in the door— me being very pushy and persistent." Both Sally and her husband were concerned about their sons' enrollment, but only Sally persistently reached out to the administration at their desired nonzoned school outside of their district. Sally's persistence reflects middle-class standards of "good mothering," which often emphasize strenuous investment of time and energy in their children's well-being.[7] Regardless of marital status or class background, mothers engaged in school decision-making labor with little help from their partners.

Working-class mothers like Camila similarly described their single-handed efforts to manage the school search process. Camila, a married Latina mother of a six-year-old, an eight-year-old, and a middle schooler and herself a part-time student, described her search for a school for all her children as a "self-made" process. Though Camila was married, she took primary charge over the school search process: "I'm more of an insider with my children's school. I like to communicate with them myself, and I do mostly all of the outreach." Camila's belief that she had to take total responsibility for the search for services and school options reflects the central tenant of the intensive mothering ideology.

New York City's habit of constantly updating the bureaucratic procedures of the school choice program has created additional burdens for these self-reliant working-class mothers. Camila found herself perpetually confused by changes to the process for each of her three children. She encountered very different procedures each time she needed to decide on a school:

> So, for me everything is different, like the oldest one is going to be thirteen, so when I started the process, everything was more of a physical contact. . . . Everything it was done by a paper trail. For my middle child the process changed because she's a child with disability, so it was more drastic and going to districts to apply for certain schools with special needs and doing paperwork for transportation. For my son who was in kindergarten everything is on the internet and I'm like a dinosaur. So, you have to apply for kindergarten through the DOE website. So, everything was chaotic. Everything was a little difficult process. And then now, I'm going to be applying for high school soon. So, it's like totally different. So, it's a different process. I'm learning. So, I'm in three different stages. I'm in kindergarten, second grade, and then in seventh grade. So, it's totally different.

With each of her children, Camila invested countless hours in figuring out how they learn and determining which schools would be good fits. On top of that, she had to learn the process of how to apply, but that information turned stale nearly as soon as she acquired it.

The emotional tool of taking on this additional labor independently affected working-class mothers' self-perception. Camila described the guilt she felt when she realized that her daughter's charter school was not a good fit:

> My oldest daughter attended from kindergarten to third grade, and she struggled. . . . The expectations were hard, and she was coming home regressing and crying a lot. So, sometimes as parents you make the mistake of trying to do things that are beneficial to us because it's the right thing and it's the coolest thing, and charter school is the hottest thing now. But you have to look within yourself and see that if it's not benefitting your child, who are we pleasing, ourselves or the kids? So, I came to the decision that pulling her out was probably the best thing.

Working-class mothers like Camila internalized the belief that the school decisions they made, particularly any "school choice errors," reflected negatively on their ability as mothers.

Whether partnered or unpartnered, working-class mothers believed "good mothering" depended on their ability to single-handedly navigate a complex school choice process. Often in isolation, these mothers engaged in additional labor to figure out application procedures, seek advice from other parents and teachers, and attend school tours; and they absorbed far more of the school decision-making burden than did fathers.

Denise, a Black, single, working-class mother who has a son in a charter school, described her struggle to research school information on her own: "It's a hard process choosing schools, it's a work in progress, you got to visit the schools you got to do a lot of research and ask a lot of questions. I did a lot of research on SUN on how they're learning. So, I really did my research on who's giving who money and what's the money going towards and everything else." Denise believed that her search for a school required ongoing research and a significant investment of time and energy.

Denise, who grew up on the Lower East Side in Manhattan, first began researching preschool options when her son was an infant. As her son approached the age for kindergarten, she toured the zoned school and felt that it wouldn't be a safe environment. She spoke with other parents in her neighborhood who didn't send their kids to the neighborhood school, and she reached out to the DOE. Denise researched and applied to several charter and out-of-zone options. She worried when she did not hear back from schools: "I was a little iffy about the charter school. But I was just like okay, I'll give it a chance because no schools had accepted him yet, and I didn't want to send him to his zoned school, so that was a big stressor. So, I said okay let's try and let's see what happens." Even after enrolling her son in the charter school, Denise continued to research school options because she feared the environment was too stressful for the kids. She explained her process for switching schools, her persistent research efforts, and her belief in her own self-reliance:

> I looked into other schools. Some of the charter schools seemed to be on shaky ground. I was reading their criteria and their credentials, and it's like hit or miss with them. I really did it on my own. I mean there's other people, but it was mostly figuring it out on my own. I kept asking myself, am I making the right choice? That was my whole thing, am I making a good decision? Will he flop or will he do well?

Denise's fears about how her son would fare and her determination to research and find school options on her own reflect the combined logics of personal responsibility and dominant mothering ideologies.

Jennifer, a working-class Latina married mother, described the sense of guilt she felt when the application process did not work out as she had intended:

I did try to apply and go through the process for the independent schools but then I realized the process was a lot harder than I thought. They require other types of paperwork, and I didn't get it in there in time. So, it was just like, I kind of just had to give up on it because it was just too much, too many requirements. So, I gave up on it. I really did want to try something different for him, a different, smaller setting. I thought maybe he might have needed that.

Married or not, the working-class mothers I spoke with expressed a belief that their own self-reliance was an indication of good mothering. Even though Jennifer was married, she searched for resources on her own. She began searching for school options for her older daughter when she turned three and settled on a community organization that provided umbrella services for adult education, mental health, and youth services and also offered early childhood education. As Jennifer described her child-centered and labor-intensive search for schools, she explained, "I was always like, engaged and stuff like that and trying to get involved as much as I could." Jennifer delved into all the resources the community organization provided. She attended guided school tours, kindergarten information sessions, and workshops and collected sheets of information on important deadlines all on her own.

With Jennifer's daughter comfortably settled in an out-of-neighborhood school, she began a similarly intensive process to find a school for her son:

Yeah, I applied to a couple of elementary schools, a couple charter schools, a lot of the same schools that I applied for with my daughter. I chose first my daughter's school but then I chose a few outside of the neighborhood and even some downtown. I don't mind just traveling as long as my son is going to get the services that he needs. You know, just to expand him so he can explore outside of the neighborhood.

Even though she knew her daughter's school was an option, she believed that she needed to put each of her children's needs front and center, even above her own. Jennifer noted that even the second time around, searching for schools was a challenge:

It's stressful because you have to be on top of it because of the deadlines and stuff. You have to get things in because the public and charter schools are different, they have different guidelines and stuff like that. And it's just about choosing schools, the right school, so you know different schools offer different things. You have to narrow it down to what's best, then you have to think, is this going to benefit my child? What are they going to learn? Is this a safe neighborhood? Or a clean neighborhood? There's a lot of things you have to factor in a lot, things you have to consider.

In addition to the stress associated with deciding on schools and considering various school characteristics, she also dealt with the daily challenges of having her children enrolled in separate schools. Because Jennifer is a part-time student and does not work full-time like her husband, she manages the work of traveling in opposite directions every day to send her children to these two schools.

Regardless of partnership status, working-class and middle-class mothers believed that achieving the standard of "good mothering" hinged on their ability to independently navigate New York City's intricate school choice process. Mothers single-handedly engaged in additional labor to anticipate their children's needs and investigate available options. This labor is closely tied to mothers' conceptions of "good parenting" and significantly influences their identity as mothers.

Mothers' Time-Sacrificing School Decision-Making Labor

In addition to the multiple ways working-class and middle-class mothers engaged in school decision-making labor on their own, mothers also described the sacrifices they made through their decision-making labor. Cindy, a Black, working-class single mother who works full-time as an office assistant, emphasized how hard and isolating it was to find a school: "There was this two-week period, where I was like "Do I have to sell a kidney or something to get him into the school?" So, when I had parent-teacher meetings, I would talk with the parents. You kind of feel alone until you have those meetings with other people." Cindy also followed the principle of maternal sacrifice to guide her search: "One person said, 'You have to find the school that fits your child, it's not what's convenient for you, just one that fits for your child.' So, I took that to heart."

Cindy was determined to find a kindergarten option that would work well for her son. After receiving letters about her zoned school in the mail, Cindy started to realize that her options might be more limited than she had hoped:

> I started crying because the DOE starts sending letters about your zone school. Well, I volunteered at my zone school and I didn't like it. The kids in my building go there. I thought, "This isn't going to work for my kid." It's like thirty kids in a class, and I don't like it. My neighbor's kids were struggling there, and I thought that if they're struggling, what's going to happen with my baby?

Cindy's volunteer efforts at the local school led her to a volunteer training at a smaller, highly rated school outside of her neighborhood.[8] After speaking with parents at the school and the leadership, Cindy ended up placing her five-year-old son there. Enrolling her son in the school outside her neighborhood required her to catch a subway and a bus from her home and added an extra forty-five minutes to her work commute. Many single, working-class mothers like Cindy made school decisions while also balancing work obligations and household responsibilities. In her exasperated statement suggesting she sell a kidney, Cindy revealed her frustration and the toll the search process took on mothers.

The uncertainties mothers experienced and the sacrifices mothers described were intensified for working-class mothers whose children were developmentally disabled. Olivia, a Latina single mother, noted the challenges of seeking out services and school options for her autistic son. Over her multiyear search, Olivia found that local neighborhood activities and school options were limited because of her son's disability. She learned that he would need early intervention services when he was only a few months old, but it took months to get access to the system.[9] The delays and difficulty finding appropriate care persisted as she searched for prekindergarten and kindergarten options for her son.[10] She wished resources were "more transparent for kids with special needs."

For Olivia, forty-five-minute transit rides became part of her basic childcare routine:

> It's hard to be a parent in New York because resources are not always available. Like, if you're applying for any single service for your child, you have to give up a day's work. You have to go to this office first to get this letter. And then you have to go to this office all the way in Brooklyn. And you have to go here, and it's a lot of running around back and forth. It's not really set up to help you.

As our conversation continued, Olivia explained how her son's zoned school did not have the resources or appropriate services that were required according to his intervention plan. Thus Olivia had to tour multiple schools to find a more suitable option. She frequently had to take time off work and adjust her schedule to search for school options.

The ideology of intensive mothering encouraged mothers across social class backgrounds to sacrifice their time and energy as they invested in the school search. Mothers like Shannon, a single Latina, working-class mother and florist who grew up on the Lower East Side, recounted how she woke up early the day school applications opened to put her daughter at the head of the line. She told me, "So, I was like, I was not playing. I wanted to get her in the school." Although all applications were accepted and reviewed up until the deadline, Shannon believed that accessing the applications as early as possible reflected her commitment to the school search.

Shannon told me that she first started thinking about schools when she found out she was pregnant: "When she was in my belly I was already thinking about the schools. Because I know the neighborhood schools. I definitely knew that I wanted her in the Globe School. I always wanted to go to the school, and my mom always wanted to put me in the Globe School. But it's by lottery. It's always been by lottery, and I never got chosen. I never got the chance to go." Shannon already knew about the Globe School, having hoped to attend from a young age. Now intending to place her own daughter there, she attended multiple school tours and took time to meet and interview with school staff, hoping these efforts might increase her daughter's chances of landing a spot at the school. Although Shannon knew that admission would be lottery-based, she did everything she could to increase her daughter's chances of admission.

Working-class mothers believed the school search required an investment of time and energy. Prior research has demonstrated that the ethic of sacrificial and individual responsibility prevalent in U.S. society and policy powerfully shapes expectations for how low-income mothers engage in care work.[11] The expectations embedded in the intensive mothering ideology similarly shape how middle-class mothers devote time and energy during the school search.[12] While middle-class mothers similarly sacrificed their time to search for schools, they benefited from an extensive network. Many of the middle-class mothers I interviewed invested time and energy to reach out to other parents, school staff, and leaders for information. Past research has shown that middle-class families use stores of social and cultural capital to engage with schools and provide opportunities for their children.[13]

Jaime, a white, middle-class mother and a part-time teacher who lives with her five-year-old son and her son's father, described how she engaged in a school search by seeking specialized information from other mothers:

> I learned from other mothers that you can really wheedle your way into a school by going to the principal and being like, "I really want to come to your school." Once you're on the waiting list, the principal has control of who comes in off the waiting list. You really can to some extent work your way in. And you hear through word of mouth which principals you can influence by calling them a lot.

Jaime found herself reaching out to complete strangers, and she eventually used this information to decide between two schools in her district: "When you're on the playground and your kid is three or four, that's the first or second question, where do you live? Where do you go to school? Where are you thinking about going to school? It's constant and it's stressful."

Jaime also invested in deepening her relationships with close neighbors who also had young children. She formed what she termed a "co-op," in which members relied on each other for babysitting support. A few years later, Jamie turned to those same relationships for information and advice about school options in and outside of the neighborhood. One mother from this friend group shared information about school seminars that helped the parents strategize about school. After learning about the intensive school search strategies her circle of friends engaged in, Jaime also invested time and energy in organizing and managing her school search process: "I actually made a huge, color-coded chart of all the schools. I went to school fairs and then ended up narrowing it down to six or seven schools that I toured."

Middle-class mothers also benefited from connections to principals and teachers—social ties that were often less accessible to working-class mothers. Vivian, a Latina mother and nonprofit director, described how she used her familiarity with school principals to make school decisions:

> So, working for Riverrun Community Services, I knew of the principals in every school, and I knew who's super passionate about this, who's not. So, having that little insider knowledge, it was nice to know these things about the principals in our local schools. And Riverrun Forums were, like, the biggest thing. And then, like, talking to people. Like, I remember talking to neighbors and them telling me about their experience and where they applied to. I try to grab advice from everywhere.

Vivian's connections extended to other mothers. She reached out to mothers in her neighborhood through a forum. She used the forum to see if there was consensus on schools in the area and to start forming a list of schools she should consider. Vivian noted that without access to these resources, her search for schools would have been a lot more challenging:

> [If] I didn't have the moms forum, the pre-K search would have been really tough. Because there's not much information. I've been to all the DOE events where they talk about schools, and the way that they present information to you is as if you're already an insider and you already know. So, if you don't know the language, you don't know what the hell they're talking about. So parents don't always know what their options are. . . . So, moms in the community are really good about identifying what programs are available to them, and sharing them within the moms group, but if that didn't exist, then where would we get our info?

Vivian's personal experience and her work for a local nonprofit provided her with access to several professional ties that aided her search for a school. Vivian's willingness to attend events and seek out information through resource groups exemplifies middle-class mothers' confidence in interacting with school staff during the school search process.[14] Social networks are a common resource for parents and inform their preferences for schools.[15] Parents learn about school reputations and generate preferences through their networks.[16]

Dawn, a Latina middle-class mother who works as a dental hygienist, described her struggle to find a school for her son:

It was a very difficult process. It's not easy with the school system. Very difficult. I hated the whole process. . . . I started going around the neighborhood and checking everything out myself and seeing. And going and doing tours and seeing what I wanted. I found like four schools that I liked. And there were like two and I narrowed it down to the Galaxy School. It was like this competition. It still is a competition to get into a school.

Dawn learned about school search resources like school tours and informational sessions. These resources helped reduce some of the challenges of the school search process. Like several of the other middle-class respondents in this study, Dawn also intensively reached out to other parents who had children attending a school she was interested in for her son:

Some of the people in his after school mentioned the school and it just kept coming up, coming up, coming up. It kept coming up every time I would do research. And I was like there comes that school again. So, when I already kind of narrowed down on a school. I would camp out at the school and ask parents. Sometimes I would prompt three questions or five questions. I would try to get them engaged.

From Dawn's perspective, selecting schools was competitive and hard work and required her to use stores of resources that could have been better spent elsewhere. "But come on," she told me, "we all know it shouldn't be this way. It's education. It's free. I still don't get it. I still don't get it." Having grown up in a lower-income neighborhood in Manhattan, Dawn attended underresourced schools as a child. Like her working-class counterparts, she invested time and energy in her search for schools to be sure that her son would be able to attend a higher-quality school than the one she attended.

Middle-class mothers sacrificed time during the school search by investing in relationships. They readily nurtured relationships with other mothers and school staff to access school information.[17] Working-class mothers also sacrificed time but emphasized their belief in the ethic of self-reliance. Regardless of class background, mothers believed that the school search was a burdensome responsibility that demanded sustained personal sacrifice. Mothers adhere to the principles of intensive mothering by engaging in time-consuming and self-sacrificing efforts to find and evaluate schools.

Mothers' Safety-Focused School Decision-Making Labor

Working-class mothers also worked on their own to identify safer school options for their children. Past research has shown that low-income mothers engage in protective care work to keep their children safe and cognitive labor to calculate needs given economic constraints.[18] Working-class mothers embrace and perform intensive mothering even as they face structural inequalities and the retrenchment of the U.S. social safety net.[19] Black mothers, in particular, calibrate their parenting strategies within the context of neighborhood crime and violence.[20] For working-class mothers, these protective strategies become part of the school search process.

Amiya, a Black, working-class single mother who works as a part-time housekeeper, described her calculated decision to remove her daughter from a local zoned school: "The first year was okay, but after a year, there was a lot of police activity, like drugs and shooting in the area. I thought my daughter was going to a good school, but I kept getting notices. So, I called the police station and took my daughter out of the school." After calling the police station for additional information, Amiya learned that a kindergartener had brought a knife to school on multiple occasions. Seeking a safer school environment, Amiya also repeatedly called the DOE in attempts to transfer her seven-year-old daughter to a nonzoned school. Receiving a transfer relieved some of Amiya's worries but created others. She worried that the disruption of transferring during the school year had interrupted her daughter's progress.[21]

Nevertheless, she was glad she had moved her daughter. The entire experience confirmed a decision Amiya had already made to leave the neighborhood: "For like two years I lived down by the school. The neighborhood was okay when I first moved there, but after a year there it wasn't. I'm glad I transferred my daughter out. I was glad she was picked to go there for her new school because I was in the process of trying to look for an apartment over there. They picked a school in one of the areas I was trying to move to anyway." Engaging in additional labor through the school search process required mothers to evaluate a range of schools. Parents' geographical preferences for schools and the sets of schools they are willing to consider for enrollment were framed by their perceptions of safety within and outside of the school doors.[22] Working-class mothers evaluated various school options to ensure their children would be safe. They also took on this search for schools with little assistance from other parents, school staff, or even their partners.

Other working-class mothers worried about the violence and criminal activity just outside the doors of the school. Shawna, a Black working-class administrative assistant, expressed her concerns about danger near her child's school after learning about a shooting during drop-off time. She began traveling several miles to school each day so that her kids could attend a school in a safer environment: "Both of my sons go to school in Manhattan. I drive them all the way from the Bronx to Manhattan. They go to schools in Manhattan because there was this one incident, my kids were going to the school near my neighborhood and one of the fathers who was dropping off his kid got shot."

Right after the shooting, Shawna pulled her sons out of the school. She felt that no one at the school cared. It seemed as if nothing had changed; if there had been improvements in safety, they had been invisible. Shawna felt determined to search for a different environment: "I just knew they weren't going to that school in my neighborhood. So, anything else was good because they weren't going there."

Finding a new school for her sons was a long fight. After months of searching online, Shawna eventually received a call from a school in Manhattan. She was relieved after finding out they could switch schools and happy that her children had a chance to see different models of success. Even so, the drive from the Bronx to Manhattan required her and her sons to wake up much earlier each morning.

Working-class mothers who were concerned about neighborhood crime and violence engaged in time-consuming labor to seek options outside of the neighborhood. Working-class families often face school options that are less safe and in more dangerous neighborhoods.[23] Yamili, a working-class Latina single mother and office assistant, worried about schools in her neighborhood because of drug activity along the streets just a few blocks from her apartment. Yamili moved into the apartment after living in a shelter with her daughter. After three months, they were placed in an affordable housing apartment building in the South Bronx. Yamili was grateful for the apartment but worried constantly that her daughter might be exposed to drug activity. She hoped, at minimum, to find a school in a different neighborhood. And because her job was located forty-five minutes from her home, she worried that she couldn't be there if anything happened at her daughter's zoned school:

> Well, I don't know much about the schools near me, I don't know enough to speak about them, like I don't want to judge. But the only reason she's not there is because I prefer for her to be closer to me to keep an eye on her. I think even if I was in a bad neighborhood as long as she was close to me, I could give her assistance if anything happened that would be the biggest factor.

For pre-K, Yamili applied only to schools near her job. She was able to enroll her daughter in a school just a short walk from her office building. Soon enough, she became worried about where to send her daughter to kindergarten. After gaining some advice from her boss, the mother of a middle schooler, Yamili applied for a school transfer that would allow her six-year-old daughter to attend a school outside her neighborhood.[24] She explained that seeking other schools required additional time-consuming labor: "I wouldn't say it's hidden but it's something that you have to really search for. For a lot of the things within the school system it's a matter of speaking out and finding an answer. So, there's not really a way of knowing what's going on."

After applying for the child exemption, Yamili sent her daughter to an out-of-neighborhood school in Harlem, about forty-five minutes by bus and two subway trains from her home. The commute was inconvenient, but sending her daughter to school in her neighborhood was "out of the question. It was not something that I wanted for her." Yamili expressed relief that the school her daughter now attended was in a safe neighborhood and close to her job, but the distance required her to wake up early and meant her daughter missed out on children's activities in the neighborhood:

> We wake up between five thirty and six in the morning and head out. Then after, she goes to an after-school program at the school, and I head out and pick her up from work. We come to McDonald's and do homework and then by the time I get home sometimes it's seven thirty or eight o clock and then it's time to get ready and go to sleep. So, I never know of any activities because by the time I get home, there's not much there.

Though Yamili liked her daughter being close to her job "in case of emergency," by the time Yamili and her daughter got home from school and work it was time for bed. Working-class mothers' concerns about neighborhood and school safety required them to travel long distances to and from schools in better neighborhoods.

Working-class mothers also worried about how the safety of environments within schools would shape their children's academic performance. Past research has found that racial background and a school's level of urbanicity shape a student's exposure to bullying.[25] Donna, a married, Black, working-class home attendant, described how a tolerance for bullying was affecting her son's education: "The whole two years he was [at the school], he was being bullied. I took him out because nobody did nothing. They didn't have counseling. They didn't have social workers. He didn't get no education and that's why he's one year behind." In response, Donna took extra steps to find a different school for her child. She walked the neighborhood and went directly to schools to see about openings. At her son's new school, teachers look out for the students. For Donna, access to mental health resources is one of the hallmarks of a "good school":

> Good schools should have counselors just in case the kid is being bullied or something is going on at home they have somebody to talk to besides the teacher. I'm talking about, like, a mental health counselor, not a guidance counselor, someone who can really help them. . . . Now these days kids get beat up and bullied and they don't tell people. So, like a mental health counselor, some kind of social worker, like within the mental health, because the bullying situation is crazy in the schools now.

Donna felt she could not count on the schools in her neighborhood to provide social and emotional support and appropriate discipline. Working-class mothers like Donna took extra steps to ensure that their children felt safe and supported in schools.

The neighborhood conditions in which working-class mothers were raising their children pushed them to actively seek schools in safer environments. This response was based on structural constraint: only eighteen of the forty-four middle-class mothers lived in neighborhoods with poverty rates above 20 percent, whereas nearly all the working-class mothers lived in higher poverty areas.[26] The single working-class mothers I interviewed had no choice but to shoulder this burden single-handedly, but most married working-class mothers also evaluated their school options on their own. Although married working-class mothers noted that their spouses were also concerned about safety, the mothers were still primarily responsible for identifying options. For working-class mothers, the convenience of local schools had to be balanced with the hope for safer environments in different neighborhoods. Guided by the intensive mothering ideology, working-class mothers searched for schools that would keep their children safe. For working-class mothers, questions of safety and security took priority.

Intensive mothering ideologies encouraged mothers across class background to invest time and energy in the search for school information. In some instances, mothers' labor strategies varied. For instance, working-class mothers believed that the search for schools required them to single-handedly find and evaluate options. Working-class mothers also prioritized safety and traveled great distances to secure safe and high-quality school options. Middle-class mothers similarly searched intensively for school information and relied heavily on their social networks. Despite these class-based differences, the ideology of intensive mothering encouraged all mothers to sacrifice their time and energy as they invested in the school search. The expectations embedded in the intensive mothering ideology motivated mothers to engage in additional labor as they identified and selected school options.

Across class backgrounds, middle-class and working-class mothers navigated the uncertainty of their school options by engaging in additional labor through the school search. Mothers' intensive labor strategies contributed to gender stereotypes about women's role in the home and their expected orientation to school matters. As common criteria for "good mothering" suggest, mothers are expected to put their children's needs first and commit to what is best for their children at all costs.[27] The demands embedded in maternal responsibility also shape expectations under new school choice systems, meaning that relative to fathers, mothers took on far more labor to search for schools. School choice policies that subtly encourage mothers' more intensified steps to mitigate uncertainties perpetuate gender inequality.

Although equity arguments in favor of school choice have sought to increase the number of high-quality school options available to low-income families in particular, school choice policies create more labor for all mothers to manage. The increased responsibility to search for a school and the increased perception of risk for selecting a low-performing school require mothers to sacrifice their time and energy. Even as middle-class and working-class mothers experience varying socioeconomic constraints, the demands embedded in maternal responsibility encourage mothers across class background to intensively search for school information.

Shifting and Minimizing Labor: Fathers' Gendered Work and the School Search

Compared to mothers, fathers across social class background engaged in less labor through the school search process. Partnered fathers shifted labor to their spouses, and single primary caregiver fathers minimized the amount of labor required to search for schools. Relative to men, women invest more time and energy to anticipate needs, identify options, and make decisions in the home.[28] Compared to mothers, partnered fathers and primary-caregiving fathers take on fewer domestic and child-rearing responsibilities.[29] Ideologies of masculinity deemphasize equal responsibility for child-rearing.[30] Gendered aspects of parental involvement also construct expectations for partnered fathers to be less involved in school matters and school decision-making.[31] In some cases, school contexts and responses from school staff also shape and may even work to undermine fathers' engagement in schools.[32] The fathers I interviewed expressed similar approaches to school decision-making and often did not see an investment in the school search process as representative of their role or identity as fathers.

Across class and racial and ethnic backgrounds, both partnered and single primary-caregiver fathers like William were overwhelmingly less burdened by school decision-making than mothers. Whereas mothers emphasized sacrifice, self-reliance, networking, and extensive resource seeking, fathers approached school decision-making less intensively. Partnered fathers shifted labor expectations to their wives.

Jean-Baptiste, a Black, middle-class married father and social worker for a local nonprofit organization, described how his wife identified the school his children now attend: "When I came to the neighborhood, we were walking and looking at signs. My wife is the one who found out. She said, 'Oh I found one, it looks clean. Everything looks very nice from the outside.' And she said that it might be very good for our children." Jean-Baptiste relied on his wife to research and identify schools for enrollment. He played only a minimal role in school decision-making. Though Jean-Baptiste had little information to share about the school search process, he did share his beliefs about education and his concerns about the environment surrounding the school. He worried that his children would be negatively influenced by crime in the neighborhood:

> For my children, they are very happy in their school because all of them are in the same school. They are doing very well. They always say, "Daddy we don't want to move from our school." They like it. But the environment is not really what I want for them as they grow up, I wish I could be somewhere else quieter. Maybe out of Harlem. But the advantage of living there is that we have a lot of resources. They have the opportunity to pursue their dreams, and they get a lot of good instruction at their school.

Jean-Baptiste believed that school decision-making was important for his children's growth and development and expressed concern about what the future would hold if they continued to attend school in the same area. Like several working-class mothers, Jean-Baptiste had concerns about neighborhood safety. Yet his beliefs about the importance of education and concern for his children's well-being did not translate into his actual behavior during the school search process. Jean-Baptiste relied on his wife to take on additional labor to search for schools. His wife took the lead in school decision-making activity. Jean-Baptiste explained that she handled the logistics of school applications and kept track of activities at their school. Sociologist Allison Daminger finds that the household work of anticipating needs, identifying options, deciding among options, and monitoring outcomes is highly gendered.[33] Mothers also hold greater responsibilities to find and select schools for enrollment.[34] As Jean-Baptiste dealt with the uncertain process for making school decisions, he relied on his wife to remember, plan, and manage the school search process.

Erwin, a Latino, married, working-class father and an administrative coordinator, explained how the decision between a few district schools for his five-year-old son primarily came down to his wife's opinion of the school:

> My wife fears for my son's safety every second of the day. So, if she's not confident or comfortable with it, she just doesn't go for it. So, when we toured that school, she was immediately comfortable and confident. So, at that point I took that as a yes and we moved for it. So, I would say it depends on the comfort level that my wife had in leaving him at that school.

Erwin attended school tours with his wife and helped her make a list of twelve schools to list on the application, but the decision ultimately rested on her comfort level with the school's perceived safety. After learning that his son had an Individualized Education Program (IEP) and would be eligible for classroom services, Erwin and his wife met with district leaders to determine the best school options. Erwin explained that he also wanted to ensure his son was safe and comfortable at the school and researched online profiles of schools to assist in their decision-making. After settling his son into the school, Erwin decided to run for Parent Teacher Association (PTA) treasurer. In this role, he planned fundraising events and felt more comfortable expressing concerns to school leadership. Erwin explained that his wife's concern about school safety influenced his involvement in parent activities at the school. Erwin's involvement in his son's school events and his involvement in the school selection process reflect what Carla Shows and Naomi Gerstel define as working-class fathers' "undoing" of gender. Erwin sought opportunities to be involved in public-facing events at his son's school and was also involved in aspects of the search for his son's school.[35]

While Erwin was involved in the school selection process and attended and hosted events at his son's school as PTA treasurer, the most important factor for deciding on a school was his wife's comfort level. Erwin engaged in labor through the school search by relying on his wife's perception of school safety to make an eventual school decision.

Noah, an Asian, married, middle-class father and financial consultant, described his wife's primary role in researching and applying to schools. At the end of the process, he encouraged his wife to consider a different nonzoned school for his now seven-year-old son: "In kindergarten, my son got into one of the citywide schools, but I guess I wasn't paying attention to the application as much. And my wife applied for several of the citywide schools, and she also included one in Queens. And they ended up selecting him for that one. And I said, 'There's no way we're sending him to school in Queens.' It just didn't make sense." Noah checked out of the school search process but then at later stages vetoed his wife's decision. Research finds that whereas mothers invest significant labor to make decisions in the household, fathers often wield more decision-making power.[36] Within his partnership with his wife, Noah held the power to alter school decisions even though he spent little time investigating options.

Noah's description of the process nevertheless emphasized how he and his wife worked together to make school decisions. Noah often used "we" to indicate his secondary role in the school search process:

> We were researching the dual language schools, and we actually met with the principal to talk about the program and we really liked the principal. . . . The friend [who told us about it] was . . . our son's friend in preschool. It was his mother that wanted to send her son to a dual language program. We were considering the same. She chose to send her kid to a different school

but mentioned that this is another school. And we explored it, and we liked the sound of that school, so we went to that.

As Noah explained what he described as their collective search for a school, he also explained how his views about school selection differed from those of his wife. While Noah's wife wanted to enroll their children in the highest-performing schools, Noah believed that most schools for elementary school were quite similar:

> We considered the different G&T programs in some of the charter schools, but my personal opinion is that at the lower ages, as long as you're in a decent school setting where there's a lot of support of parents, it's probably just as good as any G&T or charter school. . . . Even though we're going to have our daughter apply to the Science Exploratory School, it's a STEM school (and I'm not 100 percent sold she's a STEM-type person). It's a decision we're still struggling with.

Noah's description of the process differed from those of most of the other fathers I spoke to in that he emphasized how he and his wife approached the school search process differently. Noah appreciated that public school options were readily available, but he believed that taking a laid-back approach to the school search process would be sufficient for elementary school. Noah's ability to veto his wife's decision and his secondary role in the school search demonstrate the different labor expectations for mothers and fathers during the school search. Middle-class mothers engage in additional labor by intensively researching school information and networking with other parents, whereas middle-class partnered fathers engage in minimal labor by relying on their wives to manage the logistics of the school search.

Single fathers took primary responsibility over school matters for their children and minimized their school decision-making labor by focusing their attention on the basic requirements of the school search. They did not devote much more time or energy to the school search process than did married fathers. Relative to mothers, these fathers were less burdened by the school search process and saw school decision-making as a straightforward enrollment procedure. Robert, a Black, working-class single father who works as a custodian, explained how he reached out to a few neighbors for school information: "First, I found out about the school by word of mouth, people that I know locally, I see the parents coming home from school and I say, 'Where does your son go? Where does your daughter go?' And that was that. Everything was accessible." Robert described a relatively effortless decision-making process. Unlike single, working-class mothers who believed school decision-making required great sacrifice, Robert described a short and straightforward school search process for his six-year-old son. When I asked Robert if he sought advice or resources from anyone, he shared, "I did my own research. I thought about where I needed to live as far as work and what's going to be good for him." Robert's short and straightforward strategy for searching for schools was markedly less labor-intensive than the approach of working-class mothers who engaged in additional labor through the school search. While working-class mothers sacrificed and prioritized safety, fathers did not perceive the school search as uncertain and their resulting labor strategies were less intensive.

One of the unpartnered fathers I interviewed explained that he relied on the mother of his child to make school decisions. Alonso, a Black single father and painter, described how his ex-girlfriend took primary responsibility for the school search. Though he only lives a few blocks away from his ex-girlfriend and his son spends part of the week with him, he explained that "she was the one who made the decision. My son attends the school nearby her place." Alonso's son attended the school that was zoned according to his ex-girlfriend's address. Noting his ex-girlfriend's primary responsibility for the school search, he said, "The school? That's all her, that's her territory." Alonso explained that he felt the mother of his son was in charge of all school-related decisions, while his role was limited to picking up his son after school and attending parent-teacher conferences.

Other single fathers did not compare various school options or describe an intensive search for schools in his neighborhood. Jermaine, a Black, middle-class single father who works in education services, explained that he "just asked a couple of my neighbors that lived on my floor about the school." Whereas intensive standards of mothering encourage mothers to take multiple steps to protect their children from harm and monitor their children's experiences in schools, fathers devote less time, attention, and energy to these concerns. Gendered expectations around care and child-rearing responsibilities in turn shape the varying ways mothers and fathers engage in labor through the school search. The fathers in my study did not share the mothers' belief that the school search required additional labor through intensive sacrifice, self-reliance, networking, and resource gathering. Instead, fathers invested in the school search by supporting their wives and when unpartnered deemphasized the tasks required for the school search.

One single father stood out from the others I interviewed. Richard, a father of a five-year-old boy and a seven-year-old girl, was assaulted by his former partner and the mother of his children. He was forced to move to a new neighborhood and quickly enroll his children in the closest school, which he soon found disappointing. Richard spoke with dismay about his children's school: "The New York school system is a very trying system." As a member of the PTA and the school leadership team at his children's school, Richard witnessed vast differences in the resources available at his school and the school in a wealthier section of the neighborhood only a few blocks from his apartment.

Like many of the working-class single mothers in this study, Richard invested time and effort in his search for a more suitable school for his children. The school Richard ultimately found was fifteen blocks away and his daughter was not eligible for busing:

> My daughter has to go fifteen blocks to school. I have to pay, because she's not going to get any bussing because of the area. So basically, I have to get up every day, drop one child off, actually I have to drop her off first, and then backtrack and come back. So, it's actually costing me money to send her to school. I mean, I don't mind doing the hard work, but at the end of the day, realistically, it doesn't make any sense.

Richard sacrificed additional time and money to ensure his daughter had a more positive school experience. While Richard's school search process mirrored many of the same steps working-class mothers took, he was unique among the fathers in my study. Overall, mothers took primary responsibility for school decision-making and engaged in additional labor through sacrifice and self-reliance, prioritizing safety and intensively investing in school research and networks. Research finds that even when fathers are single and the child's primary caregiver, they often feel less responsible for domestic duties.[37] Investment in school decision-making is still seen as primarily women's work, and aspects of masculinity often shape how men approach child-rearing expectations.[38] Compared to mothers, both partnered and primary-caregiver fathers generally do not investigate and research schools as extensively and do not feel encouraged to self-sacrifice as they make school decisions. Unlike mothers, fathers do not connect their parenting identities to their ability to find and secure schools for their children.

Mothers perceive that the rise of school options increases the uncertainty of school admission and engage in additional labor to make school enrollment feel more secure. Fathers do not perceive that the school search requires an intensive investment of labor. Past research has demonstrated that fathers often know very little about the details of their children's lives relative to mothers.[39] Although over time fathers' participation in childcare and domestic responsibilities has increased and fathers often feel involved, they still rely on their wives as sources of information.[40] While some of the fathers in my study professed their involvement in the school search process, they were often unable to express specific details about their role in the process. Many of the partnered fathers were forthright about their minimal or secondary role in the school search process and the multiple ways they leaned on their wives to manage school decision-making. They acknowledged when their wives took primary responsibility for the school search and described their role primarily through the language of "helping." In contrast to single mothers who were self-reliant, intensively sacrificed, and searched for safe school environments, single fathers engaged in labor by focusing on the basic requirements of the school search. Their labor strategies were less intensive and did not reflect an investment of time and energy. It is clear, in other words, that the school search burden falls unequally on mothers. Mothers engage in additional labor through the school search by intensively engaging in resource-seeking activities, while fathers approach the school search less intensively, leaning on their wives or limiting their investment in the school search process. Fathers' limited engagement in the school search means that as the school search process becomes increasingly complex, the new tasks and expectations falling on families fall more heavily on mothers.

Conclusion

Across class and racial and ethnic backgrounds, whether partnered or unpartnered, mothers absorb far more of the school choice burden than do fathers. Mothers like Yolanda, Janet, and Jennifer described the emotional toll and sacrifice required to search for and enroll in schools for their children. Working-class mothers, like Shawna, described their efforts to secure a safe school in a neighborhood with low crime. Whether mothers were married or unpartnered, their stories shed light on the primary responsibility they took over the school search. Intensive mothering ideologies similarly encourage middle-class and working-class mothers to engage in additional labor through the school search. Partnered fathers rely heavily on their spouses to make school decisions, but even primary-caregiver fathers invest less effort than single mothers in the school decision-making process.

Mothers expend far more time and energy on school choice than do fathers. Because gendered expectations of caregiving fall on mothers, school choice policies in New York City mean mothers are expected to invest considerable effort in touring, researching, and rank-ordering school options. In hopes of making the uncertainty of the school search feel more secure and in an attempt to mitigate perceived risks of selecting an underperforming school, working-class and middle-class mothers intensively engage in labor through the school search. School choice policies give families more school options, but they require families to engage in increased labor. These policies also powerfully reinforce gender divisions in the household and social inequality more broadly.

2

"What I Want for My Kids"

CLASSED WORK AND PARENTING
SEARCH LOGICS

I INTERVIEWED MARGARET in a small conference room in her office building in downtown Manhattan. Margaret, a full-time development associate at
a national nonprofit, grew up in a deeply religious family and attended only
Catholic schools. Her parents were recent immigrants when she started school
in Yonkers, New York. Knowing fairly little about schools in their new city,
they decided on Catholic schools for Margaret and her siblings. Margaret
explained that her parents were not comfortable with public schools in the area.
Reflecting on her years in Catholic school, Margaret noted that the schools
she attended were academically strong, but she did not believe the school met
all of her social and emotional needs.

Years later, when searching for schools for her four-year-old son, Margaret
wanted a school that nurtured the "whole child." I asked Margaret what she
meant, and she described her desire for a school that was academically rigorous but also focused on the individual growth and development unique to
each student. From Margaret's perspective, "kids should be allowed to be kids
and learn the way kids learn intuitively." She yearned for a school that diverged
from her experiences growing up, a school that was not "all about homework
and testing and filling out worksheets and sitting at your desk and being still
and raising your hand."

Even before kindergarten, when she needed to find a daycare, Margaret
searched for a program that would allow her son to explore and learn at his
own pace. She found a local preschool modeled after the Reggio Emilia approach to early childhood education, which centers on inspiring the individual
spirit of each child and encouraging wonder and discovery.[1] Margaret explained that this approach felt like "music to her ears." The school's pedagogy
seemed to mirror "everything she believed in." Margaret longed for a school
that promoted "innovative ways of learning"—unlike the rigid structure she

experienced in Catholic school. She explained that finding schools that offered this progressive model for kindergarten was a daunting, stressful task: "I was kind of looking for any public schools that would maybe model on that curriculum or that pedagogy and really there's not that much out there in terms of that." Margaret and her husband attended several open houses, "tag-teaming" throughout the search to ensure they could see as many schools as possible. She and her husband fell in love with a progressive public school in Manhattan. According to Margaret, the school's approach was "very hands-on, centered on experiential play, with lots of field trips, and not so much emphasis on testing and the Common Core."[2] But Margaret noted that the progressive approach was one of the latest "buzzwords" in education. Many parents were just as interested in the school, and she worried that getting in would be a long shot.

When her son was eventually accepted into the school off of the waiting list, Margaret felt like the "stars aligned." Her son was selected from a pool of hundreds of families who had applied. She believed her son's school had allowed his individuality to flourish. From Margaret's perspective, the school was "into and devoted to kids learning in the way that's best for them in a nonstandardized way. My son can learn creatively in a way that works for him." Rather than her own stifling experience in Catholic school, Margaret perceived that her son gets to be himself in the classroom. Reflecting dismally on her own elementary experience, Margaret explained, "I just felt like I would've learned so much better in this way, with some hands-on experiential learning. I had my strengths, but I had more academic weaknesses. I was sitting at a desk having all this stuff regurgitated to me. Everything was done one way, and every kid was expected to get on board." Margaret noted that compared to traditional public schools where parents she knows send their children, her son's school feels markedly less punitive. He does not spend hours completing homework at night and has the independence to devote his time and energy to projects during the school day. She reiterated with joy at the close of our interview, "The stars really did align in the best way imaginable."

Parent Identity and School Decision-Making Labor

Margaret's experience searching for schools mirrored many of the parents I interviewed. Many worried about their child's future educational path from the moment the child was born. Parents spent countless hours navigating options, trying to figure out which school would be a good fit for their child, always keeping in mind that the chances of getting in would be slim. The parents I interviewed had many opportunities to select schools, but they noted that the school decision-making process also added a layer of uncertainty.[3] Parents explained that they had intense anxiety about school choice. They worried, for instance, that their child might not get selected for the school they wanted or that a school they selected might not offer the environment they anticipated. Parents also worried about their child's future and how they could possibly ensure a future path of success.

Margaret reflected on her past school experiences and found certainty in the school search by aligning her school decision with her parenting philosophy. I found that as parents like Margaret discussed the opportunities and risks of school decision-making, they worked to develop choice logics that were tied to their parenting identities. These parenting identities revealed class distinctions. For instance, to navigate a school choice system that seemed uncertain, complex, and overly standardized, Margaret, like many other middle-class parents I interviewed, focused on schools that offered an innovative approach to learning, deemphasized testing, and focused on individual development. She zeroed in on a school approach that diverged from her own experiences and felt like an improvement from the strict and inflexible Catholic school she attended as a child. This class-based decision-making logic often meant that middle-class parents selected higher-performing and more selective schools for their children relative to working-class parents.

The neoliberal turn toward the individual managing school choice means parents have to make sense of the new availability of schools on their own.[4] Parents' social class backgrounds and sense of identity shape the feelings and worries they experience through the school search.[5] Prior research has found that parents' past school experiences and information from parents' social networks play central roles in how parents narrow the types of schools they consider for their children.[6]

I argue that parents rely on class-based decision-making logics to make the complex and uncertain school search feel more secure. Across class and race, as parents described their school preferences and located their decision-making process, they cultivated decision-making logics they hoped would minimize their uncertainties.

I identify three types of decision-making logics across class and immigrant background. Of the working-class, nonimmigrant parents I interviewed, many described their *community-oriented logics*. In a rapidly changing school choice environment with many options, they focused on the traditional public schools that were grounded in their communities. To minimize the uncertainties of the less familiar charter schools and nonzoned schools, they modeled their school decisions after the decisions their parents made for them. Working-class families who expressed a community-oriented logic were more likely to send their children to zoned schools and schools that were low-performing based on state assessments. Other working-class parents and middle-class parents who immigrated to the United States as adults described their *counter-oriented logics*. These working-class and immigrant parents hoped that selecting schools outside of the neighborhood would minimize the risks of downward mobility. They pursued schools they perceived offered opportunities for advancement—schools with higher performance ratings and more favorable reviews. For these working-class parents, their decision-making logics were guided by their adverse experiences in schools as children. Many of the first-generation middle-class immigrant parents I interviewed expressed a similar decision-making logic and recounted how prospects in their native countries were bleak and that they were offered few opportunities to excel academically. Like the working-class parents who described counter-oriented logics, they also searched for highly accelerated programming that would provide their children with a competitive advantage. So, for their children, these parents sought schools outside the local neighborhood in hopes of better avenues for future success. Unlike the parents who described community-oriented logics, these parents were more likely to send their children outside of the neighborhood for schools that were more advanced and well-performing according to state ELA and math assessments.

Last, middle-class parents, like Margaret, forged *nurturing-oriented logics* they hoped would enhance their child's self-confidence. These parents were concerned about maintaining their children's social and emotional well-being and individuality. Such parents looked for schools that nurtured their children's sense of self and resisted standardization. They wanted the school to provide boundless opportunities for self-expression and broad expectations for achievement and development. Like the parents who forged counter-oriented decision-making logics, these parents also ended up enrolling their students in innovative and high-performing schools.

Parents developed decision-making logics to make sense of a confusing and complex system, but the class-based nature of these logics reproduced the very schooling inequalities school choice systems were meant to reduce.[7] When working-class families invest in the familiarity of the neighborhood school, their children attend schools that often underperform the academically competitive and innovative schools middle-class parents seek. Only some working-class families—those with extremely adverse experiences in public schools themselves—held decision-making logics that mirrored the middle class. I also found that middle-class immigrant and nonimmigrant parents were able to secure selective and higher-performing schools for their children. In fact, only 40 percent of working-class parents I interviewed enrolled their child in a school that performed above the city average on math and English language arts, compared to the over 70 percent of middle-class parents who did.[8] The decision-making logics parents develop and the resulting unpredictability they hope to minimize unintentionally contribute to broad inequities in school choice programs. Middle-class parents' focus on the individual needs of their children and working-class parents' focus on ensuring generationally consistent school experiences mean children across social class background end up in schools that differ substantially in quality.

Community-Oriented School Decision-Making Logics

Risha, a Black, working-class longtime East Harlem resident and mother of three believed that neighborhood schools were part of the fabric of the community. I met Risha in her cozy apartment in a large, low-income housing building in East Harlem. Her partner Larry also commented and interjected throughout our interview together. A longtime resident, Risha spoke fondly of her neighborhood memories. When she was a young girl, kids played in the apartment hallways and monthly fish fries with neighbors were regular events. She grew up in one of the low-income housing buildings just around the corner from where she lives now. As we spoke, she gestured frequently to the window just off of the kitchen demonstrating how close she was to her first home.

Although the conditions of her New York public housing apartment have caused her health problems for years, Risha has few options aside from her assigned unit. Frequent complaints to building managers and letters to the city have done nothing to change her circumstances. She hopes to move but also explained that this building was where she feels most comfortable—she grew up and has lived for years in the neighborhood.

Risha attended the local public school just down the block from her childhood apartment; the school continues to be an important neighborhood staple. When it was time for Risha's children to enroll, she reflected with relief that the school was still standing: "I can't believe the same school is there that I went to. It's really nice."

Risha has sent all her kids to the same elementary school she attended, just a few short blocks from her home. Her decision was grounded in what was generationally familiar and was tied to decisions her mom had made for her several decades earlier. For Risha, following the steps her mom had taken a generation earlier felt the most secure. Research finds that sociospatial ties and place attachments to neighborhoods shape how Black families make school decisions.[9]

When I asked Risha how she had decided on the school, she confidently stated, "I already knew because I was living on First Avenue. Basically, I knew the school because I went there myself. My mother put me here. I already knew this was here." Reflecting on her own mother's decision when she was a child, Risha preferred to follow a similar path for her children. Easily drawing a mental geographic map of the school and other community services, Risha explained her ongoing comfort with "her" school. For Risha, the school in her neighborhood is a "social anchor"—a key landmark that links her and her children to the neighborhood.[10]

Risha preferred the school not only because of its proximity but also because she felt she received a good education. Risha expressed hope that her children will receive the same: "That's what I want for my kids. You want your kids to have the best. You want your kids to deal with a teacher that got your kid's best interest at heart. Because that's the way to get them to learn. Because if the teachers are not into it obviously the kids are not going to be into it, right?"

Risha worried about the unfamiliarity of other school options in the neighborhood and schools that were farther from her home. She noted her concerns about her older children, who are in middle school and high school: "My older daughter takes a bus and a train to school, so I worry every day. I'm not comfortable until everybody is in this house. I'm on pins and needles because all types of stuff is happening in this world. I cannot relax."

Risha expressed appreciation that the local elementary school is just a short three-minute walk away. She can visit frequently, check on her kids during the school day, and speak with teachers and staff. Never one to bite her tongue if something is amiss, Risha explained, "If I see something is not right, I'm going to speak on it. They already know me. I'm really familiar with the school." Many of the administrators know her by name, and some even worked at the school when she was a child. Risha shared her appreciation for her closeness to the school staff because someone is always watching out for her daughter: "If something goes on with my daughter like if she's doing something she shouldn't be doing, they'll say I'm going to tell your ma, and she'll straighten right up. Ms. Watson and Ms. Joyce keep her on her toes."

Risha feels closely linked to the school that was such a familiar part of her childhood. Over the years, she had enrolled her children in the neighborhood school because of its proximity and comfort and reminders of her own childhood. Risha forged a community-oriented choice logic that was deeply tied to her familiarity with the neighborhood school. Black parents rely on their experiential knowledge of school settings and their place-based attachment to neighborhoods to make future enrollment decisions for their children.[11] To manage the uncertainty of an increasing number of school options, many of the working-class parents I interviewed forged community-oriented decision-making logics. These decision-making logics are grounded in their experiences living and growing up in neighborhoods and their familiarity with traditional neighborhood schools.

Jeffrey, a Black, working-class married father, also described how social and historical space contextualized his school decision for his daughter. He believed schools were grounded in neighborhoods. Like Risha, Jeffrey grew up attending New York City public schools across the Bronx and Brooklyn. He spent his early adolescence and teenage years in Brooklyn and has lived in his current affordable housing complex for more than a decade. We met outside his apartment in Brooklyn. Dressed casually in jeans and a brown jacket, Jeffrey sat with me on a bench outside the entrance. Jeffrey serves as the building's maintenance worker and is well-known in the neighborhood—neighbors greeted him fairly frequently as we spoke. Jeffrey shared that he plays an active role in keeping the neighborhood safe and knows who belongs in the building, which hallways are clean, which doorways are secure, and which buildings are better kept up than others.

Jeffrey's familiarity with his building and with the community extended to the school decisions he made for his daughter. His longtime neighborhood friend John, who has a few older children, told him about the local school nearby. John and Jeffrey have been friends for years and barbeque in their courtyards during the summers. Thinking back to those summers, Jeffrey explained, "My man John told me. He said, 'Hey man let her come here.' So, I walk her to school every day." Although there are also charter schools and out-of-zone options nearby, Jeffrey felt a sense of community by sending his daughter to the school his close friend in the neighborhood had suggested. He explained that the school "stuck," as in the school was sealed in his mind once he knew that friends in the neighborhood also sent their kids there. Jeffrey's "selective solidarity" with his neighborhood friend helped him make important decisions for his daughter.[12] Research has shown that schools bring residents of the same community together and may help reinforce neighborhood social ties.[13]

This shared sense of community has always been important to Jeffrey: "You get to know people, and they get to know you and you trust them, you really trust them." He felt deeply tied to his neighborhood as a child and chose to create the same tradition for his daughter. They play in the parks near the low-income housing units, and she has made a few neighborhood friends.

He remembered that his parents did the same when he was a child. He reflected that growing up, "it was always the neighborhood school." He recollected how, for his parents, "there was no sitting down, making a decision, for every neighborhood we were in, it was the neighborhood school." When deciding on a school, Jeffrey found security in the familiar: "My parents used to do it like this, where whatever neighborhood we was in we went to that school, I did the same." Jeffrey thought about schools in a way akin to his parents.

The neighborhood school gave Jeffrey a sense of comfort and reminder of his own childhood experiences. He described the school with happiness: "It's a good home atmosphere. Being a Black person, you can feel the love. You can feel that they care about the kids. They gather the kids like a herd of sheep."

The local school also provided Jeffrey a sense of belonging and a climate to nurture his daughter's socioemotional well-being.[14]

When thinking about schools, Jeffrey—like Risha—blended two histories. He thought about his more distant past and the steps his parents took when deciding on schools for him. He also thought about his more contemporary history—his connection to the neighborhood and his friends in the community. For Jeffrey, who had developed friendships in the community over the years and attended the neighborhood school growing up, sending his daughter there meant he was investing in the familiar, putting faith in what he knew best. Jeffrey leaned into his local connections and relied on his place-based attachment to the neighborhood. He believed that schools were social anchors, connecting children to their neighborhoods, and invested in the familiar neighborhood school that mirrored his experiences as a child.

As sociologist Eve Ewing notes about schools in Chicago, public schools are the hearts of communities.[15] Schools bring community members together and help orient parents' understanding of the neighborhood.[16] Schools are shared institutions, and as some of the working-class parents I interviewed note, they are an integral pathway for children to connect to the community. Parents who invested in the familiar through the school search drew connections to their experiences as children, reflecting on their school's role as the social anchor that grounded their childhoods. They reflected fondly on their neighborhood schools and chartered similar paths for their children by enrolling them in local schools that they could visit frequently. By investing in the familiar, these parents managed the uncertainty of the school search and avoided schools that were unknown. Communal bonds between neighborhood schools and local families can enhance the educational experiences of Black students.[17] Historically, sociospatial attachments to neighborhoods have been vital for Black families' sense of community, familiarity, and identity.[18] Schools play an essential role in nurturing place attachments and strengthening sense of belonging and collective identity.[19]

I argue that when parents speak about their geographic preferences for school and generational connections to neighborhoods, they are forging community-oriented school decision-making logics. The working-class parents perceived that neighborhood schools could hold generational significance and link children to family traditions.[20] They also believed that schools played an important role in building community and reinforcing and fostering neighborhood connections. Working-class parents also felt that sending their children to the local school extended their parents' legacy and grounded their children in the neighborhood.[21] These parents found a shared connection in the neighborhood school and saw the school as a landmark of familiarity.

Despite recent increases in school choice, many of the working-class parents I interviewed invested in the traditional neighborhood school. While working-class parents emphasized maintaining consistent school experiences across generations, middle-class parents tended to prioritize the specific needs of their children. As a result, children from different social classes end up attending schools that vary significantly in quality. The parents who expressed community-oriented school logics often unknowingly settled their children in underperforming zoned schools in their neighborhoods. The contrasting decision-making strategies parents used inadvertently contributed to widespread inequalities in school choice programs.

Counter-Oriented School Decision-Making logics

Other working-class parents I interviewed held very different perceptions of neighborhood schools. These parents forged counter-oriented choice logics and strategically avoided neighborhood schools. Often describing negative experiences in neighborhood schools growing up, these parents hoped to identify nonzoned schools that would offer more opportunities. They fled schools in their neighborhood that they perceived were underperforming and pursued higher ranked schools outside of the neighborhood.

Helen, a Latina single mother of three, grew up in the Bronx and had a rough childhood. Holding back tears, Helen described her tumultuous home life with her father, stepmother, and two siblings. Her mom fell ill when she was nine years old, and she went to live with her father, who didn't give her the attention she needed. She suffered physical abuse by her stepmother for years. After moving out of the house when she was eighteen, Helen vowed to do things differently for her children: "I told my father I didn't want to raise my daughter the way he raised me growing up. We would go to school, come home, and clean and cook, and that was so cruel."

Helen's experience as a student at the neighborhood school was no better than her home life. Helen was heavily influenced by kids in her neighborhood who went to school with her. She frequently cut class, did not turn in homework, and rarely paid attention to her teachers. Her dad was never concerned about the type of school she went to and did not encourage her to join activities. Helen reflected sadly, "One of my hang-ups with my dad is he just sent us to the school across the street, the neighborhood school. But because we went with the same kids and some of them cut school, I would follow them because I grew up with them." Helen feared that if she sent her children to the neighborhood school, they would experience similar peer pressure.

Helen's troubled past and limiting experience in the neighborhood school motivated her to seek schools farther away for her children. She noted that for her prospects were bleak; few students in her high school graduated and hardly any continued to college: "All I got to make it to was high school being with my stepmother and father. I didn't get there, but my kids will."

These experiences colored Helen's impressions of the neighborhood schools, and Helen actively considered out-of-neighborhood alternatives. Research has found that perceptions of risk motivate parents' decisions to exit district schools.[22] When Helen left her father's home, she worked in a cafeteria in an elementary school in an affluent area of Manhattan. During the years she spent working at that school, she saw parents organize social outings for their children and involve them in a host of extracurricular activities. Adopting a style modeled after the parents at the school, Helen has tried to provide a similar experience for her three children. She takes her kids to the parks, museums, and movies and reads to them daily.

In contrast to her father, who she noted thought less carefully about the schools she would attend, Helen spent countless hours studying her children's school options and researching schools outside the neighborhood. She relied heavily on school performance data and informal networks like parent coordinators at local schools and administrators she met at open houses. She used the DOE resources directly and spoke to other parents who had children attending the schools she was considering. Helen found new opportunities for her kids through public school options:

> I didn't want my kids to grow up with the same kids from the neighborhood. I didn't want that because when you go to school with the same kids that live in your neighborhood you get in trouble with them. You either become a bully and pick on other kids or you start cutting, and I didn't want that. I didn't want my kids to grow up in that environment. I wanted my kids to see out of the box, that there was more. That it's okay for you to take a train and go to school.

When it came time to narrow her options and decide on schools for her children, Helen avoided schools that were near her home. She believed there were more opportunities and better funded schools outside the Bronx. Despite the complexity of the school choice process and the time sacrifice, Helen expressed confidence that her efforts would pay off: "I rather take two trains and a bus. I rather sacrifice because I got to do what's best for my daughter."

Helen scoured books from the DOE to see how the school was rated and to look for indicators of bullying and suspensions. Reflecting on her decisions for all of her kids Helen explained, "I'm glad that they went to different schools far away and that they have a mind of their own." In hopes of opening new doors for her children, Helen enrolled her youngest daughter in a highly rated out-of-neighborhood school that provides after-school programming. Helen trucks her daughter forty-five minutes each way to her elementary school in East Harlem. Despite the long distance and exhausting commute, Helen is proud of her decisions. Her older children are college graduates and have had opportunities to travel and explore careers that she never did. Helen explained that leaving the neighborhood for school has given her children new directions beyond what they may have encountered in their neighborhood. She shared that they are pushed to reach their full potential. They don't have to worry about many of the barriers she faced in school. "I looked for schools in places that were in a good environment where my daughter would feel safe and where I know she is going to be okay."

Helen perceived that underperforming schools hold a great risk and can limit opportunities for the future. Considering her own experience, Helen forged a counter-oriented school decision-making logic. She closely examined indicators of school quality, hopeful that more highly ranked schools would lead to better outcomes for her children. Black and Latina/o parents have historically experienced unequal access to higher-performing schools and like Helen describe various factors that push them away from traditional neighborhood schools.[23] As families face an increasingly arduous school decision-making process, parents rely on their own schooling experiences to narrow down the types of schools they select.[24] Parents forge counter-oriented decision-making logics as they seek to disrupt the educational disadvantages they experienced as children.

Like Helen, Latrice also had a tough childhood and hoped to diverge from the school decisions her parents made for her as a child. Latrice mainly grew up in a small, one-bedroom apartment with her mom in East Harlem. Latrice's mom and dad abused drugs during her childhood. She described how they moved frequently—at times they lived in the Bronx, sometimes in Manhattan, and at one point she was sent to live with extended family in South Carolina. Latrice described her neighborhood in Harlem as severely "crack and drug infested. It was rough, it wasn't the easiest neighborhood." She shared that to this day she is not close to her mom or dad and feels that even her extended family are rarely reliable: "My circle is extremely, extremely small. I don't have a good support system."

Latrice's parents sent her to the neighborhood school in each place they called home. She went to several different neighborhood schools between third grade and junior high school. When reflecting on the quality of the schools, Latrice noted that she "could've gotten a lot more. I think if I was guided a lot better, then I could've gotten a much better education." She felt that the schools in her neighborhood failed to prepare her for graduating high school and making it to college. She wished that she had received more guidance from her school and more insistence from her mom to perform better academically.

Latrice disapproved of the education she received at the neighborhood school and her parents' lack of involvement in her education. Reflecting on her parents' school choices for her, Latrice explained, "Unfortunately for me it was the neighborhood school. It was like you live in the neighborhood; you go here. But I don't believe in that. My parents raised me, and I don't knock them for that. They did the best that they could with what they had, but I think I could've gotten a lot more."

Now raising her son in the Bronx, Latrice explained that she wanted to make better decisions than her parents had for her. Latrice forged a counter-oriented school decision-making logic by reenvisioning new school options for her son. She was concerned about the students who attended the neighborhood school and the peer pressure her son might experience: "I knew that I didn't want my son to go to the neighborhood school because I saw how the neighborhood kids were, and I knew that they went to those schools, and I didn't want my son around those kids."

While Latrice feels safe in her neighborhood, she noted that there remains a lot of poverty. She sees the same people hanging around the neighborhood when leaving for work and returning. Latrice expressed fear that her son might be influenced by youth in the neighborhood: "I didn't want my son around that. I want more for my son. I knew that I didn't want my son in that neighborhood, and I didn't want him playing with the kids. It's not like I think I'm so much better, it's just that I don't want that for my child."

Latrice looked for schools outside the neighborhood that she hoped would provide better educational outcomes. Latrice explained that she was willing to commute to a well-performing school. From Latrice's perspective, sending her son outside of the neighborhood would provide more opportunities: "He needs to have every opportunity to be the best that he can be. I'm big on that and that wasn't given to me, and I promise that that's going to be given to my son and so his education is everything you know it starts there but it starts with me, but then that's the second thing so he needs to be able to have a decent education."

Latrice applied to several schools outside of the neighborhood for pre-K and ended up enrolling her son in a school in Manhattan. She loved the teachers and the curriculum for the year, but she soon learned that her son was not guaranteed a spot for kindergarten. Knowing that she did not feel comfortable with the neighborhood school, Latrice called the DOE to see what her other options might be. She explained her strategy: "I went to the Department of Education. I'm a straight shooter. I didn't want my son to go to the zoned school. I know that it's a failing school. I looked it up online. I just told them I know that my son has a zoned school, but my son was at another school for pre-K, and I really like that school, and I don't want to take anything less." Through that conversation, Latrice received more information about availability at a new charter school developing in the Bronx. Latrice sent her son to the school for a month before a space opened at the original school he attended for prekindergarten. She explained that she was willing to do whatever "footwork" was necessary to advocate for him.

Reflecting on a school and home life that offered few opportunities for future advancement, Latrice approached school decision-making deeply concerned about the risks of academic underperformance. She forged a counter-oriented decision-making logic as she searched for settings that would ensure her son was academically engaged and would provide models of success beyond the confines of the neighborhood. Latrice forged a decision-making logic that intentionally diverged from her experiences as a child. As past research has suggested, parents rely on their school experiences to make decisions for their children.[25] I argue that parents use these past experiences to cultivate search logics through an uncertain and complex school search process.

Neighborhood concerns and fears of school quality also shaped how Martha, a Latina single mother of two boys, forged her decision-making logic through the school search. Martha grew up on Manhattan's West side. She noted that in current times the neighborhood is virtually unaffordable for working-class single parents: "The neighborhood and the schools are much better now. And it's because of the type of people that are living there now. That's what changes it. And now it's a very, very expensive neighborhood." Even while reflecting on neighborhood changes over the year and the influx of wealthy new white residents, Martha still noted that she loved her neighborhood as a child and was able to attend a school that pulled in low-income children from an affordable housing development and children from more affluent families on the Upper West Side.

Martha moved to the Bronx as a young adult and had lived in her home for twelve years. She loves her apartment building and feels lucky to have secured such a large space for which she pays according to her income. Over the years, she has formed friendships with a few other women in her building who she feels are like sisters. Although she feels safe in her building, she noted with disappointment that the neighborhood remains riddled with poverty. Martha rarely takes part in activities in her neighborhood or along her block and often travels to Manhattan for activities for her youngest son. She explained that the schools in her area are similarly poor in quality: "I just don't like the schools in my neighborhood. I wish the schools were better."

The mother of a six-year-old and a twenty-seven-year-old, Martha reflected back on what a difficult time her elder son had going to schools in the neighborhood: "It's really sad, I have a twenty-seven-year-old and it was very rough for him going to the neighborhood school. He had a really bad experience in the public schools near me."

When her younger son was a toddler, Martha decided that she would do what she could to ensure he could attend schools in Manhattan: "I've been traveling with him since age two. He started at a very good school I found in my old neighborhood." Martha noted that back when she was in school and when her elder son was in school, zoning requirements limited school options. Martha wanted to pursue other options when she realized how much her elder son was struggling in school, but she was limited by the zone: "I always knew there were better schools in Manhattan, but when I was trying to get my older son into certain schools, they would reject him because they said it wasn't his zone school."

Martha expressed worry about the schools in her neighborhood: "They're failing the children. The reading percentile scores are very low. The children are not learning. They're failing. If you go onto the website, you can see they have an F for failing. The children are not passing." Martha believed the schools in her neighborhood limited her older son's educational future and had not improved. Concerns of poor academic quality and safety and negative stereotypes in educational settings often encourage Latino parents to exit traditional public schools.[26]

Similar perceptions of schools shaped Martha's school decision years later when her younger son was ready for kindergarten. Martha learned that new policies meant she could apply to schools across New York City, so she applied to twenty different elementary schools for kindergarten. She looked through the New York City schools directory that, at the time, provided a letter rating system for schools. Martha also looked at performance percentiles to determine how enrolled students were performing. She filled her list with schools from Manhattan.

Martha did not get her first choice but then got a call for a school she had ranked fourth on her list. Martha decided to move forward with that school in Lower Manhattan. Since then, she has been impressed with the extracurricular activities her son has been able to pursue and how he has advanced through the curriculum. She noted, much more at ease, that "it's a beautiful school, they provide support, and they're giving him extra help if he needs it. He's being well rounded so I would give it a high ranking."

Though Martha loves the school, the commute has been hard on her and her son. They wake up at five every morning to travel to a school more than an hour away from their home. Martha explained that while she would have loved to stay in her neighborhood, the schools near her home were unreliable: "I would've loved to have a school right near me with the right programs. It doesn't matter where. I even applied to schools in Brooklyn. Just as long as they're providing the right education and that the children are not failing." In her school search for her younger son, Martha reflected on her experience dealing with poor-quality schools two decades earlier and determined that school achievement levels were her most pressing concern. Martha sought to minimize the risk of underperformance and pursued schools that offered an assurance of upward mobility. Sifting through school rankings and percentile data offered a sense of security that her youngest son would be offered more academic opportunities.

Working-class parents who relied on counter-oriented search logics believed that the task of making school decisions required more vigilance compared to a generation prior. They hoped to minimize uncertainties by securing seats at higher-performing schools in more affluent neighborhoods. Noting the limitations they experienced from elementary through high school, they worried that neighborhood schools would lead to underachievement. They forged counter-oriented decision-making logics by selecting schools that diverged from their past experiences and by reenvisioning new school options for their children. They perceived that school choice provided more possibilities that would lead to better outcomes than the school settings they experienced decades earlier.

These working-class parents' perceptions were often correct, and their children were more likely to be enrolled in out-of-neighborhood schools that were better performing on state assessments. Working-class parents who forged counter-oriented school decision-making logics used what resources they could to chart a *different* path, applying to schools outside of the neighborhood that offered more activities and received high rankings based on information they researched.

Many first-generation middle-class immigrant families shared a similar logic. They were also concerned about school quality and wanted to ensure that their children maintained a competitive advantage in the United States. They were heavily invested in their children's academic success and hoped their school decisions would promote upward mobility.[27] Research has shown that immigrant families hope to provide better opportunities for social advancement and hold high expectations for educational achievement.[28] I found that the immigrant parents I interviewed similarly relied on counter-oriented school decision-making logics by anxiously searching for high-performing schools that would provide a strong foundation and promote upward mobility.

Bundled in a light jacket against the springtime winds in downtown Manhattan, Violet reflected on her experiences growing up in Ukraine and her parents' financial limitations: "In my home country, I went to regular schools, my parents were not able to afford any private schools." Violet was a top student, but with little money and ongoing corruption, she was unable to further her education in the way she envisioned. "I had all A's. I was valedictorian. I wanted to always go to a great college even when I was a child, and it never happened because it's a very corrupt country unless you have money." She recognized that growing up she did not benefit from many enrichment activities and craved schools that support academic development for her son.[29] After marrying her husband and moving to New York City, Violet felt hopeful that she would be able to find better educational opportunities for her son.

In search of opportunities for her son, Violet took him in and out of four schools for the first six years of his life. She described herself as someone "always striving for better. It's okay to be okay but if you're choosing education, it's not okay to be okay, it's better to strive for better." Reflecting on the limitations she experienced growing up, Violet found many of the schools her son attended to be mediocre. She said with dissatisfaction in her voice, "The school was fine. It was a nice community school. It was a public school, and they were teaching them what they were supposed to know. But it's really hard for a person who strives for better to accept."

After learning about New York City's G&T program, Violet signed her son up for the test and eventually had him transferred to the citywide G&T school. Since the school transfer, Violet had been happy with her decision. She connected her constant battle for the most prestigious school to many of the constraints she experienced as a child in Ukraine. Research has demonstrated that immigrant parents' educational aspirations and expectations for their children are adaptive responses to migration-related losses.[30] Violet's educational aspirations were influenced by her educational limitations in Ukraine.

When researching schools, Violet paid careful attention to graduation rates and, for K–12 schools, college enrollment rates. Unable to access her ideal college as a young person, Violet searched for schools that would hold more promise for her son's future.[31] She explained confidently, "I was looking at the percentile of kids who graduate and get great grades and ELA and where they were accepted after and their colleges. So, I guess this stems from what I didn't accomplish when I was younger. I wanted to go to a good school, so if I didn't, I want my children to be able to."

She reflected happily that her son's school was very different from hers in Ukraine: "Well we never had a 3D printer. We had very scarce supplies, and we never had a counselor to help you with choosing the right path in your life. This is totally different." Violet thought back to her educational trajectory as a child to explain her search for better opportunities for her son. Rigid educational structures in her home country limited her options as an adult, so for her son Violet valued schools that taught advanced thinking and would provide him with more than what she had. For immigrant families, past educational limitations and economic constraints motivate their pursuit of upward mobility for their children.[32] Violet urgently searched for schools that could provide greater educational benefits than she experienced. She forged a counter-oriented school decision-making logic in hopes of expanding her son's educational trajectory. Immigrant parents were anxious about being able to successfully access top schools because they saw their search process as a conduit to social advancement.

Jean-Baptiste, whom we heard from in chapter 1, is a refugee from Cameroon and a married father of three young children in East Harlem. Like Violet, Jean-Baptiste also immigrated to the United States as an adult. He envisioned a strong grounding that would secure his children's educational futures. He explained that when he was growing up there were many students in the classroom and the teacher often had limited tools to teach lessons. After elementary school students had to pay for schooling, and many of his classmates could not afford to continue their education. He noted with dismay, "In the middle of our education, we had to start paying for the school, and that discouraged a lot of people because they didn't have the means." As an adult refugee, Jean-Baptiste managed to continue his education in the United States and now works in the nonprofit sector as a case manager. Reflecting on his time in Cameroon and his career now, he shared that he remains acutely aware of how poverty shapes educational access. Jean-Baptiste's reflection on the limited educational access growing up motivated his counter-oriented search logic.

Now Jean-Baptiste worries about his children's future trajectories, especially because crime and drugs have a foothold in his neighborhood: "The thing I don't like much about my neighborhood is the people, dealing with people and seeing people on drugs. There are many single-parent families who are on public assistance. There are a lot of children hanging on the streets, doing nothing and cursing." Jean-Baptiste lives in the neighborhood because of its affordability, and he received a sought-after income-based subsidy for his apartment unit. He appreciates the convenience to subway stations, stores, and the public library but worries constantly that the surrounding neighborhood will not provide a strong foundation for his children's academic progress. He offered, "I worry about it because my kids they are very little. I'm very scared as they grow up. I don't want them to get influenced by the kids who drop out early from school and get involved in drugs. They might imitate the fashions on the street and the bad words. And I'm very scared because I don't want them to get involved in those types of activities."

For Jean-Baptiste, school decision-making is a way to limit his children's contact with neighborhood behavior he disliked. Jean-Baptiste's concerns and associated counter-oriented logic also reflect African immigrants' ethnoracial identity work. Research on African immigrants suggests that African immigrant youth draw intraracial ethnic distinctions based in part on parenting values.[33] Jean-Baptiste sought a school environment that would shelter his kids and provide a more positive alternative. Rather than the downwardly mobile trajectory he anticipated for many kids in the neighborhood, he saw the school as a way to broaden future opportunities. He was concerned about his children as they reach their teenage years, that they might be influenced by other kids' behavior in the neighborhood. The challenges associated with leaving one's home country and attempting to adapt to an unfamiliar new environment are commonly reflected in migrant narratives.[34] Jean-Baptiste feared that as his children adapted to life in the United States their academic trajectories might decline.

Jean-Baptiste and his wife decided on a charter school that he described as both "rigorous and strict." For him, the school provided a structure and orderliness to balance the less than ideal elements in the neighborhood: "They have that structure and being in a place where we are surrounded by homeless and surrounded by kids and projects, they really need that. A lot of kids don't go to school, and they get involved in drugs and everything. We need a place where our children could be there to study. A place where they have everything and the structure they need."

The small school provides a close-knit community for his children to grow. Jean-Baptiste described it as a very successful school offering a good balance of discipline and care. Jean-Baptiste cultivated a counter-oriented school decision-making logic by reflecting on his immigrant background and seeking school options that offer academic rigor and a strong foundation.

Like the working-class parents who forged counter-oriented school decision-making logics, the middle-class immigrant parents I interviewed also worried about ensuring the best academic opportunities for their children. The parents reflected on their immigrant experiences and attempted to mitigate the riskiness of the school search by identifying schools that would promote upward mobility and offer opportunities. They searched for schools that provided a secure path for the future and a competitive advantage for their children.

The middle-class immigrant parents also forged counter-oriented decision-making logics in hopes of reducing the uncertainties of academic and career success in the United States. These families searched for schools that were well-known for academic rigor and would ultimately promote upward mobility. In contrast to the working-class parents who forged community-oriented school decision-making logics, these working-class and immigrant parents were more familiar with the criteria for academic excellence and could effectively evaluate the various factors that contributed to a school's academic rating. The families were also able to navigate school choice strategically despite the complexities of the application process. Their children in turn ended up in higher-performing schools that provided a competitive edge for future opportunities. Few working-class families ascribed to the counter-oriented logic, and few ended up in high-quality schools compared to the majority of middle-class parents. Even as school choices expand, class-based disparities in educational enrollment persist, resulting in widespread differences in school quality for students across social class backgrounds.

Nurturing-Oriented School Decision-Making logics

I found that most middle-class parents assuaged their concerns about the uncertainty of school decision-making by searching for schools that would nurture their children's individuality, creativity, and personal interests. While these parents similarly hoped to promote upward mobility, their central goal was focused on developing their child's unique identity and prioritizing emotional well-being and individual strengths. They identified schools they hoped would have adaptable approaches and be responsive to different learning styles. The parents who forged nurturing-oriented school decision-making logics were concerned about school fit and wanted their selected school to provide boundless opportunities for personal development and growth. Research has demonstrated that parents' notions and perceptions of fit are socially constructed and influenced by race- and class-based assumptions of school quality.[35] Past research has also found that privileged parents often select schools that will maintain their social advantages and promote social mobility for their children.[36] More recent research has identified that not all advantaged parents choose schools that prioritize academic outcomes. For example, Mira Debs and colleagues identify a subgroup of advantaged parents who seek schools that prioritize social-emotional well-being.[37] Due to recent shifts in parenting away from traditional measures of success, parents in privileged positions have expanded their definitions of high-quality schools.[38] Some advantaged parents opt instead for schools that emphasize nonacademic factors such as wellness, social justice, and individuality.[39] These parents were certainly concerned about upward mobility but hoped to find niche schools that focused more on student individuality rather than solely on academic rigor.

I argue that irrespective of recent shifts in middle-class parenting values, when middle-class parents seek schools that promote individuality and free-thinking, they are hoping to make the school search feel more secure and maintain their children's social class standing. They forge choice logics that center on nurturing-oriented approaches and search for schools that will deemphasize competition and promote social-emotional well-being. In an increasingly competitive society with less predictable paths toward success, these middle-class parents perceived that a school that encouraged individuality rather than uniformity would allow their children to nurture their unique talents and develop a multifaceted skill set. With more school options that seemed to bring both opportunities and risks, parents believed they could find niche school environments that would help their children discover and nurture new skills and abilities.

Middle-class parents' individualized concerns for their children and central focus on finding hard-to-access, innovative programming reproduced inequality in education. These parents had the time and flexibility required to apply to and search for competitive schools and were extremely familiar with evaluating school quality. Unlike the working-class parents who forged community-oriented logics, the middle-class parents who forged nurturing-oriented logics were more strategic in their school choice planning and enrolled their children in exceptionally well-performing schools.

Renata, a middle-class mother of four, expressed specific expectations for how schools should meet the individual needs of each of her children. Renata was born in the Philippines and as a middle school student moved to Long Island, where she attended Catholic schools. She appreciated that her parents sought better educational opportunities for her, but like Margaret her time in Catholic school also shifted her thinking around the type of education she wanted for her children. She explained grimly,

> Catholic school is a very traditional way of teaching. You sit down, the teacher lectures, you pretty much memorize. The exams were more like you repeat back to the teacher what was said to you. It was very traditional, and I think it was pretty much that way throughout elementary and high school. We had nuns as our teachers. It was just really like, "This is what you learn, this is it." The information is given to you, and you just throw it back at them. That's pretty much what it was. There wasn't a lot of discussion about what we were learning.

Renata gained a newfound appreciation for flexible teaching methods as she researched and toured schools for her children. In hopes of promoting her children's individuality, Renata searched for a school culture that was open and exploratory in nature. She perceived that more latitude and flexibility in teaching approaches would encourage her children to develop without constraints. Renata valued metrics other than standardized test scores and, as research suggests, had a more expansive definition of school quality that emphasized the social and emotional components of the school environment.[40] Renata also searched for a school that would nurture her children and allow them to learn in an open and accepting atmosphere.

> So not until my kids started going into school did I realize, oh, there is a difference in the way people are taught and learn. It's important to have teachers who care about more than just the academics of a child. They should be concerned about the whole child, the mental, physical, academic,

social/emotional of the child. There is such an incredible sense of community between the staff and the parents, and our kids are thriving. The teachers are attentive, they're nurturing to the kids. . . . Each child is different, so I've learned. . . . I have four children at four different schools, because I realize that no one school is the best fit for each child because they have different personalities. I think because with four kids, you look at all the schools that you could possibly look at just to see which one is the best fit for your child.

While Renata experienced the rigid and traditional Catholic curriculum in grade school, she has tried to find a more nurturing learning environment to help her children develop their unique talents and abilities. Over the years, with each of her four children she has found niche environments that suited their needs and learning styles. For instance, when she learned that a school did not seem to be a good fit for her son, she immediately transferred him to a school that aligned with his learning needs:

> Even though my daughters were fine there at that time, for my son, it wasn't the right fit. With my son there was a lot of difficulty in the class, and I didn't think he was learning as much as he could at that time, and he started not listening, because it was like we're all getting into trouble anyway, why do I have to listen if I'm going to be punished, so he was just joining in. So, I thought, "Oh, no, no, no, this is not going to happen." We've got to find another place for you. I just knew he had to be out and go into a new environment.

Renata firmly believed that schools should take the whole child into account. Renata sought a new school environment for her son because she was invested in finding a school that would promote "hands-on-learning" and individually support her son's development. Guided by a nurturing-oriented logic, she perceived that these broader expectations for personal growth and social emotional development would provide a freer and more inclusive trajectory toward future success.

Deidre's recollection of her elementary school years on Long Island mirrored Renata's accounts. A Black, middle-class, divorced mother raising two daughters in Harlem, Deidre also believed schools should promote discovery and nurture the "whole child." When searching for schools for her two daughters, she envisioned a school environment that would support her children's growth beyond academics. Deidre noted, "You know as a child I think I did have a good education but as an adult, I think it could have been a little more progressive. I think other things could have been added to help you as an adult."

She explained that she liked schools that "deal with children's emotions, you know, having them have a morning of reflection or a yoga type of meditative moment to let the kids center their understanding of how they're feeling for the day." She looked for a school that would provide more openness for her daughters to thrive while also learning more about themselves as learners. She wanted them to "learn how to deal with the world that's waiting for them beyond just arithmetic, social studies, and the arts."

To find schools that provided this particular niche environment, Deidre connected with other parents through online groups. Deidre explained that the process felt scary at first. Although from Long Island, Deidre was not familiar with the complexity of school selection in New York City: "I'm not from here, so I don't even know neighborhoods. It was a little like 'woah wow!' now I have to figure it all out." Deidre began her search for schools at a charter school orientation meeting. She was a bit taken aback by the rigor and strictness: "It was a little too much. I understand that getting good grades is important, but you also need to expose the kids to learning different things. I just don't think that they need as much pressure as that academy puts on." From her perspective those methods might actually "weed out intelligent children" who learn in different ways. She believed that schools should instead focus less on competition and spend more time building self-awareness. After attending a few more orientations and tours, Deidre settled on a neighborhood school just outside the bounds of her catchment zone.

Deidre appreciated the school leadership and admired how the principal had an "open-door policy." According to Deidre, he "embraced everyone in a really cool manner. Everyone loves everyone, and the students are nurtured." She felt that the school inspired her daughters to be true to themselves and to develop self-expression. The school supported Deidre's perspective of the "new generation we live in." Deidre believed that modern times required a less "methodological" and more "artistic" and open approach to teaching for students to grow and thrive. She noted with pride that her girls had made strides: "They're developing, they're happy, they're healthy, and they are learning."

Stella, a Black middle-class mother, sought a similar nurturing school environment for her multiracial son. Stella was born in New York but grew up in an affluent suburb in Massachusetts. The school setting from kindergarten through high school was highly competitive. She described how, in junior high school, "people would do things like keep library books" so other students would not be able to use them. According to Stella, the environment in high school was specifically geared toward getting into an Ivy League college. In the younger years, Stella noted that her school lacked racial diversity: "I didn't know anyone who looked like me from the area. By junior high school, all of the other kids who looked like me were bused in from other areas or one of the other lower income cities." Stella's youth was marked with stark racial divides and an intensely competitive school culture.

For her son, Stella wanted the school to deemphasize rigor and promote creativity. From her perspective, "teachers should enjoy teaching and encourage their students to enjoy learning. They should love that curiosity in children and have a desire to teach." She hoped to find a school that valued different learning styles and an environment that encouraged teachers to find ways to connect with students to promote their growth and development. Giving examples, Stella explained that some children might be "more visual or more tactile, or more physical." She believed the school should nurture these individual characteristics.

Stella worried about the risk that her son might be exposed to constant testing from an early age. She was concerned about what this might mean for his creative spirit: "One of the things that really frightens me about the New York City school system is the emphasis on testing." Stella believed that the increased focus on testing took away from other aspects of the learning experience.

After settling on a neighborhood with her partner, she felt that the zoned school would not provide the approach they were seeking. From interactions with other parents who had older kids in the neighborhood school, they had the perception that it was just a place for "parents to park their kids for a couple hours while at work." To Stella, it seemed like "there wasn't a focus on development, and it didn't seem like it would be the right fit." Stella believed that the zoned schools tended to be too regimented, saying jokingly, "They live within the Common Core and the kids can probably recite from memory." She was looking for a more open and flexible curriculum that was not so standardized. Stella believed that with less structure, her son's personality could flourish and that he would not be hampered by stringent lesson planning.

After months of searching, Stella found a suitable school that seemed like a great fit, but a few months into the year the school suddenly faced a host of issues and families began withdrawing. Many of the parents then enrolled in a nearby school. Stella did the same but felt the second school was a poor fit: "It's a uniform school and they really love the Common Core. They give homework to kindergarteners." Stella was not hopeful for her son's future at the new school, already seeing how his personal style and individuality were at odds with some of the school's policies: "He chooses to wear funky ties and socks and you're not supposed to, but he likes it and he does it to stand out because that's him and he wants to be himself."

Even though the school is well-resourced and the staff and teachers are kind and welcoming, Stella feels she cannot get behind a school that does not provide learning flexibility. From Stella's perspective, adherence to the Common Core is the school's main focus: "They are very into Common Core and following it and teaching to the test." At the same time, Stella worried that in the end this might be their best option. The school selection was uncertain and left many aspects unknown. She hoped her son wouldn't have to stay but explained, "The lottery is such a crapshoot that I don't know, he may stay there and then for first grade transfer somewhere else." Stella was determined to find a school that was academically rigorous but also flexible in its approach. She worried that strict adherence to the Common Core might hurt her son's creativity in the long run. She feared that teaching to the test so directly would limit his ability to learn in a way that would meet his needs.

Some parents sift through options that meet the tailored needs of their children and provide individualized instruction. Rather than aiming for specific expectations for success, parents who cultivate nurturing-oriented school decision-making logics want schools to encourage a broad understanding of achievement.[41] I found that this segment of middle-class parents were deeply concerned that rigid academic structures and narrow views of academic success could limit their children's possibilities. At the same time, they were still acutely concerned about maintaining their children's social standing and searched for schools that were well-performing. They forged nurturing-oriented school decision-making logics in hopes that schools with flexible structure and broad understandings of learning styles might lead their children toward success. The parents found it important to fully support a wide range of ambitions and viewed schools as settings in which their children could develop passions and explore unique interests.

Even when middle-class parents espouse nontraditional interests in progressive schools that are focused on nurturing their children's individuality, their actions still reflect their privileged class positions. They more easily evaluate top school options that offer advanced curriculum. Relative to the community-oriented logics of the working class, their search logics lead them to higher-performing schools and schools that provide their children with a competitive advantage. The contrasting logics of the working class and middle class contribute to the very inequalities school choice policies were meant to reduce. Among the middle-class families I interviewed, over 70 percent sent their children to high-performing elementary schools. When middle-class parents rely on decision-making logics that point them to well-resourced and more advantaged schools relative to working-class parents, children end up in schools that vary in quality according to their social class background.

Conclusion

Parents form preferences for schools and enact various decision-making logics that are deeply tied to their past school experiences and parenting identities. By relying on these search logics, parents also hope to resolve their experiences of uncertainty.[42] Parents use a variety of strategies to reduce the risks that come with making school decisions. These strategies represent how parents invest labor through the search process. Parents are concerned about the uncertainty associated with the school search and the unpredictability of their children's future and academic success. Parents' class-based decision-making logics through the school search process mean children end up in schools that vary in quality and mirror their social class backgrounds. Among the parents I interviewed, working-class parents were more likely to send their children to lower-performing schools, even though many of these parents opted out of their zoned school. In contrast, middle-class parents' decision-making logics led them to schools that were higher performing. The complexities of school choice policies that result in unequal search pathways mean school choice policies reinforce class-based inequalities in school enrollment.

As the stories from the parents demonstrate, vast economic and social differences shape how parents forge their decision-making logics and how parents experience the uncertainty of school decision-making. Parents' social class backgrounds shaped the types of school risks they perceived and the search logics they used to make school decisions. For instance, some working-class parents were concerned about the risks of unfamiliar schools, while others were concerned about school underperformance and downward mobility. Middle-class parents' perceptions of risks also varied. Immigrant middle-class parents worried about status reproduction and wanted to be sure that their children had access to an advanced curriculum. Other middle-class parents worried about school uniformity, standardized testing, and their children's ability express their unique identity. Parents' search logics were also shaped by neighborhood inequalities and perceptions about the availability of quality schools in their neighborhoods, a topic that is explored in greater detail in chapter 4. Middle-class parents often lived in more affluent neighborhoods and were in closer proximity to higher-performing schools relative to working-class families.

All the parents I interviewed believed that the quality of the school would influence their child's ability to get ahead in life. Parents managed the uncertainties of school decision-making sensitive to what their school decision would mean for their child's future. However, middle-class parents selected schools for enrollment that were better performing relative to working-class parents. Persistent differences in how parents conceptualize and manage school decision-making resulted in unequal school outcomes. Many working-class parents sent their children to neighborhood schools that often underperform local charter schools and nonzoned schools. Middle-class parents were often able to access resources and information from networks to identify high-performing schools and schools that offered innovative learning environments.

TABLE 4. Sample characteristics across class background ($N = 102$)

	Middle class ($n = 48$)	Working class ($n = 54$)
Household income		
<50,000	6	54
>50,000	42	0
Race/ethnicity		
Asian	11	1
Black	13	28
Latina/o	11	21
White	13	4
Type of school		
Not zoned by address	35	28
Zoned by address	13	26
School academic rating		
ELA rating > City average (41%)	35	22
Math rating > City average (38%)	34	20
Distance traveled to school[a]		
<0.5 miles	12	19
>0.5 miles	36	35
Decision-making logic		
Community-oriented	1	29
Counter-oriented	11	25
Nurturing-oriented	36	0

a. Distance categories selected based on New York City transportation eligibility parameters (NYC Public Schools, "Transportation Eligibility").

Clear distinctions in parents' choice logics and school preferences can be directly linked to the increased responsibility parents have to search for schools. Given this new requirement, we must take seriously how school choice policies reproduce inequality. School districts must invest in providing broad access to high-quality public schooling for all families. Doing so will ensure greater equity for parents making school decisions for their children.

3

You Don't Really *Feel* the Diversity

FUMI IS A BLACK, middle-class, divorced mother of a seven-year-old and a five-year-old and a law school administrator. She grew up in London and moved to New York as a young adult. Fumi loves New York City's rich cultural diversity. She deems her section of Inwood—a neighborhood in northern Manhattan—"a mosaic, a traveler's paradise." Fumi hoped her son's school options would reflect New York City's racial and ethnic diversity. Soon after she began her search, however, Fumi realized her options were highly segregated. The more racially diverse schools in her zoned catchment area were underperforming. The well-performing schools she considered had very few students of color:

> A lot of Caucasian schools have better infrastructure and better-quality schools. A lot of Black kids don't have that except to go to charter schools. And I did consider it. It was either a charter school or the Gifted & Talented exam. And we went with the Gifted & Talented program instead. But I don't think that's fair. With the amount of Black and Hispanic kids that I see in the city, how can it be that in a class with twenty kids, my son is the only Black one and there are no other Black and Hispanic kids? That just doesn't seem right to me. There isn't as much integration as there could be.

As Fumi searched for schools, she came to the frightening realization that, while certain schools might be a better option academically, the schools often lacked racial diversity. Based on a recommendation from her son's former teacher, Fumi decided to have her son tested for the G&T exam. Her son's teacher noted that he was not challenged in his former class and that "he was way above his peers." After painstaking consideration, Fumi decided that the G&T program was the best option.

Fumi faced a trade-off many Black, Latina/o, and immigrant parents in my study also faced: she wanted her son to receive a high-quality education, but she did not want him to be the only Black student at his school. Fumi appreciated the school's friendly atmosphere and the principal's strong leadership, but she constantly worried that her son might feel marginalized: "I don't like the fact that he's the only Black one in his class. The Gifted & Talented classes are mostly white and the other classes for his grade are more diverse. I think the school, the whole system needs a heck of a lot more help than it's getting. Because my son is in the G&T classes, it's different for us. But I have eyes, and I see what's going on." The lack of diversity within the G&T class left Fumi uneasy about her son's engagement with his classmates. Since he started at the school, her son has had ongoing issues with bullying, and Fumi feared that he was being targeted because he was the only Black student in the class. Fumi also worried about how he would fare in these segregated classes during the rest of elementary school and beyond.

Fumi's search for a school demonstrates one of the ways parents of color engage in ongoing racialized risk assessments as they search for schools. Black parents' school choice decisions have historically been restricted due to the injustices of segregation.[1] Today, families of color continue to face trade-offs even as school options have expanded.[2] Linn Posey-Maddox and colleagues explain that concerns of anti-Black racism are central to Black parents' educational decisions.[3] They describe the experiences of parents like Fumi who worry about the impact of potentially harmful school environments on their children. When searching for a school, parents of color must incorporate a host of race-based concerns into their decision calculus, including school demographics and how anti-Black racism may shape teaching and disciplinary practices at the school. Black parents also search for schools that will embrace Black identity and promote a racially affirming environment.[4] Parents' racial and class backgrounds intersect to shape Black parents' daily strategies to find high-quality and culturally inclusive schools.[5] This decision-making process is indicative of the intensified labor Black, Latina/o, and immigrant parents take on as they search for schools.

Choice-based school policies have increased the options available at the elementary level in New York City. These policies have significantly amplified the uncertainty and complexity of school decision-making for all parents, yet families of color must make these choices against the additional backdrop of anti-Black racism and persistent residential inequalities. America's long history of racial discrimination in educational settings shapes how Black and Brown parents engage with New York City's school system today. The steps parents of color take to estimate various trade-offs intensify school decision-making labor. Parents of color across class backgrounds engage in racialized work that spans well beyond the enrollment process. I identify three types of racialized work parents take on during and after enrollment.

- *Racialized gauging*: Parents of color first initiate their school searches by gauging. They attempt to estimate the relative trade-offs in their search for schools by balancing academic rigor and cultural diversity. They engage in racialized work by searching for schools they hope will build a sense of racial comfort.
- *Racialized auditing*: After their children are enrolled in schools, Black, Latina/o, and immigrant parents continue to monitor racial climates within schools by auditing. They track their children's experience in schools to manage possible risks and threats to their children's racial identity.
- *Racialized resistance and deflection*: As parents of color take steps to evaluate the prospects of various schools and monitor their children's experience in schools, they encounter racialized resistance, a process in which they endure their own marginalizing experiences from school staff and other parents in schools. To counteract these experiences, some parents of color work to *deflect*, a process by which they work to overcome their own racialized treatment in schools.

Black, Latina/o, and immigrant parents have responded to the transformations in risk and uncertainty brought on by new school choice policies by steadfastly searching for schools that balance racial inclusivity and academic rigor and by acutely monitoring their children's experiences in schools. Yet they absorb additional labor during the school choice process as they navigate marginalizing interactions with school leaders, teachers, and other parents. Even with increased school options meant to promote greater equity, Black, Latina/o, and immigrant families still face a school system that is racially segregated and limited by neighborhood residence. Race-based discrimination in schools and continued residential segregation shape how Black, Latina/o, and immigrant parents approach their school decisions and which schools feel safe for their children. Black and Brown families experience these educational inequalities regardless of income background and despite the increase in school options in New York City. Conceptualizing the school decision-making process for parents of color as racialized labor makes clear the inequalities that persist even as school choices expand.

Prior research has demonstrated that white families also consider the racial composition of schools as a method for excluding certain schools for enrollment. White parents' avoidance of predominately Black and Latina/o schools exacerbates segregation levels across schools.[6] I similarly found that the white mothers I interviewed were more likely to avoid schools in which over 75 percent of the student body was Black and Latina/o.[7] I also found that many of the white mothers I interviewed believed that exposing their children to diversity would provide an added long-term benefit. Unlike the parents of color who engaged in intensified racialized labor to make school decisions, the white mothers conceptualized diversity as a form of racial socialization—an opportunity to facilitate interracial acceptance.[8] While white families generally assessed diversity at a single moment during the school search, I found that parents of color continuously evaluated schools after enrollment, which required significantly more labor.

The majority of Black and Latina/o families in my study selected schools that were over 75 percent Black and Latina/o. Only 20 percent of white families and 30 percent of Asian families selected schools that were over 75 percent Black and Latina/o. Families of color and white families in my sample selected schools that differed in their levels of diversity. At the same time, these numbers mask a lack of diversity at the classroom level. While the Black and Latina/o families in my sample selected schools that appear diverse based on New York City DOE data, if their child enrolled in a G&T class or a dual language program, the classroom environment was often predominately white. For instance, Fumi selected a G&T program and enrolled her child in a school that was 77 percent Black and Latina/o, however the class her son attended each day was predominantly white. Similarly, for the white parents I interviewed, a school that is 20 percent Black and Latina/o may be even less diverse depending on their children's specific classroom.

Although the schools that parents of color sent their children to were often predominately Black and Latina/o relative to white and Asian families, they still engaged in extensive labor to apply to and search for schools. Nearly 60 percent of the Black and Latina/o parents I interviewed sent their children to schools not zoned by address.[9] Parents of color invested labor to gauge the academic quality and diversity of the school, monitor their children's experience in schools, and resist and deflect marginalizing experiences from teachers, staff, and parents.

Racialized Gauging

The parents of color in my study searched for schools they hoped would offer diversity and high academic quality. On one hand, they worried that schools that lacked racial diversity would hurt their children's sense of racial pride; on the other, they worried underperforming schools would limit their children's future academic prospects. Even post–*Brown v. Board of Education*, the United States' long history of residential segregation, funding disparities in education, and systemic barriers to access to high-quality schools has resulted in schools that are rarely racially diverse and higher performing.[10] Prior research has explored the various ways that this history severely constrains how parents of color make school choices.[11] Dawn Dow finds that middle-class Black mothers screen for racial intelligence when searching for schools.[12] Camille Wilson Cooper's research introduces the concept of "positioned choice" to demonstrate how race, class, and gender influence how low-income African American mothers construct their school decisions.[13] Concerns of race and anti-Black racism shape how Black parents choose and assess schools for enrollment.[14] As parents of color consider schools for enrollment, they use race-based assessments to anticipate measures of belonging.[15]

I find that searching for a school as a parent of color requires families to engage in racialized gauging. Important class distinctions driven by structural inequalities in New York City schools and neighborhoods shaped how parents attempted to gauge their children's school options. Middle-class parents of color often considered a wider range of schools, were more persistent in their efforts to find school alternatives, and were willing to switch their child from one school to another if they felt they found a better fit. Working-class parents also worried about the quality of their children's school, but due to geographic and transportation constraints and the limited number of high-quality schools nearby, they often focused on a much smaller range of schools. Unlike middle-class parents whose income and educational background eased the search process, working-class parents often adopted less meticulous methods in advocating for their children and in many cases believed their options were restricted to the neighborhood zone. Despite these class distinctions, both working-class and middle-class parents of color used methods of racialized gauging during the school search.

Tamar, a middle-class immigrant mother and a public schoolteacher, expressed concerns about finding diverse high-quality schools. Tamar was born in Israel, her husband in Antigua. She wanted a school that would support her child's racial and ethnic identity: "I think a huge element also of what makes a good school is the idea of nurturing and supporting kids to become advocates for themselves and others. So, there should be a focus on social justice and really preparing our children to be strong individuals and appreciative of their differences." After moving farther north to Washington Heights, a predominately Dominican neighborhood that featured more ethnic, racial, and cultural diversity, Tamar found the search for schools more challenging than she anticipated:

> Well, I would say something that I'm embarrassed to admit because I'm a New York City DOE teacher is that I don't think we considered the school opportunity as much as we should have. Just having easy access to a high-quality zoned school wasn't a reality in the places that we could afford. I'm very familiar with how these things work, but I really believed that the choice option was more real than clearly it is.

Over the years, Tamar saw other families send their children to schools outside of their neighborhoods. She believed she would be able to do the same. Tamar's remarks demonstrate how the school choice system demands intensified labor, yet parents are not guaranteed a favorable outcome. Tamar felt especially hopeful about New York City's new universal pre-K program.[16] Unfortunately, her daughter was wait-listed at nearly all the schools she listed on the application, except for the local zoned school:

> It's very clear that where you live affects your neighborhood school. . . . There are only really two or three decent schools. And those schools are on streets or between streets that are really unaffordable to us and people like us. So, the majority of kids that go to those two or three decent schools are white and the rest of the schools are a majority of kids of color. The school down the block from us is majority of kids of color and it has really struggled academically, socially, and it just doesn't do well in terms of student support and resources. And we felt like there was no way we could send our daughter there.

Through a process of racialized gauging, Tamar continued to search for available schools the entire summer before pre-K: "I was . . . in the office begging secretaries to just add my daughter's name to the list. And I was rejected almost every single time." Tamar searched for a school in the hopes that she could strike the right balance, yet she found it nearly impossible to maximize educational opportunity and racial diversity:

> We cannot find a school in New York City that has predominantly kids of color, predominantly staff of color and that is well resourced and supported and where teachers are happy and there's not a high turnover rate and is successful and that's a problem and that's what we want and that's what we should be able to get regardless of where we're living. It's of the utmost importance that our kid is not the only Black child in the school. It's also really important that our kid is not one of three Black children in the class or the school, that they don't go to a school with white teachers and administrators. She has to go to a school where she'll see people like herself and not be an anomaly.

Eventually, after weeks of searching, calling, and visiting schools and a brief stint in a school that appeared to be a good fit but actually wasn't, Tamar managed to enroll her daughter in a new school. As Tamar finished sharing her experience searching for schools, the exhaustion in her voice was clear. At the same time, she was relieved to have found a school with socioeconomic diversity and high academic ratings:

> The school is very diverse. About 70 percent of families are families of color and 30 percent are white. Socioeconomically I think it's about 60/40. It's

Title 1 so at least 70 percent of the students receive free and reduced lunch. The administrators are people of color. About half of the teachers are teachers of color. Maybe even more than half. Her class has a lot of kids of color.

But even with this outcome, Tamar explained that her feelings of relief were only temporary. Even though her daughter's current pre-K has been a good fit, she felt in "limbo" about the future. Enrollment in the pre-K class would not guarantee enrollment for kindergarten, and Tamar would need to search again for school options the following academic year. For Tamar, racialized gauging was not a one-time process but rather an ongoing project of evaluating and reevaluating alternatives in search of a diverse and high-performing school environment.

Even when middle-class families of color like Tamar's access high-quality schools, they may find that better-performing schools are also schools with increased levels of racial inequality.[17] Tamar closed out our time together explaining the racialized labor involved in making such decisions:

> The fear that families of color have when it comes to sending their children to school is a fear that lots of people in New York City don't have and it doesn't even cross their mind if a school is going to have kids that look like them. This is something they've never had to contemplate before. . . . They're just choosing a school because they hear it's good. We don't have that option and we're not sending our kids to an all-white school, so we have a lot of sleepless nights. We have to think about the long-term effect that this will have on her life and her identity and how she will feel about herself.

Tamar gauged options as a form of racialized labor through the entire school search. In the long-term, persistently segregated school environments negatively impact student performance.[18] Parents of color search for schools that they hope will affirm rather than marginalize their children's identity, while they also aim for schools that will support their children's future academic prospects.

Trisha, a Black, middle-class single mother, also weighed the relative trade-offs of schools that were predominately Black and underperforming versus schools that were higher performing but less diverse. Trisha grew up in Harlem and attended public schools. After finding out that one of her sons is autistic, Trisha began searching for services and school options, only to find limited options near her home in the Bronx: "I moved to Harlem because I learned my son had autism. When we lived in the Bronx, I looked for services and therapy and they didn't offer a lot. It felt like almost all the good services and programs were in Manhattan so I knew I had to get to Manhattan somehow so that was my decision to move to Harlem. It was about the services and the schools."

Although Trisha believed there were more opportunities in Harlem relative to the Bronx, she perceived that schools in wealthier downtown school districts would offer even more opportunities:

> I feel like schools up here in Harlem don't offer as much funding as schools downtown. . . . District 2—that's where all the money is. That's where all the resources go is District 2. A lot of wealthier people live in that area, so the schools are better because they get more funding and have more resources down there. So, I wanted them to be in a diverse group, I feel like they would get more out of it, more experiences with the diverse population and not being around just minority children in that atmosphere.

A year in a District 2 school, however, changed Trisha's assessment of her boys' needs. "I felt like minority families didn't get treated as well as Caucasians there. I felt like when they did something. it was more of an issue than when someone of a different ethnicity did the same thing." Her interactions with her sons' teachers were strained, and she didn't feel like the teachers understood her children, especially her autistic son:

> Some really important things that I think the schools are lacking is a really caring input. He's been to school downtown, and I feel like the schools downtown tend to be more diverse. You don't want your kids to be just around their color, you want to mix them up and diversify them a little bit. But as far as the schools downtown being able to teach our Black students, I don't feel that they can. So now he's in a charter school, which is really great because they really have structure, guidelines, and they have a behavioral system in place that I think he's really adapting to. So that's why I chose to bring him back up here and put him in a charter school.

Trisha took her kids in and out of multiple schools in search of the right balance and fit. Many working-class Black, Latina/o, and immigrant parents in my study shared similar concerns about balancing academic rigor and racial diversity. Even though working-class Black and Brown families could not rely on social and economic resources to steadfastly research school options like their middle-class counterparts, working-class parents still experienced intensified concerns about their children's well-being in schools. Ariana, a single, Latina, working-class mother who works in a fast-food restaurant, explained that exposure to racial and cultural diversity was important for her. At the time of our interview, Ariana was living in a shelter system. She explained that she had her own apartment in the Bronx for ten years, but she had given that up when a close friend convinced her to move to Upstate New York for a job opportunity. But she had to leave Upstate New York quickly after learning that the friend who convinced her to move there was abusing her child.

Unfortunately, because her friend was not her partner, she did not qualify for housing through domestic violence assistance, and when she returned to the city, she lived with her sister for a week and then entered the shelter system. She struggled emotionally, continuing to feel guilt over the situation, and worried constantly about how her daughter was faring.

Ariana was thankful for the School-Based Student in Temporary Housing (STH) liaison who let her know about the elementary schools in the area and helped her pick one appropriate for her daughter. Ariana was concerned about finding both a diverse school and a school that would support her daughter academically. She knew that her resources would be limited, and she was counting on the school to provide as much support for her daughter as possible. Ariana recounted how she expressed these concerns to the liaison: "I said you know she's very smart she needs something that's going to challenge her and a place where she can be herself too. And she said, 'Well we can put her in pre-K right there down the street.' And I was like all right what about the other schools and she said they're good, they're all right too." In addition to providing an intellectually stimulating environment for her daughter, Ariana wanted a school that would make her daughter feel included and would expose her to diverse perspectives:

> Some of the schools are not as diverse as the other ones, and I wanted her to experience every culture not just one. I toured one school, and it was nice, but it's more one-sided, more of just one kind. I wanted her to see more diversity and more cultures. Before the Christmas break, she asked if we can celebrate Hanukkah and Kwanzaa. She said my friend celebrates Hanukkah. I told her we would find out more from her friends and maybe next year she can celebrate with them. So that's really one thing that I love that she's so open to different things, and she needs that.

Ariana appreciated that her daughter was in a safe and academically focused environment that embraced the neighborhood's rich cultural diversity.

Some families lived in neighborhoods where the schools were significantly underperforming, and higher-performing options seemed to be completely beyond reach. Although these parents of color intensively researched schools for environments that were both diverse and high-performing, they often had to settle for an option that was significantly undesirable.

Richard, a Black, working-class father, whom we heard from in chapter 1, quickly learned that his address in a low-income housing apartment limited the schooling options available to his daughter:

> I went to about eight schools, seven of which were within a four-block radius. But she was only slated to go to one particular school that had a 65 percent turnover rate. This school is actually closing at the end of this

year. There's a lot of schools. It's just hard to get into some of them, because it's a lot of charter schools and then there's a lot of public schools, but there's only certain ones that you are either zoned to or allowed to go to. So that gets frustrating.

In the wake of Richard's assault by his partner, he moved to a new home in East Harlem with his two children. The emergency move occurred during the middle of the school year, which meant that he missed many of the deadlines for charter schools and out-of-zone options. Noting geographic constraints, Richard explained that the charter school his oldest daughter attended in Brooklyn was no longer a feasible option for enrollment.

After learning that his daughter's new zoned school in the neighborhood had low academic ratings, Richard kept looking, only to find that other schools nearby with higher ratings would not admit his daughter: "So, I did my homework on the schools, and I said, 'Well, this is the school I want my kid to go to,' and they were like, 'Well, you're not zoned here.' And I was like, 'Well, what does that mean? You're only two blocks away from my house. I could throw a rock and hit the side of your building. Literally. Why can't my child go here?'" Even in an era of increased school choice options, Richard found that his options were limited. He could not, according to his communications with school staff and school leaders, enroll his daughter in a school that was not in his specified catchment area. Richard put in the effort to gauge his relative options, only to find that his address restricted his options:

> Sometimes I just wish I didn't live in this particular district, because it's just that once you go uptown, you're kind of stonewalled. It's almost like legalized segregation of children, because there's like a big barrier there. You can't get into the district, even if your child is there. I realized it's the real hard fact of segregating of kids. It still goes on today. It's disgusting. It makes me furious. My children have been subjected to subpar schools, subpar teaching.

Though Richard was upset about his inability to get his daughter into a higher-performing school, he began volunteering at her current school. He served on the School Leadership Team (SLT) and was also a PTA member. Through his involvement with schools across the district, Richard became even more aware of the stark inequalities between his school in East Harlem and other schools on the Upper East Side:

> You have certain zones, like Ninety-Sixth and above. They eat up all the funding, and then in these neighborhoods where the schools aren't great, parents might be more apprehensive to fight when something's going on with their kids. Versus if you go Ninety-Sixth and lower, they have everything. The last time I checked, public schools were public, which means that

it's free. It doesn't mean that you get all the funding, and you just suck it away from everyone else.

Schools south of Richard's East Harlem school were able to raise hundreds of thousands of dollars from their students' families to support learning and extracurricular activities. In contrast, parents in Richard's low-income and mostly Black and Latina/o neighborhood did not have the financial means to create these opportunities. Volunteering made the disparities obvious to Richard. He saw how teachers and staff members at his daughter's school struggled to provide students with a positive learning environment while the students themselves were often experiencing a host of issues at home:

> There's a lot of kids at the school who are displaced. Families get displaced in shelters. People move around. Kids come in the middle of the school year or kids come two months before the school even ends. And it affects them. It affects their little brains. They want to come to school, they want to have fun, they want to learn. They shouldn't have to deal with real-life adult situations like parents fighting to get them in a better school.

Richard's zoned school was surrounded by low-income housing developments and filled with children, like his, who had previously lived in the shelter system. Richard was well aware that schools only a few blocks away did not have to accept children from low-income public housing. These schools could prepare lessons and activities without having to address the myriad social issues that the children at his daughter's school experienced daily.

Richard's growing awareness of the vast disparities in schools within a single district clarified for him how students continue to be segregated according to racial and class background: "It's pretty disgusting that, as much diversity that's here, that we segregate the children. There are no white students whatsoever in this school. But the neighborhood is diverse. You see Caucasian people here, but they're not sending their kids here. But how do you get in there? Is there a pass for the color of your skin? Is there a pass?" Richard's advocacy and volunteer experience helped him understand the vast inequities in schools across New York City. After learning more about the G&T Exam, Richard had his daughter tested, and she scored well. For the upcoming school year she would have access to a better school. This was a relief to Richard, but the two of them would have to travel fifteen blocks each day to reach the new school. It would have been much easier to send her to the well-funded and higher-performing school only a few blocks away.

Other working-class parents like Richard and middle-class Black, Latina/o, and immigrant parents struggled to search for schools across heavily segregated school districts. Parents engaged in intensive racialized labor to find school options even within the restrictions of segregated school zones. For many parents, the needs of balancing these various trade-offs over academic rigor and cultural diversity extended their school search across multiple academic years. Structural inequalities shaped by the intersections of race and class significantly impacted how families of color searched for schools and intensified their concerns. Even when middle-class marginalized families relied on economic and social resources to access schools, they, like their working-class counterparts, worried about how anti-Black racism would shape their children's experiences in schools. America's legacy of racial discrimination in schools shaped how parents, regardless of class status, evaluated their options.

Racialized Auditing

For parents of color, the school search process does not end with choosing a school. Given the United States' long history of systemic racism in education, Black parents are compelled to vigilantly evaluate racial biases that may shape their children's experience in school.[19] Parents of color look for schools that will offer culturally relevant pedagogy and an unbiased school environment.[20] They also hope schools will be inclusive and culturally affirming.[21] Once their children are enrolled, Black, Latina/o, and immigrant parents absorbed an additional school search burden that required them to continually reevaluate the racial climate at schools. Previous research has found that parents of color regularly monitor how their children are faring in schools and routinely assess school disciplinary policies and practices.[22] To constantly watch over their children's experience in schools requires parents of color to repeatedly engage in racialized labor as part of the school choice process. Parents of color audited school racial climates and discriminatory incidents to ensure their children would feel welcomed and affirmed.

Lisa, a Black, middle-class, married mother of a six-year-old daughter and nine-year-old son and a chief information officer, described her ongoing process of monitoring her children's experiences in their schools. Lisa, a native New Yorker, was born in Queens and grew up on Long Island. Lisa shared how her mom always made sure she understood her position as a Black woman and how this shaped expectations for how she needed to perform in school. Lisa has since shared this same wisdom with her own children: "My mom always told me because of my race and because I was a female, I always had to work twice if not three times as hard as everyone else which is something that I instilled in my kids. I tell my kids all the time, why they have to behave a certain way." Concerns of anticipated discrimination in schools shape how Black parents assess their children's schooling experiences.[23] Parents relay their concerns about race by regularly giving their children messages at home about how to navigate school.[24] Lisa's understanding of her own positionality and the future experiences of her children informed her search for a school. She described an arduous and uncertain school search process: "No matter what zone you're in, you have to fight to get your kid into the school that you want to get them into anyway. So, it really didn't matter where I lived, I would still try and figure out a way to get them into the school that they need to be in." Rather than put all her "eggs in one basket," Lisa applied to every school available:

> I literally went to twenty open houses for elementary schools. And my kids definitely did the G&T tests. I applied for several charter schools, everything, I was like, I'm just going to apply for everything and then see my choices and I'll make my choice from there. To me I didn't want to make the choices beforehand and I was like, I'm just going to throw everything on the wall and what sticks, sticks. There are a lot of schools out there that a lot of people want to go to.

Through Lisa's persistent efforts, she ended up with a choice between a dual language program, a charter school, and a G&T class in a traditional public school. Lisa and her husband decided on the charter school, and her son seemed to do well, at least initially.

First grade was another story. The principal at the school hired a new teacher for first grade, and the class ballooned to thirty-two students. As the year progressed, Lisa explained that the teacher's ability to manage the class declined and impacted her son:

> So, what ended up happening was the teacher placed blame on my son for something that he had never had an experience for in previous years. She said he was being disruptive, but there were thirty-two kids in the classroom, and she didn't have good classroom control because she was a new teacher. She ended up, without letting us know, sending him to a social worker. She said he was an at-risk kid. Meanwhile my son has top grades in school. He's always done well. None of his previous teachers have had any problems.

Frustrated with the school's response and their "nonchalant" attitude, Lisa decided to speak with the DOE about her experience. These conversations seemed to make little difference. She reflected on one of her phone conversations with a DOE administrator:

> I got really disheartened with the DOE, and I realized that there is a deep sense of just inequality that's acceptable within the system. Someone at the department said, sometimes the DOE basically says that Black kids who are doing well in school are high risk. They say it's still abnormal for Black kids to have good grades, that they actually consider them high risk. And,

in the end, they didn't do anything about it. There was no disciplinary action on the principal for taking my child out of the classroom without my knowledge to a social worker.

Ultimately, Lisa's experience with the school and the DOE motivated her to seek out new options for her son: "I just realized that I needed to just take him out. And if I had a million dollars, I would totally have sent him to a private school and been done with the public school system and I think a lot of parents probably feel that way and they're trapped."

Lisa described going through the school search process a second time around. This time, her son enrolled in a dual-language school. While Lisa appreciated the teachers and staff, the school was more racially divided than she anticipated:

> The school is diverse because there is a French program and a Spanish program. But when you look at the class, it doesn't look diverse. I've seen articles about the school and they tout that there's diversity but in reality when you're a Black person walking in there, you don't really feel that diversity. . . . And it becomes really hard to figure out that point in time when you have to tell your kid that they are a minority, and they could be treated differently.

Lisa continued to audit discriminatory incidents for the next several years. When her daughter scored within the 99th percentile and was accepted into a prestigious citywide G&T school that was "infamous for not having enough people of color," Lisa also began monitoring her daughter's experience. She worried about the lack of diversity at her daughter's school:

> When you walk into a school and you see that—that's a lack of diversity, it's physical, physical attributes of diversity. And I ask myself, why don't we just create the algorithm to benefit them more since they're disproportionately not involved in these schools Right? And that's been happening for years, and it hasn't improved. It seems like nothing is happening, nothing is changing.

Lisa experienced ongoing uncertainty about her enrollment decisions upon confronting unexpectedly stratified racial and ethnic classes at her children's schools. Lisa closely monitored how her children were treated in school because she feared for how segregated school environments would shape her children's experiences in the years to come.

Parents also increased their racialized auditing if their children reported being bullied. Deborah, a white, middle-class mother married to a Dominican Afro-Latino husband, closely monitored bullying at her children's school.

Deborah is part of a blended family, and her husband's older daughter from a previous relationship in the Dominican Republic also lives with them and her two younger children. Deborah's stepdaughter moved to the United States in fourth grade and began attending the same school as her two younger children.

While most of the white working-class and middle-class mothers I interviewed did not monitor racial climates to assess racial biases at their children's school, Deborah described the ways she advocated for her stepdaughter when a racially charged incident occurred at her school. Deborah knew that the transition would be challenging for her stepdaughter, who needed to learn a new language and adapt to life in New York City. At first Deborah believed the school offered an ideal learning environment for her stepdaughter:

> The kids seemed to be very diverse mostly. I always tell people you never really know the makeup of your neighborhood until you go to a school. School is the one time when everybody's got to come together at one spot. At eight o-clock everyone's there. So, I would say the majority are probably Middle Eastern, Asian, and Eastern European. And the teachers, I would say the majority are white or Russian.

While Deborah appreciated the school's cultural diversity, she recalled that some parents in the neighborhood were uncomfortable with the school's racial diversity. Hearing these kinds of comments heightened Deborah's concern, but she nevertheless believed the school would be a good fit for her stepdaughter because it provided additional services for English language learners.

Deborah's stepdaughter began learning English quickly. After her stepdaughter had been at the school for a few months, however, Deborah grew increasingly concerned about bullying and racial discrimination:

> Earlier this year a little boy, two little boys actually called my bigger daughter a burnt marshmallow. And then they said a few other things. Interesting thing is that they are Brown as well. So, it was like where did you hear this and what do we do? I think that growing up here and knowing the history of things that happen is different than people who come here and don't necessarily know it. And especially a child, I think thankfully a lot of it was lost on innocence. It's unfortunate that the little boys probably heard it at home and were just repeating it.

Deborah worried about the racial climate these interactions created for her daughter. After the incident, she audited the school climate more vigilantly and sought a direct conversation with the other parents involved: "As soon as I brought it up to the school, they were on it. But they don't allow parents in to talk to one another. The principal says the reason they don't do that is because you never know the temperament of parents and he doesn't want to have to end up calling the police to come in and deal with parents. . . . So, I do wish that they had a way to facilitate conflict resolution." Deborah engaged in additional racialized labor for her daughter by reaching out to the parents on her own and more closely monitoring how the school approached discipline.

In some instances, after hearing about incidents of race-based school bullying, parents of color decided that removing their child from the school was a better option. Deja, a single, Black working-class mother and a childcare provider from East Harlem, described the challenges she faced in trying to find a racially inclusive space for her daughter. Deja grew up attending private schools in the southern United States and New York City, and so her first thought was to enroll her daughter in a private school, with the support of scholarships. Deja quickly realized that while the schools were academically strong, they did not feel racially inclusive:

> She's been in very, very good schools and majority of the time it's predominantly white with only a few people of color. It's difficult for me to explain that because you're Black and this person is white, this might happen. I try not to impose certain things on her. I need for her to grow as herself as an individual and to form her own ideas. But it's hard when you meet parents, and you meet other people, and they don't teach their kids about race.

Deja perceived that other families at her daughter's school rarely initiated discussions about racial differences, and she felt this negatively shaped her daughter's experience in school.

Months into the school year, when her daughter experienced race-based bullying, Deja felt the school did very little to support her daughter or respond to her concerns:

> A few kids at the school bullied her. They put thumbtacks in the chair. One of them tried to push her down the stairs. I was there pleading with the principal to do something, threaten them with the suspension, call the parents. She did nothing. So, I called all the top people. I pleaded with this principal, and she begged me not to do anything. You don't take matters into your own hands and then this? Like what do you want a parent to do?

When Deja had exhausted her efforts at addressing bullying at the private parochial school, she tried out the local zoned school. Her daughter's school experience improved, but Deja was concerned about the quality of the curriculum. Deja's racialized auditing extended to an additional academic year, as she next placed her daughter in a predominately Black charter school that she hoped would safeguard her daughter from discriminatory experiences. Since switching schools, Deja has felt that her daughter is much more comfortable.

The school has a strict antibullying commitment, and her daughter has been supported academically.

Children's experiences with racism and bullying in schools pushed parents to approach school environments more critically, taking time and extra steps to audit school climates to protect their children from discriminatory incidents. The steps parents of color take to audit school racial climates and investigate instances of discrimination extended the labor required to search for schools and finalize school decisions.

Racialized Resistance and Deflection

By design, school choice policies prioritize individual decision-making.[25] In practice, this concept of "consumer-citizenship" requires parents to engage in intense relational work to learn about their school options and to access schools for enrollment. Persistent segregation and racial discrimination within schools can make the task of deciding on a school more challenging for Black, Latina/o, and immigrant parents. As part of the school choice process, parents of color engage in racialized deflection as a means of offsetting experiences of racial bias. When parents of color experience opposition to their racialized labor, they describe measures they take to redirect and manage their own experiences of racial exclusion from school staff, teachers, and other parents.

Talita, a single, Black middle-class mother who grew up in a small, predominately white neighborhood just outside of Seattle, Washington, described the constant prejudgment she experienced from school staff as she became involved in her children's elementary school. Reflecting on her own childhood, where she was one of just a "handful of the minority students" at her school, she recalled that she didn't receive the support she needed. When it came time to decide on schools for her children, the school providing a "sense of belonging" was key. While Talita appreciates the rich cultural diversity of her Washington Heights neighborhood and the many local amenities like restaurants and hair salons, she realized that many of the schools in her neighborhood were underperforming.

A fellow church member who regularly cared for Talita's children offered to share her address so Talita could enroll her children in a better-performing school on the Upper West Side. While she felt her children were receiving a better education at the school, she encountered constant resistance from teachers and school staff when she tried to advocate for her children:

Most of the faculty are white, including the teachers and the principal. And I think the way that they interact comes with this prejudgment. . . . The way that they came at me was like she looks young, and she might not be as educated. So, their actions showed that. So, they may already have this idea that whatever they say goes. And then they don't listen. So, there's definitely class and racism issues that do exist in that environment.

Talita recognized how staff members' perceptions about her identity shaped how they treated her. She noted that the staff and teachers were "hostile" to her and many other parents of color at the school.

The school was located near a low-income housing complex. Talita believed that many teachers and school staff assumed that all the families of color at the school were poor and did not value education. Talita explained the horrific ways students were disciplined at the school and how this shaped how teachers interacted with her: "So, I've seen cases where kids, fourth graders were escorted by four cops in handcuffs. So, I think they . . . feel like they're higher." Talita also had concerns about racial segregation across classrooms at the school. For Talita, the separated classes and discriminatory treatment of students of color shaped her interactions with leadership and teachers at the school. Her experiences illustrate the deep contradictions and inequalities parents of color experience as they engage in racialized labor for their children. Parents of color seek opportunities to advance their children's interests, yet they face resistance from school administrators when exercising their strategies for engagement. Talita responded to the opposition she experienced by deflecting her treatment and redirecting her efforts to advocate for her children. She described her constant communication with her son's teacher to ensure he was supported in his class.

> I feel like I constantly have to step in and talk to the teachers and help them counsel and help them mediate situations. So, I find myself staying on top of the teachers. It's constant, on a weekly basis I've set up to make sure that we're all on the same page and that I'm doing everything I need to do as a parent to make sure my son is maximizing his potential at the school. . . . I'm a huge advocate for my children's education. My children have to feel like the school is a place of belonging and I need to feel safe as their mom.

Talita's own negative treatment as a parent at the school compelled her to focus her efforts on ensuring her children experienced a positive learning environment.

Immigrant mothers also shared experiences in which teachers and staff marginalized them. A combination of limited resources for parents who did not speak English and dismissiveness from teachers who were reluctant to interact with them challenged their ability to build relationships at their children's school. Immigrant mothers attempted to evaluate school options and interact with teachers and school staff, but many of them consistently felt excluded from their children's school community.

Yan, a middle-class Chinese immigrant and a stay-at-home mom, lived on the Upper West Side with her husband and daughter, having moved from France a few years earlier. While Yan enjoys the upper-middle-class amenities her neighborhood offers, she noted that "it's not very racially mixed. We are family that is mixed. My husband is French, and I'm Chinese. Here, I think the neighborhood is quite 'white.'" Yan's experiences of racial exclusion in her neighborhood extended to her experiences at her daughter's neighborhood school.

Yan described how they first enrolled her daughter in a private Catholic daycare connected to the Catholic church they attended regularly. The amount of information seemed overwhelming to Yan, who had limited knowledge of the school system: "It was like a full-time job to apply for kindergarten for her. I only moved here only a couple of years ago. So, I was not familiar with the school system, and the society, or even the language and culture of things. I felt that I was excluded." Yan considered the citywide G&T schools but settled on the G&T class at the local neighborhood school.

Overall, Yan has felt satisfied with her daughter's school. She felt, however, that her immigrant background as well as cultural differences in expectations of involvement have made it more difficult to build relationships at her daughter's predominately white school:

> I think there's a cultural difference because it's completely different. In China, the parents are not involved in elementary school. It's 100 percent managed by teachers and the principal, so the parents are not allowed in the school. During the day or on field trip, there are no parents, and there are not parents for pickup and drop off. So, we don't really talk to teachers like the way it is for my daughter's school.

During her daughter's first year at the school, Yan tried to adapt to these new expectations. She became involved in school activities, but often still felt excluded: "So, I'm very active in my daughter's school. I was a class parent, and I was the auction cochair. So, I did a lot for the school, and I'm always there when the staff meet the parents or if they need a financial aid donation for our teachers. I was always the first to volunteer. But I still felt that I was a little bit excluded compared to some of the other mothers." Yan's feelings of exclusion have shaped her comfort at school events and her interactions with school staff and parents. Yan noted that she primarily interacts with another Chinese family at her daughter's school: "There's not much exchanges with most of the mothers, we don't talk much. The kids can still play together, but we don't exchange a lot of what we really feel. So, it's a little bit delicate to talk about this kind of stuff. But the two or three that I could exchange with are also Chinese, so we feel closer." Like Talita, Yan's experiences of exclusion limited her ability to interact and build relationships with school staff and teachers. Despite her feelings of isolation at the school, Yan deflected and built strong relationships with other Chinese families.

Other working-class immigrant mothers like Manuela experienced exclusion because few services were offered in their native languages. Manuela grew up in Mexico City and moved to New York City when she was twelve. She searched for progressive schools in Washington Heights, where she attended middle and high school. Manuela was delighted and relieved when her daughter was accepted into her top choice school. After a year, she found the school to be marginalizing for Latina/o parents: "But every school has pros and cons it has great in terms of education, but I feel like they don't count us, the minority. Like Spanish people we don't count for them because the majority is white, and they are rich, and they have good jobs not like us low-income families. The principal always listens to what they say but, when it comes to us, we have to just deal with it." Although Manuela found it difficult for her and other Latina/o families to make their voices heard, she responded by becoming more involved, both as a way to learn more about programs and resources and to advocate for other Latina/o families at the school. In partnership with a few other parents at the school, Manuela brought some of these issues to the attention of the principal:

> A couple of us parents got together, and we went to the principal, and we said we feel unwelcome here. We come to the PA [parent association] meetings and there's no one translating there. It's so disrespectful. And she said "sorry," and she said she would do something, but she never did, so we stopped going. But I talked to my friends and the next incoming PA is going to be us. . . . So, I ended up being the vice president and my friend was the treasurer.

Manuela's daughter also experienced marginalizing treatment at the school. She shared that she believes school staff favor white children and parents at the school in both obvious and subtle ways:

> My daughter was bullied by one kid for a long time. And I figured out that because she was white, they were finding excuses for the kid because there was another girl who bullied kids, and she was Colombian and they had no problem suspending her all the time. Every time she did something. But this one because she was white, all they did was give excuses like "Oh she's been through a lot." I told them, "I feel like because my daughter is Hispanic and she's white you give preference to the other girl."

Manuela's involvement in the parent association gives her the confidence to advocate for her daughter and point out punishment discrepancies.

Even so, most of the parents Manuela feels comfortable communicating with on a regular basis are Latina/o. She expressed difficulty in trusting and interacting with the school staff:

> Most of my friends at the school are Hispanic, I found them at the school. Now that I'm more involved, I can talk more to the principal. But she is like a woman with a thousand masks. She can give you one face right now when she needs you but then other times not pay attention. Now the superintendent is Dominican and so now when he comes to the school, she asks me to help because he's coming and she wants to show her support for Hispanic people.

Manuela explained that the principal seems to care about diversity and the perspectives of the Latina/o community at the school only when it serves her. She and other families at the school can tell that this interest is inauthentic. Even though Manuela appreciates the school's academic environment, she constantly deals with discrimination and exclusion.

The experiences of the Black, Latina/o, and immigrant mothers demonstrate the forms of marginalization parents of color experience as they attempt to communicate and interact with teachers and school staff. These marginalizing experiences with teachers and school leaders challenge parents' ability to advocate for their children. Communication challenges and race-based discrimination in schools intensify the school search process for Black, Latina/o, and immigrant mothers. Despite the ongoing isolation parents of color experience, they continue to engage in racialized labor by deflecting attention away from their own marginalizing experiences and redirecting their efforts to make sure their children feel supported.

Symbolic Diversity Intentions

For Black, Latina/o, and immigrant parents across all class backgrounds, concerns about racial inclusion were at the forefront of their school search process. In contrast, only a few white mothers noted concerns about diversity. Prior research has found that white parents often avoid predominately Black and multiracial school settings.[26] Similarly, over 80 percent of the white mothers I interviewed selected schools that were less than 75 percent Black and Latina/o, compared to the majority of Black and Latina/o parents I interviewed who selected schools that were predominately Black and Latina/o. Although most white mothers in my study often did not express concerns about a school's level of racial inclusivity directly, their school preferences indicate that they excluded schools with large numbers of Black and Latina/o students.

I found that the white mothers who mentioned concerns related to diversity were the few mothers who also sent their children to schools with more racially diverse student bodies. As prior research has suggested, these mothers desired to expose their children to diversity.[27] For white, middle-class parents, diversity represents an opportunity to enrich their children's lives.[28] This approach to what Megan Underhill has called "exposure to diversity strategies" stands in marked contrast to the ways parents of color engage in racialized labor before, during, and after school enrollment. The white mothers in my study often described a school's diversity as an added benefit for their child, but they did not hold the same fears for their children's racial comfort and safety that Black, Latina/o, and immigrant parents had. I focus here on the white mothers who sent their children to schools with larger numbers of Black and Latina/o students.

Jaime, a white, middle-class mother of a kindergartner, for instance, hoped to prepare her son for an increasingly diverse nation. She saw her school decision as an intentional "social justice" decision and wanted her choice to reflect a stance for greater school equity. Jaime loved being able to raise her son in a place as diverse as New York City. She explained with gratitude, "I wasn't aware, wasn't aware of half of the things my son is aware of growing up in the city. He is able to see that there are different ways to be a family. . . . The neighborhood is diverse, socioeconomically it's also diverse racially. All kinds of people which is one of the things I like about the neighborhood." Jaime shared that the city's diversity provides an added social value by facilitating interracial contact for her son. Jaime also thought about her son's exposure to diversity when making decisions about the school he would attend. However, Jaime found that parents she had befriended from very early in her son's life had vastly different perspectives about schools and racial and ethnic diversity. Jaime pointed toward a significant tipping point in one of these relationships:

> One of the things I realized going through the process is that you also stop talking to people who don't have the same goals as you. I ended up learning a lot about the things that other parents value. Our neighbor downstairs put their daughter in the Gifted & Talented program, but they had a private tutor who prepped her for the tests. A lot of parents did that, and I wasn't willing to do that. We were not going to test our son for the Gifted & Talented exam because I think it's keeping our schools segregated by socioeconomic status and race. And I decided I really don't even believe that kids should be heterogeneously grouped.

Jaime grappled with her relationships to other families and her beliefs about equality in education as she searched for schools. Having attended schools in the South that were integrated through mandated busing, Jaime hoped for a similarly racially diverse educational experience for her son.

After going on many school tours and attending seminars, Jaime realized that the only way her son would experience more diversity was if he attended a dual language program. She narrowed her search down to schools in her district that offered dual language classes, only to find that tracked classes in the school she toured still reflected stark racial divisions: "It's frightening to see that the Gifted & Talented classes are majority white kids, the dual-language classes almost all Hispanic, and the Gen Ed is more of a mix but they're predominantly African American. I didn't want my son to grow up with that because kids when they're little they are impressionable and they're going to form these ideas." Jaime ended up finding a school for her son that better reflects the diversity of the city. She felt better about the makeup of the school and her son's classmates:

> It feels diverse when you walk in. We are probably in the minority as a Caucasian family. There's also a very international student body. There are a lot of West Africans and Hispanics, and then there seems to be some Eastern Europeans, some European parents like from France. . . . The school feels warm, and the PTA is small and active. It has the feel of a neighborhood school.

In an increasingly diverse nation, some white middle-class parents were concerned about a school's ability to promote equity.[29] Jaime's own approach to diversity moreover emphasized a different set of issues than the racialized labor Black, Latina/o, and immigrant parents took on during the school search. Instead of racialized gauging, auditing, or deflecting, Jaime worried primarily about the possibility that her son would form stereotypes at an early age if he saw stark racial disparities in his school.

Research has indicated that members of the middle class attempt to express ease when interacting with people from different ethnic and racial backgrounds as a way of achieving class distinction.[30] Yet there are limits to white parents' commitment to racial inclusion, at least when it comes to their children's education. White parents' school enrollment decisions often reflect their avoidance of schools with high numbers of Black students.[31]

Other white middle-class mothers, like Chelsea, similarly believed that diversity was important in school environments, but she did not believe that a lack of diversity would harm her child's identity. Accordingly, once she decided on a school, she did not audit racial incidents at her child's school. Chelsea attended a magnet elementary school and elite private middle and high schools in her Upper West Side neighborhood. She appreciated that her elementary school helped her recognize her privilege compared to her classmates, an experience that she credits with giving her an understanding rather than a fear of social differences. She contrasted that spirit of inclusion with the sense of entitlement on display at her former high school:

> I found that the two private schools that I went to, the message I got was you are the elite, so you've got access to things. You're lucky to be here because what you're getting is better than what anyone else is getting. It was this pecking order type attitude, as opposed to the way I felt in elementary school. And so, I guess my takeaway was that a school has to have enough academic resources, but that the sense of community, the values of the school that pervade the school has to be healthier and more beneficial. It should reflect the diversity of the world. The school should reflect that we're all in this together, and let's learn from each other and learn together.

Now, as a parent, Chelsea believes in the importance of creating an environment that supports her value for community and togetherness in selecting a school. Chelsea explained how she had to resist efforts from the staff at her son's private preschool who encouraged her to consider elite private schools. Even when her son scored high enough on the G&T test to be considered for a variety of G&T schools, she specifically turned away from schools that seemed to promote classroom homogeneity and tracking:

> We liked this school better, because we didn't like the way that the Gifted & Talented class was separate at the others. I didn't think that was a great message. I like that the teachers are able to do differentiated learning, like they teach to kids who have different strengths, and everyone is challenged in their own way. And I philosophically agree with that.

Chelsea's educational experiences growing up have motivated her to seek out a school environment for her children that values social diversity while also promoting a sense of community and togetherness.

White mothers also experienced significantly less friction in their interactions with school staff, both during and after their search, than did the Black, Latina/o, and immigrant families in my study. The experiences of Patricia, a white, working-class mother, are typical. Patricia "scouted" for schools around the neighborhood, "so I basically just went into a few schools and talked to the principals and did the legwork." Patricia felt comfortable throughout all aspects of her search and knew that she could ask for assistance along the way. She navigated interactions with schoolteachers and administrators with ease, and she felt confident reaching out to other parents for help. Patricia also explained that she received a lot of assistance and advice from teachers at her daughter's daycare, even without asking: "They were extremely helpful and extremely knowledgeable. They actually were the ones who pushed her to take the G&T tests, and they provided the open house dates for the different schools so parents could go and see what was happening. So those teachers were very helpful." Once her daughter was enrolled in school, Patricia continued to feel at ease communicating with the school administration: "I really like [that] things are set in stone, the rules are the rules but it's like life itself, we have to be flexible. Conflicts occur, things happen, but everybody works on it together and the resolution is always there. So, the administration is very open to parents' input and they encourage parents to become a part of it, which we absolutely love." When I asked Patricia how comfortable she felt expressing concerns at the school, she enthusiastically said, "Totally, absolutely." Patricia also described positive everyday interactions with her child's teacher: "Basically every time I pick her up, I see them, and I ask is everything going okay? Is there anything we need to do? How was the day?"

Compared to the Black, Latina/o, and immigrant mothers who described marginalizing encounters with school staff, Patricia felt comfortable and confident interacting with parents and school administration. She found the staff to be welcoming and accepting of her ideas, and she felt at ease communicating with teachers and advocating for her daughter. Patricia experienced "moments of inclusion" as she built connections at her daughter's school.[32] In contrast to the Black, Latina/o, and immigrant parents whose queries were dismissed or ignored, Patricia's attempts at engagement were supported and welcomed.

To the extent that white mothers like Chelsea, Jaime, and Patricia mentioned diversity at all, their interest was driven by a desire to enrich their children's experience, rather than to protect their children's safety and self-identity. My findings suggest that white families have different ways of conceptualizing diversity. For instance, most white mothers I interviewed rarely considered schools with a majority Black or Latina/o student body. The white mothers who did consider more diverse schools believed doing so would have potentially positive long-term life outcomes for their children. In contrast, Black, Latina/o, and immigrant parents expressed great concern for how their children would fare in schools. They continuously engaged in racialized decision labor in their search for schools. The stark racial differences in how parents approach the school search process highlight the racialized burdens that school choice policy has placed on parents of color.

Conclusion

Black, Latina/o, and immigrant parents engage in additional racialized labor to make sure that schools provide a sense of racial comfort and safety for their children. They approach school decision-making with deep concerns about how schools will support their children's racial identity. Parents of color search

TABLE 5. Sample characteristics across racial/ethnic background ($N = 102$)

	Asian ($n = 12$)	Black ($n = 41$)	Latina/o ($n = 32$)	White ($n = 17$)
Household income				
<50,000	1	31	22	6
>50,000	11	10	10	11
Type of school				
Not zoned by address	10	23	20	10
Zoned by address	2	18	12	7
Distance traveled to school[a]				
<0.5 miles	7	9	10	3
>0.5 miles	5	32	22	14
School racial composition[b]				
>75% Black and Latina/o	4	31	21	3
<75% Black and Latina/o	8	10	11	14
Home neighborhood racial composition[c]				
>50% Black and Latina/o	6	30	24	8
<50% Black and Latina/o	6	11	8	9
Home neighborhood poverty composition[d]				
Low poverty (<20%)	7	6	6	9
Above average poverty (20–30%)	5	32	21	8
High poverty (30–40%)	0	3	5	0

a. Distance categories selected based on New York City transportation eligibility parameters (NYC Public Schools, "Transportation Eligibility").

b. Data retrieved from NYC Open Data ("2013–2018 Demographic Snapshot School") provided by the NYC Department of Education. Racial composition data are based on percentages from 2016–17 school year when the majority of interviews were conducted.

c. Racial composition estimates modified from the U.S. Census Bureau interpolated intercensal population estimates, 2000–2021.

d. Poverty levels retrieved from the American Community Survey and augmented by NYC Opportunity ("Poverty Measure").

intensively for schools they feel will appropriately balance academic rigor and racial diversity. Once their children are enrolled in schools, they intensively monitor racial climates to protect their children from discriminatory incidents. But as parents engage in racialized labor through the enrollment process for their children, they simultaneously experience marginalizing treatment from school staff, teachers, and other parents. Together, these additional efforts demonstrate the intensive racialized labor strategies Black, Latina/o, and immigrant parents employ to protect their children. Parents' investment in these strategies demonstrates the amplified structural inequalities marginalized families experience as they engage in school decision-making.

Black, Latina/o, and immigrant parents have always had to engage in additional labor to raise their children, but the task of deciding on a school in the current school choice environment poses new, increasingly unpredictable challenges. For the parents of color in my study, the additional school options under New York City's school choice system also meant additional potential risks—that their child might end up in a school with few other children who looked like them or that they might endure racial experiences that challenge their racial identity. Black, Latina/o, and immigrant parents moreover encountered these risks within the context of persistent racial and ethnic inequalities. School options have increased, yet stark variation in school quality and school racial and ethnic composition have remain unchanged. Segregated school environments and neighborhoods create challenges for parents attempting to find racially balanced and high-quality schools. Teachers' and other parents' racial biases shape how parents are treated when engaging with schools and shape their children's everyday experiences in schools.

There are vast racial and ethnic differences in how parents experience the risk of school decision-making. White parents did not approach the school search with concerns about their children's racial identity, instead viewing a school's racial diversity as an added enrichment opportunity or perhaps a stance for racial justice. Black, Latina/o, and immigrant parents, in contrast, encountered the school search process as an intensive exercise in gauging, auditing, and resisting various forms of exclusion. The school search is a racialized process—one in which parents of color search for schools that are racially inclusive and that will support their children's growth and development, all while experiencing active resistance from school staff.

If parents of color are increasingly charged with searching for schools in a high-stakes environment, we must take seriously how school choice policies reproduce inequality.[33] The nation's legacy of discrimination in educational settings and the perpetuation of segregated neighborhoods continue to constrain how parents make choices and create an unequal school choice landscape.

4

Dealing with the World
Outside the Door

COMMUNITY WORK AND CULTIVATING
NEIGHBORHOOD ENGAGEMENT

ABOUT A DECADE AGO, Kimberly, a Latina middle-class mother, and her then-fiancé moved to Sunnyside, Queens, in hopes of building a community for their kids. The couple originally lived in Manhattan, but her soon-to-be husband's law school journey brought them to Queens. They liked the space available in Queens and ended up staying. After a few years, they had their son and later their daughter and eventually bought a house in Sunnyside.

Kimberly shared her appreciation for the neighborhood's strong sense of community and its rich history in contrast to her childhood growing up just outside of D.C.:

> I studied history at Columbia, so I really liked the history of Sunnyside Gardens because it was built as kind of like a community for the working class. And I like the history behind the community too. There's still the community aspect that is there that survived for the past almost hundred years. Here it feels like you know your neighbors. It's like kind of something that I didn't have growing up that my kids run next door and go see their friends who may go two doors down and their friends are there or around the corner. So, there are a lot of kids who are my children's age.

As her kids have gotten older, however, Kimberly has found it challenging to maintain that same community feeling. Kimberly had hoped that her kids would attend the neighborhood school, to better develop long-term friendships with other children along their block. Kimberly had her son take the G&T exam, with the intention that he would attend the G&T class at the local school. But when she learned that he would have been in a class with forty other kids, she changed the plan. Her son would attend a citywide school with a strong G&T program. Most of the other parents in the neighborhood made similar decisions for their kids: "None of the kids that my son knows in the neighborhood went to our zoned school. They all went to other G&T programs across the district or across the city or they went to Catholic school, or they went to charter schools. And for my daughter, most of them didn't go either. They were all being bused to other places."

Kimberly moved to this neighborhood, in part, because she wanted her kids to have a stronger sense of community in the neighborhood. This hasn't necessarily happened—and Kimberly blames school choice. She has met a lot of parents in the neighborhood, and she feels comfortable and close to other parents she met when her children were young, but the relationships are different now that her kids don't have strong neighborhood friendships. School zoning changes, new DOE policies, and better school options outside of the neighborhood have meant that her kids rarely interact with other kids in the neighborhood.

In hopes of maintaining stronger neighborhood connections for her daughter, Kimberly enrolled her daughter in the local neighborhood school. Eventually, however, her daughter scored high enough on the G&T exam to be admitted to the same school that her brother attended. The decision to change schools was easy for Kimberly and her husband: not only would sending both of their children to the same school ease logistics, but the fact that it was a K–12 program meant that they wouldn't have to worry about finding a new school for either child until college. Her daughter was less happy with the decision and begged to go back to her old school in the neighborhood.

> And so, I've been on the fence about sending her back even though I love the new school. She has a lot of anxiety issues, and I guess like I've also learned after being at the citywide school, it's really hard to have a community within the school. Kids live all over. My daughter misses her friends because she had a lot of friends, not just in her class but a lot of friends from her neighborhood. They all went to the school, and they were in other classes, so she saw all of her friends. She misses going to school with kids who live near her.

The very community Kimberly had hoped to cultivate by moving to Queens had virtually disappeared as her kids and her friends' kids traversed different neighborhoods each day to attend schools. This chapter examines how parents like Kimberly reevaluate their relationship to their neighborhoods in the context of school choice. In the sections that follow I describe the context of school choice across New York City neighborhoods and parents' neighborhood engagement strategies. I highlight how the expansion of school choice and persistent inequalities across neighborhoods shape how connected families feel to their neighbors.

School Decision-Making and Neighborhood
Ties in New York City

The growth of school options has occurred as traditional neighborhood schools have seen decreased enrollment across every borough in New York City.[1] As the sheer number and availability of school options have increased, parents' connections to their neighbors have also shifted. The new labor of school decision-making requires parents to simultaneously manage the search for their child's school and their engagement in the neighborhood. Because my interviews focused on parents with elementary-aged children, parents often described residential decisions that preceded their search for their child's school. Once their children reached kindergarten age, however, parents re-evaluated their neighborhoods in relation to their child's school.

The few middle-class parents at the top of the economic spectrum living in wealthy neighborhoods and high-performing school districts rarely had to decouple their neighborhood and school decisions.[2] Instead, these parents were satisfied with their neighborhoods and felt comfortable sending their children to the neighborhood zoned school. New York City data support this pattern as zone retention rates are the highest in District 2, one of the wealthiest districts in New York City.[3] However, most parents I interviewed felt they did not have this option and decided to enroll their children in schools outside of the neighborhood. Nearly 70 percent of the parents I interviewed traveled over a half a mile from their home to their child's school.[4]

The experiences of the parents I interviewed also mirror broader decision-making patterns for parents of elementary-aged children across New York City. In recent years nearly thirty thousand kindergarten students have left their homes every morning to attend schools outside of their residential school zone.[5] Since 2000, the number of elementary zoned schools has decreased while the numbers of charter schools, nonzoned schools, schools with a dual language program, and schools with a G&T program have all increased. Over this same period, Black, Hispanic, and free-lunch-eligible students have been less likely to attend their zoned schools and more likely to travel farther from their home to their school relative to white students.[6] Families living in predominately low-income school districts are more likely to leave their home districts to attend school elsewhere, creating additional travel burdens and weakening how closely connected working-class children are to their neighborhoods. The persistence of segregated neighborhoods in New York City means all families do not have the same access to high-quality schools in their home neighborhoods.

Pursuing higher-quality alternative schools and exiting the neighborhood is a burden that parents of color and working-class parents must increasingly take on as school options expand and as New York City neighborhoods have experienced decades of divestment.[7] While many areas in New York City experienced rapid divestment in the 1970s, neighborhood gentrification has brought middle-class families back to the city and increased the competition for schools.[8] Parents who move to newly gentrified areas often do not select the same schools or engage in the same activities as long-term residents.[9]

Neighborhood reputation also shapes the schools parents consider for enrollment and parents' access to resources about school options.[10] Parents often conceptualize available school options and frame their school decisions based on how they perceive the built environment and their own communities.[11] In parents' assessments of their neighborhoods, local organizations and schools often serve as landmarks and social anchors that link parents to their communities.[12] Local connections to fellow parents and community members can shape parents' perceptions of the neighborhood and their sense of community.[13]

The expansion of school choices often means parents are pulled in different directions outside of the neighborhood and schools are no longer local anchors.[14] Sociologist, Julia Burdick-Will finds that parents who have a child attending the local neighborhood school report stronger social and spatial connections to their home neighborhoods relative to parents who travel for school.[15] For parents of color and working-class parents deepening connections to their child's school community may mean they and their children have decreased connections to their home neighborhoods. I argue that because school choice expansion in New York City continues to operate within a segregated school system, parents develop different strategies for interacting within neighborhoods and selecting schools. These strategies vary according to their social class background and place of residence.

Many working-class parents lamented the loss of community and the safety of community schools. They described severely restricting their neighborhood interactions through *neighborhood distancing*. They withdrew from their neighbors and neighborhood activities, instead seeking opportunities and schools outside of their home communities. These parents knew few of their neighbors but forged friendships with many parents outside of the neighborhood. Other working-class families, and some middle-class families living in lower-income neighborhoods, *selectively engaged* in neighborhood activities to manage fears of community loss. They strategically selected whom they and their kids would interact with in the neighborhood and sent their kids to schools outside the community or local zoned and nonzoned schools that attracted kids from across the city. These parents had a few neighborhood friends and a few parent friends from their children's schools. Inequalities across neighborhoods shaped parents' access to ties and comfortability interacting with neighbors. School choices expand where children attend school and inevitably scatter and weaken local community ties for low-income families and those living in low-income neighborhoods.

Last, many of the middle-class parents I interviewed who lived in higher-income neighborhoods managed their fears of community loss through *inclusion strategies*. They bridged friendships and hoped to re-create a sense of community for their children. These parents often searched for charter schools and nonzoned options that were in their local communities. Some middle-class families, especially middle-class families of color, attempted to exercise similar strategies but found their options constrained by a variety of circumstances, particularly their residence in relatively lower income neighborhoods.[16] These families drew closer to neighbors and extended great effort to organize playdates and activities for their children. They often sent their children to schools well outside the bounds of their home neighborhoods. They struggled to juggle friendships with parents in and outside their neighborhoods and engaged in *inclusion strategies with constraints*.

In my interviews, parents noted a variety of non-school-related factors that influenced their attitudes about their neighborhoods. For instance, parents discussed how transportation concerns and work constraints were instrumental in their decisions about schools. Research also has demonstrated that parents' geographic preferences for schools are tied to their notions of space and place and their ideas about parenting, identity, and child development.[17] This chapter specifically focuses on the consequences of school choice and the school-related factors that drive and shape parents' neighborhood interaction strategies. As Kimberly's experience suggests, parents' relative closeness to neighbors and to the broader community shifts as children attend school outside of their residential neighborhood. I argue that Kimberly's experience also reflects how parents' experiences are deeply tied to the structural inequalities plaguing neighborhoods and the uneven access to quality schools across neighborhoods.

As we shall see, the greater availability of school choice options not only complicates how parents make school decisions but also challenges parents' ability to build neighborhood connections and foster a sense of community for their children. This chapter helps us understand how parents make sense of their school decision-making and their children's neighborhood experiences at a time when school choice policies have expanded traditional neighborhood boundaries.

Neighborhood Distancing Strategies

I met with Christopher, a working-class Black father and Bronx native, at a local Starbucks. Christopher works as a security guard just outside this neighborhood, where he has lived for most of his life. He lives with his wife and their

four-year-old daughter and seven-month-old son. Growing up, Christopher's
family sent him to schools across his neighborhood, hopeful for better educational opportunities. During our conversation, Christopher lamented that the
neighborhood was changing and becoming unsafe and crime-ridden: "I would
say if you have to live in the Bronx, where I am is pretty much better than a lot
of places, a lot less volatile. But the environment is starting to go down a little
bit, just the whole surrounding area."

Christopher's immediate family started moving out of the neighborhood
about five years ago. Now, with hardly anyone left, his ties to the community
are limited. Christopher has also restricted his interactions in the neighborhood
because he feels his neighborhood is not conducive to raising a child. He feels
uncomfortable bringing his daughter to playgrounds and finds it difficult to
find safe play areas. Worried for his daughter's safety, he exits the neighborhood when looking for activities for her. He feels like outside areas are better,
a conclusion he reached after visiting his relatives who moved out of the city:
"The environment is a bit more conducive to the welfare of a child. Seeing my
cousins who have moved and went to certain schools, they were able to have
more. The environment was better, and they had more offered to them like
sports, and they thrived. I want that for my children."

Christopher's hopes for a stronger community life—his strategy for achieving neighborhood security—center on exiting the neighborhood. He's waiting
for the right time to move, but for now he and his wife have decided to send
their daughter to a school outside of his neighborhood. Christopher feels happy
with the decision and has formed connections with the school administration
and other parents at the school. His social ties are increasingly embedded in
these school networks, unmoored from place, rather than neighborhood proximity. Christopher's shifting social ties also demonstrate how neighborhood
disparities increase feelings of isolation in lower income communities.

Donna, a working-class Black mother and home attendant whom we heard
from in chapter 1, describes similar limited interactions with residents in her
neighborhood. Donna grew up in a low-income housing development in
Brooklyn and nearly two decades ago moved to Manhattan's Lower East Side,
where she now raises her two sons. Like Christopher, Donna laments the loss
of community in her neighborhood. She sees how sections of the Lower East
Side have improved over the years but still finds it difficult to trust people in
her community: "Basically, I stay by myself in this neighborhood. Because the
people are not genuine. The block is all right if people stay to yourself and
leave people be. But the neighborhood has changed over the years. . . . Like
the building I used to live in, I knew everybody and now I don't really know
the people that's moving in." Donna's comments reflect how long-term community residents experience gentrification.[18] She finds it difficult to trust the

new people in the neighborhood and struggles to adapt to a changing community culture.[19] Research has demonstrated that the process of gentrification can disrupt the social fabric of neighborhoods, making it harder for residents to build social connections and leverage networks for social support.[20]

Amid all this change, Donna has withdrawn from people and activities in the neighborhood because she feels this is the best method for protecting her children. As she explained, "You don't know what your kid is doing when you're not around." Donna's limited interaction with her neighbors is a proactive buffering parenting strategy meant to safeguard her son from neighborhood harm.[21] Donna's strategy also reveals how neighborhood disadvantages drive parents' decisions to limit interactions.

A yearlong bullying incident at the local school her son first attended also shifted Donna's sense of closeness to the community. Donna switched her son to a school outside of the neighborhood that she feels is much more supportive. Her son fell behind at his last school because of the constant bullying, but his new school has what Donna calls a "hands-on" approach. She said the school is "more for the kids."

With her son's move to a new school, Donna has accelerated her distancing from the neighborhood. She now participates in fewer community activities and interacts less frequently with neighbors as she spends more time at her son's school. At the same time, she has shifted her social ties to her son's new school.

Shamara, a working-class Black mother of three boys and a package handler, similarly relies on her son's out-of-neighborhood school for connections to other parents and more suitable interactions. Shamara grew up in the Bronx and moved around frequently as a child. She raises her three sons in a low-income housing development in the Bronx. Like Christopher and Donna, she maintains her distance when interacting with people in the neighborhood.

> For the most part I'm always in and out of my building. So, I don't know anyone there. I mean it's still the projects, but it's quiet though. I think it's good that we don't know anyone. We're just in and out, in and out. . . . They're a whole other different breed. I mean because for me, I'm not saying I'm antisocial but I'm just about being in and out, in and out. So, even if my kids want to hang out, we go back to my old block. I feel like the neighborhood we're in now is not so good. It feels like it's falling apart.

Shamara explained how she knows very few people in the community because she does not spend a lot of time in her home. She feels that the people in her apartment building do not model the type of behavior and lifestyle she likes, so she limits her time there. She doesn't feel a strong sense of closeness to other neighbors. Sociological research suggests that Shamara's experience of retreating from social life is not uncommon in poor urban neighborhoods.[22]

Shamara's time in the neighborhood is focused on keeping her children safe and providing her children with more opportunities than she had as a child. All three of her sons attend high-performing schools outside of the neighborhood. After her oldest son was hurt at the neighborhood school, Shamara searched for alternative options in other neighborhoods and made similar decisions for her two other sons. Shamara proudly shared how well her sons have done at their schools:

> My older son is graduating. He goes to school near where we used to live. So, he has to take two buses or the train to get there. And my middle son, this was his first year in high school and that's downtown on Fourteenth Street so that's off the 5 train. So, he's the last stop. And then for my youngest, he was in school right where we lived about two blocks up, but the teacher recommended a new school, so he just started there. He's past my other son, it's a stop off of the 4 train or 5 train.

Each day, Shamara's kids traverse the city to get to their respective schools. But traveling such great distances also limits her sons' interactions with their peers in the neighborhood.[23] To Shamara, who worries about the neighbors, this is a positive outcome. Shamara remains overwhelmingly happy with their progress in school and the friendships they've formed outside of the neighborhood. Shamara fondly described the sense of community she feels at her youngest son's school:

> It's a nice community, and the teachers are really like family. They really respect each other. The teachers are really there for them. I feel it too. I've gone to the school plenty of times for parent teacher conferences, for meetings, and I feel like they really know me there. You come in and the office is right there. They're friendly. They always have the door open. You can come in if there's a situation. And they talk to you. They always seem to be there for you.

Shamara engages more often with people from her son's school than she does with other families in the neighborhood. She feels lucky to have found one other parent in her neighborhood whose son also goes to the same school. They have exchanged numbers and feel a connection because of the school. For Shamara, the school is an important social anchor that links her to other parents and a friendly community of educators. Her connections at the school and perceptions of neighborhood insecurity pull her away, socially and spatially, from her home neighborhood.

Parents who hold negative perceptions of their neighborhoods withdraw from neighborhood life and limit how frequently their children engage in neighborhood activities. As prior research has suggested, Christopher, Donna, and Shamara have shifted their connections in the direction of her child's school.[24] Compared to parents living in advantaged communities, parents in lower-income areas assess neighborhoods to reduce threats to their children's livelihoods and more strictly monitor and supervise children.[25]

Parents' strategies for withdrawal reflect their methods for making their neighborhoods feel safe for their children. These strategies also illustrate how neighborhood inequalities restrict parents' engagement in neighborhood life. I found that most of the parents who implemented distancing strategies were working-class parents who lived in lower-income neighborhoods.[26] Many of the parents who withdrew from neighborhood life also opted out of the neighborhood school. Parents' school decisions and movement out of the neighborhood also altered and often restricted their relationships with proximal neighbors. With declining neighborhood connections and a belief that their neighborhoods were deteriorating, these parents felt more comfortable investing in school ties. As options to leave the neighborhood school increase, working-class parents like Christopher, Donna, and Shamara may continue to experience community loss and may struggle to deepen their children's connections to the neighborhood. Limited neighborhood opportunities and persistent residential segregation create additional challenges for working-class families and constrain their ability to form relationships in their communities.

Neighborhood Selective Engagement Strategies

Some parents hoped to make their neighborhoods feel more secure by engaging in their neighborhoods, albeit selectively. Unlike the parents who created distance from their neighborhoods, these parents did not completely withdraw from neighborhood life and did not describe widespread distrust of their neighbors. Instead, these parents forged selective relationships with some community members. Sociologist Danielle Raudenbush coined the term "selective solidarity" to describe how community members in an African American public housing development managed feelings of distrust while still maintaining meaningful exchange relationships.[27] Some of the parents in my study used similar strategies when interacting in their neighborhoods. While they believed that many people in the neighborhood could not be trusted, they strongly held to the importance of cultivating a community network for their children. These parents might or might not have sent their children to a local school—for them, everything came down to specifics. Parents' selective engagement also stemmed from vast disparities across New York City neighborhoods. While white families living in more advantaged neighborhoods rarely discussed selectively engaging with neighbors, Black and Brown families across class background used selective engagement strategies to navigate low-income neighborhoods.

Imani, a working-class Black mother of two elementary schoolers, grew up between the Lower East Side and Harlem. She enjoyed experiencing the rich cultural diversity of both neighborhoods. When she had children of her own, she intentionally returned to the Lower East Side with her mom so that her children would share this experience of cultural richness:

> I really appreciate the neighborhood because of the diversity, being here and growing up uptown. I been down here since around eleven years old and it's such a great melting pot. Like how New York City is, the Lower East Side truly speaks to that. You can go a certain amount of blocks and there's like Chinatown and there's Little Italy but then there's the West Village and you get these different cultures.

Imani explained that she also likes her neighborhood because she identifies with the people who live there. She hoped to build this common thread of identity for her children in the neighborhood. When I asked Imani what she liked about the neighborhood, she explained, "My people so to say, because I'm very comfortable in my skin. And I think that the neighborhood that I am in, people are more adaptable. We are adaptable in the sense that . . . it's the saying, if you can make it in New York, you can make it anywhere. And when you grow up a certain way with certain conditions, it kinda makes you more resilient." Imani is proud of her identity as a New Yorker. Having grown up in the neighborhood, she feels connected to her neighbors who share her racial background: they are "her people."

Still, Imani dislikes certain aspects of her neighborhood and makes sure to keep her children from these negative elements. Imani explained that she dislikes the type of people that hang around and "don't do anything with their time." She said of the immediate area surrounding where she lives, "There's an abundance of ignorance [chuckles]." She strategically avoids areas of the neighborhood that do not set positive examples for her children. Unlike the parents who create distance and withdraw from the neighborhood, Imani engages selectively by making sure her kids are involved in the right kinds of neighborhood activities. She has friends who live nearby, her kids enjoy the neighborhood, and she has become friendly with local parents. Imani's kids are involved in swimming and go to local museums, but Imani explained that her kids are more involved in school-based activities than neighborhood organizations.

Imani's selective engagement also extends to the school decisions she makes for her children. Imani's daughter attends a charter school outside the neighborhood, but her son attends a nonzoned school in her neighborhood. At both schools, Imani has built strong ties with parents. When discussing her son's school, she described how she appreciates the sense of community she feels with the school administration and other parents:

My son's school is community-based, and it has like a Montessori-themed environment. My son is very happy there. His friends, the family, the parents are really involved. I feel like he's really thriving there. It feels like a family. I'm saying hello to almost everybody I'm walking by. The children are very interactive like a little family. At the office, they know your kid and they know you and are very responsive to things. I appreciate that it's just a warm environment for me.

Though her son's school is nonzoned, with students from inside and outside the neighborhood, Imani appreciates the rapport she has developed with other parents at the school. Imani feels a similar closeness at her daughter's charter school, but she wishes her daughter's school was more conveniently located. Both of her children have strong social ties at their schools. Their limited connections to children in the neighborhood are structured by Imani's selective engagement with the neighborhood's kid-friendly activities and neighbors she can trust. Through her selective engagement, Imani can build social bonds for her children while maintaining distance from negative aspects of the neighborhood.

Jermaine, a middle-class Black father who works in educational development, lives with his seven-year-old daughter in the South Bronx. He similarly described how his neighborhood is "a hole in the wall" and can "get pretty wild." Like Imani, however, he selectively engages by trusting and relying on a few people in his building to provide a sheltered environment for his daughter:

Everyone I know mostly lives on my floor. Now there's a couple of people that I may say hi and bye to that I don't really know by name. But I know everybody that lives on my floor. There's only like five apartments on each floor. So, the kids sometimes during the wintertime we let the kids outside in the hallway and they play and stuff like that. So, everyone watches each other's kids.

While Jermaine identified negative aspects of his neighborhood, he also cultivates friendliness and community with his immediate neighbors who also have young children.

Jermaine relied on these trusted connections to make school decisions for his daughter. Unsure of the local public schools, he asked his neighbors in his building for advice when he first moved in:

Well, there's one charter school and another private school not in our neighborhood but in the Bronx that I thought about for her. But then I asked a couple of my neighbors that lived on my floor about the school. My neighbors were telling me, you know all their kids went there. And even the older lady said her grandkids went there. So, she said it's always been a pretty good school. So, I told myself I would just give it about a year. And she loved it. So, she stayed there. So, it's working out.

Since this first conversation about schools, Jermaine has stayed close with families in his apartment building, and his daughter is close friends with the kids there. The school serves as an important social anchor that links parents in his building together. Jermaine explained that he appreciates the neighborhood school's small, community feel:

> I really like that they have smaller classes so it's not that many kids on one teacher. I appreciate that they have a really good after school program. So, if she needs extra help or something she can stay after school and connect with her teacher. The teachers really keep you informed with what's going on. They even make phone calls at home if something is going on. It's a small neighborhood school.

Jermaine feels confident in the selective relationships he has built with parents in his apartment and with teachers at the local school. Instead of describing a sense of pervasive distrust, like people who forge distance, Jermaine creates an intimate sense of community with the people he and his daughter see on a regular basis: "We know the guys that own the bodegas. And I know the lady at the laundromat because I dropped me and my daughter's clothes off every week so she could wash them. I know the guy at the barbershop. They call me by name. I think over the years people see you and stuff like that. I think I've gotten pretty comfortable in the neighborhood over the past couple of years." For Jermaine, knowing the local workers in the neighborhood and staying connected to families in his apartment are integral parts of his experience in the community. He hopes this experience is an added benefit for his daughter. Though Jermaine has created a sense of community, he is nevertheless careful to keep some relationships at a distance:

> For advice I would go to family or something like that. First of all, I don't think I would get all personal with my neighbors and stuff. I just wouldn't do it. But let's say something happened at school. I know the babysitter can shoot by and get her. The babysitter lives two blocks from us. I'm glad that I have help from my friends and the babysitter when I'm at work. I know that she is being taken care of.

Jermaine nurtures relationships that help build close-knit connections to the neighborhood even as he limits his interactions with his fuller set of neighbors. His selective engagement helps to build a sense of community for his daughter in their low-income neighborhood.

Brianna, a working-class Latina mother, also primarily socializes with other residents in her building. Brianna is originally from Mexico City and moved to New York City when she was five years old. While Briana has lived all throughout Harlem, she has lived in her current home with her daughter for about seventeen years. Brianna is very familiar with everyone in her building;

she rarely sees strangers. When I asked Brianna to describe the people who lived in her building, she explained that they all share a common identity that helps make her and her family feel comfortable: "I don't know everybody personally, but I know people [who] have been my friends for a long time. My building is mostly Spanish, they're all families. A lot of working families. We know each other for a long time. One of the neighbors' daughter goes to the same school as my daughter. . . . My friends live here. Some of my neighbors are very good, and if there's anything, they're there for you." Brianna expressed a sense of closeness with other families in her community, a closeness reinforced by a shared immigrant identity and the children's associations from school.

While Brianna feels that she and her daughter are connected to other neighbors in her building, she must also contend with neighborhood disorder. Brianna clearly distinguishes whom she associates with in her neighborhood as a means of protecting her daughter from harm. When her daughter was younger, for example, she didn't give the liquor store next door much attention. Now that her daughter is older, she tells her daughter to ignore the drunk people outside. She knows that her daughter notices them anyway.

Brianna is also careful with how her daughter travels throughout the neighborhood. After learning about a higher-performing school that her sister-in-law selected, Brianna switched her daughter to another charter school a few blocks away from the local neighborhood school. Brianna is happy with the school, but she chooses their route to traverse the neighborhood carefully. She explained, "I don't let her walk to school, I don't even let her go to the store because I don't feel so safe about her going by herself to the store." But while Brianna keeps a close eye on her daughter's movement in the neighborhood, she feels much more secure about the school itself. She said of her selective engagement with other parents, teachers, and staff,

> There's a lot of contact. You have the teachers' phone number, and you can send them a text message about anything—if you have any questions about homework or how to help your kids, you can directly contact your teacher. It feels like a community-based school. I can come here freely anytime and see anyone anytime. All the teachers say good morning and shake your hand. I always feel welcome. Everyone knows my daughter and I know that if there's a problem, she feels free to tell them right away. The teachers really care for the students. They are bilingual. Almost everyone speaks Spanish, and they help you a lot.

Brianna feels a strong social connection to the school, and she believes her daughter benefits from this connection. Brianna's neighborhood network incorporates her social contacts in her immediate neighborhood and larger network of school contacts. Brianna's selective engagement in the neighborhood means she strategically balances contacts in proximity and connections away from her home. For instance, Brianna makes sure her daughter is involved in tons of school-based activities, including the afterschool program, school festivals, and tutoring events. Over the years, Brianna's neighborhood interactions have primarily focused on a few close friends and families in her building and parents, teachers, and staff at her daughter's school.

Some parents who hoped to selectively engage in the neighborhood struggled to find contacts in their immediate neighborhood. The struggle to access and find these positive role models—to "deal with the world outside of the door"—is at the center of the ambivalence parents who selectively engage in the neighborhood feel. Fabiana, a middle-class Latina mother who works in business development, discussed the uncertainty and challenges she experiences raising her son: "For me, the most challenging thing in this city is raising my son and dealing with the world outside of the door. The diversity here is beautiful, but it's challenging because you need to explain how to have an open mind and an understanding that not everybody is the same. And you don't know if the rest of the kids have that information, so it's really difficult."

Just as parents who distance themselves from neighbors withdraw from neighborhood life, parents who selectively engage in the neighborhood also strategically evaluate how to make their neighborhoods safe places to raise their children. Fabiana, for instance, described a few of the things she dislikes in her neighborhood and how it may negatively influence her son:

> I wish that people didn't smoke right in front of our building. It seems like people don't understand there's things that you don't do in front of the kids. Because when you do it, you're teaching them how to do it. So, if I have to change something I would definitely change that. I don't smoke, and I don't like alcohol. I'd rather not show my son those kinds of things. I'd rather that people around don't teach him those kinds of things.

Fabiana worried about how negative aspects of the neighborhood would shape her son's attitudes and experiences. She selectively engaged with neighbors in her building whom she felt she could trust. At the same time, she hopes to guard her son from some of the poor conditions in her neighborhood.

Fabiana's selective engagement also shaped how she sought information about schools when her son turned four. When Fabiana searched for kindergarten options for her son, she asked other parents at the park about various school options. She ultimately listed eleven schools, all in the neighborhood, on her application. Although her son is happy at the neighborhood school, she worries that it wasn't the right decision:

> There are so many kinds of kids, people coming from everywhere. People with different cultures, people with different backgrounds. What is good for me as a parent, maybe it's not good for someone else. Not everybody is

going to think the same and the kids are not the same. And sometimes they don't have the best example at home. And so sometimes it's hard to explain to my son why it's hard to get along with all types of kids.

Fabiana worries about her son's well-being, both in the neighborhood and at school. Although her son's school is highly rated, she noted that not all children are raised in the same way and not all parents share the same commitment to education and fairness in the classroom. Fabiana struggles to selectively engage with trusted neighbors and shelter her son from poor neighborhood conditions and potentially negative behavior at school.

Parents who selectively engage in the neighborhood hope to identify trustworthy neighbors, spend their time with resource-rich organizations, and select spaces that they believe will counteract the neighborhood's negative influences. Research has shown that parents also use neighborhood resources to insulate their children from harm and forge beneficial settings by connecting with community members and local organizations.[28] Parents' strategies for selective engagement often required tremendous and demanding efforts, particularly related to schooling.[29] For instance, parents who selectively engaged strategically searched for school options outside of the neighborhood or local nonzoned options. They in turn balanced friendships with school communities and neighborhood friendships. Often these social circles did not overlap, and parents invested additional energy to ensure they and their children benefited from a variety of carefully selected contacts. Neighborhood structural inequalities are reproduced when families living in low-income neighborhoods must undertake selective engagement strategies or withdraw from the neighborhood entirely. As I demonstrate in the next section, parents living in more advantaged areas rarely took on this additional labor.

Neighborhood Inclusion Strategies

Parents living in higher-income neighborhoods forged community-building strategies and cultivated feelings of shared membership in their neighborhood. In contrast to parents who withdrew from the neighborhood or selectively engaged in the neighborhood, parents living in safer and wealthier area invested in community activities and resident relationships. Parents' inclusion strategies were driven by unequal access to neighborhoods in New York City. Middle-class families living in more advantaged neighborhoods could more easily develop strong social ties with neighbors. They were able to derive a sense of membership and safety through meaningful engagement with their neighbors. Driven by fewer concerns about neighborhood poverty and safety, they encouraged their children to nurture community ties and sought local school options within their districts. While few parents decided on the traditional neighborhood school, these parents prioritized schools that were close to home.

Janet, a white, middle-class mother from Queens whom we heard from in chapter 1, described how she intentionally became involved in community activities to build relationships with other families. She formed an online parent group to learn about local schools and connect with other parents, and she has tried to form a similar group at her youngest son's preschool:

> I run a program for toddlers in the neighborhood. So, I'm the Google group manager of my youngest son's online baby group. So, there's groups in my neighborhood where mothers, fathers, and caregivers get together. They've been going on for almost a decade now. They're split up into three months. So, probably in our group, we have about twenty-five moms. . . . I occasionally get involved with the community board, and I wanted to start up like a PTA at my son's preschool, but so far, the preschool director told me they just don't have a PTA. Other than that, as far as involvement, I mean, like a couple of years ago, I was involved in the local theater company for kids.

Janet has drawn closer to other parents through her community involvement. She intentionally engages in neighborhood activities that bring her in contact with other parents with young children. Research has shown that the kinds of intracommunity ties that Janet describes help parents feel connected to their neighborhoods.[30]

Janet appreciates that her community is family-oriented and multicultural. Having grown up in the neighborhood, she has seen the neighborhood shift. She noted that there is less crime and that more families move in each day. She feels comfortable interacting with other parents and regularly brings her children to activities in the neighborhood: "We have a playground and there are lots of different types of classes to take my kid to, like taekwondo next week. But there's so many different types of classes, like dance classes and music classes. There's the local library, it has like story time." Janet appreciates the neighborhood and feels that her children benefit from it. She and her husband made the decision to move to their current neighborhood five years ago in hopes that they would be zoned for higher-quality schools. Janet listed twelve schools on her son's application and prioritized neighborhood proximity and language programs.

Janet's community-building strategies encouraged her to forge connections with her neighbors and look for local schools with innovative programs. Any time that Janet is looking for school advice, including which schools to list on her application and even whether she should hire a tutor for her son, she connects with other parents in her neighborhood. She also shares advice with newer moms who join the online group.

Over the years, Janet has cultivated strong neighborhood friendships:

> We built our friendships over the years, in these past four years. I didn't
> know anyone from before. I even have best friends in my neighborhood,
> but their children are like a year older. They're like some of my closest
> friends now, but they're only people that I've met in these last few years. As
> far as close friends, people that I talk with regularly they're all moms. I think
> everyone's a mom because if they're not a mom, it's hard to relate right now,
> because it's all-encompassing and challenging. And so, I started this pro-
> gram here in the neighborhood for toddlers and I just felt like I was able to
> get closer to these moms because we could actually see each other and be
> in each other's presence like every week. And that was really nice.

Janet believes that drawing closer to her neighbors gives her and her kids a
strong support network in the neighborhood. Her close relationships shape her
daily interactions and inform the school decisions she makes for her children.

Parents who view their neighborhood favorably derive a sense of comfort
and security from knowing familiar faces in the community.[31] Middle-class parents' higher social status and position in higher-income neighborhoods enabled
them to more easily invest in community-building activities and enhanced their
ability to foster social cohesion and promote inclusivity. Susan, an Asian,
middle-class mother and program director, admitted to feeling close to her
neighbors and putting in more effort to develop relationships specifically for the
benefit of her children, even if she doesn't necessarily see them as her closest
friends. After Susan and her husband bought their home in Washington Heights
nearly a decade ago, she sought to create a sense of community and to develop
a close-knit environment for her children. Reflecting about what she enjoys
about her neighborhood, Susan described the family-friendly atmosphere:

> It's really like a small, local community. Everybody shops at the same shops;
> everybody goes to the same areas and stuff. Very family-oriented, which is
> really rare in Manhattan. You don't really see a lot of neighborhoods that
> are just family-oriented. Lots of parks. That's the way I would describe
> it. And one of the main reasons that I moved to Washington Heights was
> that I knew I was going to have a family. I wanted to start a family, but I
> wanted to stay where I could be close to work but not be feeling like I'm on
> top of each other. I feel like because of the parks and the playgrounds, it
> doesn't feel like I'm in Midtown with all the big high rises.

Susan loves the feel of her neighborhood and sees how her kids benefit
from parks and small-town feel of local stores and restaurants. At the same
time, Susan worries about how quickly the neighborhood is changing as rents
are increasing. As a long-term resident, she feels that the rising housing and

commercial costs of the developing infrastructure mean she will lose out on the local amenities she has used for years.[32] Susan also worries about how an influx of new residents will change the family-oriented atmosphere that she has tried to cultivate for her children. Susan makes sure that her kids are involved in community events so that they have a chance to get to know the unique cultural history of the neighborhood: "We do a lot of after school activities in the neighborhood, and we specifically stayed in the neighborhood, one, because we wanted to help the small businesses and we wanted to get that *community feeling* for our kids. They might not all go to the same school, but they live in the same building, or they live in the same blocks, so that at least they have some commonality." Susan described how creating this "community feeling" for her children is challenging in a neighborhood undergoing changes and considering that her children go to a variety of nonzoned schools across her neighborhood. Susan has made an effort to find quality nonzoned schools in her community, but this means her kid's friends live all over New York City. To ensure her children feel a sense of closeness in the neighborhood, Susan focused her school search on schools in her neighborhood and district and schools with strong community and parent involvement. She ultimately decided on a high-performing, progressive school known for attracting families across Washington Heights.

Even though Susan decided on nonzoned schools that admit students across the larger neighborhood, she still made sure the schools were within a few blocks of her home. She has also tried to be involved in the school along with other parents. As part of her community-building strategy, Susan commits to developing a strong school network and a strong network in her immediate neighborhood.

Louise, a white, middle-class mother who lives in Queens, also described how she benefited from drawing closer to young families with children over the years. She distinguished her time before and after becoming a parent to demonstrate how over time she has relaxed social boundaries with her neighbors:

> Through becoming a parent, I've gotten to know a lot of families in the neighborhood. I think before, I was one of those people who just didn't really hang out in the neighborhood. So now, I know more about some of the wonderful things in the neighborhood. Like there are only two private parks in New York City, and one of them is here. So it's pretty special and unique, it's just sort of like our backyard for my daughter. We don't have a backyard, so that becomes the backyard.

Louise draws closer to organizations and play areas in her neighborhood, deepening her connection to the community. Over time, the strong friendships that Louise has formed with other families, particularly in a baby-sitting co-op, have been essential for her search for schools. She gathered information from the other parents in the group on kindergartens, compiling a sheet of information on each school. Ultimately, Louise decided on a school outside of the community, in Manhattan, for her daughter. Though the school is far from her neighborhood, Louise noted that it feels local because a few moms from her neighborhood also send their children to the school. While Louise worries about whether her daughter will still build community bonds, she reiterated that her family's investment in community organizations and parent groups makes community relationships possible:

> I mean all of my friends, all of our kids go to different schools. So, it's not always easy to connect. So many different schools. But we do know a couple of people who live in our neighborhood and go to our school. We've gotten to know some other parents just through me really making an effort to do playdates. But it doesn't happen on its own for sure. It's different from how I grew up. But they are still able to play with kids in the neighborhood. And we are still able to get to know people with kids in her neighborhood. And she does piano and theater and basketball in the neighborhood.

Louise invests in community relationships so that even though her daughter travels out of the borough for school, she can still feel connected to her neighborhood.

Parents who implement community-building strategies rely on a variety of neighborhood resources and build trust with neighbors to cultivate a strong and supportive environment for their children, regardless of where their children attend school. To be sure, many of these middle-class parents benefited from higher incomes and flexible jobs that allowed them to strategically select their neighborhoods and be more involved in the community. The middle-class families did not face the same structural constraints working-class families experienced. They lived in relatively safer neighborhoods and felt comfortable investing in their home communities. Middle-class parents' higher social status helped facilitate their regular and repeated conversations with neighbors and their familiarity with other families with young children. They were able to more easily develop and maintain strong community-based relationships through local community schools. Unlike parents who withdraw from the neighborhood or who only selectively engage in the neighborhood, parents who forge community-building strategies make intentional efforts to link their neighborhood and school communities and to take advantage of local neighborhood activities. Parents used informal and formal methods to deepen their relationships in the community.

Neighborhood Inclusion with Constraints

Many middle-class parents believed that drawing close to neighbors was a key strategy for forging a sense of neighborhood security. However, not all middle-class parents were able to draw close with ease. This was particularly the case for middle-class parents of color whose children either attended schools outside their neighborhood or went to local nonzoned schools that attracted children from throughout the city. Unlike parents who withdrew from neighborhood life or who selectively engaged with neighbors, these parents desired to draw close to their communities but found that doing so required strategic effort and a repeated investment of time and energy.

Veronica is a Black, middle-class single mother who works as a college career counselor. Veronica lives in Brownsville, one of New York City's poorest neighborhoods.[33] She continues to stay in Brownsville because of its affordability, but finding people to connect with in her neighborhood is a constant challenge. She would like to draw close to her neighbors, but the neighborhood conditions often mean that many families are living just within their means with limited free time. Yet still Veronica believes that great things can come from even the poorest of neighborhoods: "Although we live in these low-income neighborhoods, there's great things that come out of it. So, I feel like I am at a place where it's like maybe getting a little too rough, maybe we should leave, but at the same time I think there is a shift happening all over Brooklyn. So, I think if I sit long enough it might be a benefit." Veronica is hopeful that over time the neighborhood will improve, and she will be able to deepen relationships with newcomers. She puts effort and intention into her engagement. As part of that effort, Veronica organizes community events and tries to involve her daughter in local activities in the community. Yet due to concerns about safety and the poor ratings for schools nearby, Veronica knew she could not select the local neighborhood school for her daughter. Now that Veronica travels outside of her school district for higher-quality schools, her daughter has hardly any friends in the neighborhood.

Many of the parents in this study described their closest social relationships as emerging from their children's school. Parents, after all, come to know other parents. Since Veronica's daughter attends school elsewhere, Veronica has attempted to facilitate spaces where other parents in the neighborhood can interact, regardless of where their children go to school. She described her attempt to develop a forum directly in her neighborhood:

> Last year, I had a forum for single moms, for single parents and mothers raising the children alone because sometimes they're married, but they still feel like they're alone. I wanted to have it in East New York because the

whole purpose of the forum was to let them know that although you're doing it by yourself, it's still possible to create the life of your dreams. And I just couldn't do it because I didn't have the space. I couldn't work with people in the neighborhood, so I just ended up taking it somewhere else. So, it's just hard to, to collaborate with people in the neighborhood.

Veronica is passionate about creating opportunities in her neighborhood, even though this activity requires her to invest in her neighborhood as well as her daughter's school community. As with the parents who embrace neighborhood inclusion, she is very open to sharing resources and bringing people together. Yet Veronica faces constant constraints that limit her ability to build social cohesion in her neighborhood.

Veronica has also struggled to build connections with the other parents at her daughter's nonzoned school. Over her daughter's two years at the school, she has become closer to just two parents. Veronica described the ways that she actively seeks and maintains close relationships. She believes this relationship-building is beneficial for her and her daughter. While parents who draw close with ease described how community relationships seem to form organically, Veronica noted that her relationships require a significant investment of time and energy. She puts in double the effort—she works to build local relationships in her community and build friendships outside of her community at her daughter's school.

Veronica also described the challenges of helping her daughter maintain friendships when she goes to school far from her neighborhood:

So, my daughter has her friends at school and because she lives so far away from the school, her friendships with them don't go beyond texting or the face time, things like that. She would like me to be friends with her friends' moms, but I don't have time. She had a very close friend at the charter school she went to, and that was her really good best friend. So, I really try to keep them together because they don't get to go to school anymore. So, on the weekends if I'm doing something with her, I always bring her along to keep their friendship together.

In the same way that Veronica struggles to maintain friendships with the parents she'd like to be in community with, Veronica's daughter has few face-to-face interactions with her friends outside of school. Her daughter's interactions are limited because her daughter's friends live all over the city. Veronica believes strongly that cultivating these friendships is extremely important for her daughter's well-being and takes extra steps to help her daughter bridge these relationships when she can. From Veronica's perspective, we see how drawing close requires repeated and sustained effort. Veronica hopes to balance relationships with her daughter's school and her home community, but she struggles to maintain both. Unlike middle-class families who live in advantaged neighborhoods, Veronica experiences increased structural constraints that challenge her ability to engage in her community. Persistent inequalities across neighborhoods contribute to differences in social cohesion and community inclusion, shaping how families and their children interact in neighborhoods.

Lisa, a Black middle-class mother whose story I shared in chapter 3, described the steps she took to draw close to neighbors. At the time of our interview, Lisa and her husband had recently bought their home in Brooklyn. Lisa loves her new community and feels she can trust her neighbors. Lisa described her neighborhood's rich cultural tradition and how she hopes this bolsters her children's experiences in the neighborhood:

> The neighborhood is very tight and most of the people who are there have been there for years, which is why I love it. It's also a Black Caribbean neighborhood with people who are very conscious. And that's kind of how I was brought up. And so, I like the neighborhood because of that. And when I first came to the neighborhood, I think I had no less than five of my neighbors come and knock on my door and say welcome to the neighborhood. I mean, every time I have a grocery load in my car, my neighbor comes out and helps me out and so that's the kind of neighborhood that we live in. I feel close enough and we're not best friends, but if my kids were on the street and there were other adults out, I would totally trust them to be able to watch my kids and they'll be safe. So that's a high level of trust because of my kids.

Even though Lisa has only recently moved to her neighborhood, she has already identified close-knit social ties that remind her of her own childhood and the type of environment that she finds suitable for raising her own children. Lisa finds this sense of community embracing and supportive as she and her husband raise their children. She also feels that her children benefit because they feel welcomed, and she can rely on her neighbors for support. For Lisa, the neighborhood's ethnic history provides a strong foundation that she hopes her kids also embrace.

At the same time, Lisa also notices how gentrification is shaping and reshaping her Brooklyn neighborhood each day. Even in the short time that she has lived in her home she has noticed the constant change of residents. Just in the past year, three of her friends have announced that they're moving. She worries about how gentrification may, over time, break down the bonds she has just started to cultivate with her neighbors.

As dedicated as Lisa is to her new neighborhood, she has struggled to develop and maintain close relationships with other parents. Her current group of friends, largely developed through school connections, are scattered across the city:

> Most of my friends are actually outside of the neighborhood because I moved there three years ago. My kids have been in school longer, so a lot of our friends are from the schools that they used to go to, and they don't currently go to schools in the neighborhood. And so, we either are friends with the parents who were their friends at the previous school or in the current school and neither of which are in the current neighborhood.

Lisa attempts to maintain all the friendship groups from all the schools her children have attended in just a few short years, but this requires a great deal time and energy.

Lisa wishes her kids' schools were in the neighborhood. She recognizes how this would more easily facilitate relationship-building:

> If we had a really great school in our neighborhood, we would know the neighborhood kids. So, the kids miss being able to hang out with the kids on your block. Because of all the options of schools in different neighborhoods, you don't get that as much. One kid down the road is going to a charter school and that kid is going to this school and I'm going to school in the city. And so, you lose that, right? So, you don't know them as well as the kids you go to school with. The kids who lived on my block went to school with me. We knew each other really well. And so yeah ideally, I'd love for my kids to be in the neighborhood, so then we'd have the neighborhood community.

Lisa recognizes how much easier it would be to develop and maintain community bonds if she did not have to traverse the city every day, in opposite directions, to bring her kids to school. She would benefit from stronger connections to the neighborhood school, and her kids would benefit by feeling closer connections to other neighborhood kids.

Lisa works diligently to maintain her kids' friendships at new schools, at the old schools, and across neighborhoods, but doing so requires an investment of time and energy. For parents like Veronica and Lisa who are attempting to forge neighborhood inclusion within a context of constraint, holding on to school and neighborhood social contacts is a challenge. They value their neighborhoods' rich cultural diversity and want to invest in relationships, but they experience constant constraints that limit their ability to forge meaningful connections. Whether these Black families live in extremely poor neighborhoods, like Veronica, or in gentrifying neighborhoods, like Lisa, drawing close to neighbors requires strategic investment. Neighborhood inequality is reproduced when families must invest additional effort in building social ties. The city's persistently segregated neighborhoods and continued economic disadvantages shape not only how parents select schools but also parents' interactions in their neighborhoods.

Parents of young children occupy a distinct residential position and are often expected to traverse distant geographic spaces to meet their children's needs.[34] Parents, for instance, may reside in one neighborhood, send their children to school in a different neighborhood, work in yet another neighborhood, and even visit public amenities in yet a fourth location.[35] Parents' evaluations of their neighborhoods influence child-rearing patterns and ultimately shape children's experiences within neighborhoods, quality of life, and chances of upward mobility. My interviews with parents demonstrate how the expansion of school choice, combined with persistent inequalities, can weaken the sense of community among families. The greater number of school options not only increases the labor required to make school decisions but also disrupts local social networks and perpetuates economic and racial divides.

Parents' neighborhood perceptions and experiences are shaped by persistent structural inequalities across neighborhoods. Families living in higher-income and low-crime neighborhoods were more often middle-class and were more easily able to draw close to neighbors. Parents who drew close to neighbors increased their neighborhood connections and were more likely to enroll their children in high-performing nonzoned schools near their neighborhoods. They benefited from strong local connections and a greater sense of neighborhood trust. Their children had stronger emotional connections to their neighborhood and benefited from more close-knit ties. In contrast, working-class and even middle-class families living in poorer neighborhoods faced constraints when connecting with neighbors and withdrew from the neighborhood altogether or invested in strategic interactions. Parents who withdrew from neighborhood life experienced social isolation and often opted to send their children to schools outside of the neighborhood. With few local school connections, their children were unable to develop strong community bonds. Research finds that connections to a greater number of residential neighbors can have important social consequences for children. For instance, knowing fellow community members can promote higher academic performance and cognitive development in children, increase interpersonal trust among families, and give parents access to social resources.[36]

Many of the working-class parents I interviewed heavily restricted neighborhood interaction and withdrew from the neighborhood in search of family-oriented activities elsewhere. Parents hoped to protect their children from perceived neighborhood dangers and for some this meant sending their children to schools outside of the neighborhood. Christopher, for instance, described his constant worries at local parks and noted that he and his wife decided on a school outside of the neighborhood for his daughter. Many of the working-class parents lived in low-income neighborhoods, which likely shaped their perceptions of their neighborhoods and their unwillingness to engage with neighbors more regularly.[37] With school options readily available outside of the neighborhood, parents felt comfortable distancing from neighborhood residents and connecting with their school communities instead.

A mixture of working-class and middle-class parents selectively engaged in their neighborhoods. These parents strategically demarcated safe and unsafe areas and monitored whom their children interacted with while also cultivating neighborhood connections. They brokered interaction to counter negative influences in the neighborhood and to bolster their children's neighborhood experiences. The parents who selectively engaged sent their children to schools located either within or outside the neighborhood. These parents often described how a shared identity encouraged them to form friendships with select neighbors who had similar backgrounds.

Mostly, middle-class parents implemented community-building strategies by drawing closer to neighbors and encouraging their children to build a sense of community in the neighborhood. These parents viewed their neighborhoods as close-knit and cohesive and engaged in the neighborhood so that their children would benefit. They cultivated a sense of community with their fellow neighbors. These parents created close-knit ties with other residents and developed high levels of neighborhood trust, familiarity, and resource-sharing. Middle-class parents engaged in informal and formal organizations to facilitate connections. These connections were often instrumental in their search for local schools.

Some parents, especially Black middle-class parents, attempted to draw closer to neighbors but experienced significant constraints. These parents had to invest considerable effort in strategically organizing playdates and taking extra steps to cultivate relationships for their children. Like the parents who selectively engaged in the neighborhood, these parents also sent their children to a mixture of schools within and outside the neighborhood. Because these middle-class parents often lived in lower-income neighborhoods relative to some of the white parents I interviewed, they often felt the local neighborhood schools were not an option.

Existing research, as well as my own, has found that the increasing expectation that children attend schools outside of the neighborhood decreases the level of closeness parents feel in their neighborhoods. Efforts to engage or disengage in the community are also deeply tied to neighborhood inequality across New York City. The variation in parents' neighborhood interaction strategies has important implications for the school decisions they make for their children and how families perceive urban neighborhoods. Traditionally,

TABLE 6. Sample characteristics across class and neighborhood ($N = 102$)

	Middle class ($n = 48$)	Working class ($n = 54$)
Household income		
<50,000	6	54
>50,000	42	0
Race/ethnicity		
Asian	11	1
Black	13	28
Latina/o	11	21
White	13	4
Type of school		
Not zoned by address	35	28
Zoned by address	13	26
Distance traveled to school[a]		
< 0.5 miles	12	19
> 0.5 miles	36	35
Neighborhood engagement strategy		
Distancing	0	28
Selective engagement	16	20
Inclusion	27	6
Constrained inclusion	5	0
Residential status		
Homeowner	20	0
Renter	28	27
Low-income housing development	0	27
Time in neighborhood		
>10 years	21	30
<10 years	27	24
Neighborhood poverty[b]		
Low poverty (<20%)	14	6
Above average poverty (20–30%)	33	38
High poverty (30–40%)	1	10
Neighborhood borough		
Bronx	4	16
Brooklyn	9	4
Manhattan	28	33
Queens	6	1
Staten Island	1	0

a. Distance categories selected based on New York City transportation eligibility parameters (NYC Public Schools, "Transportation Eligibility").

b. Poverty levels retrieved from the American Community Survey and augmented by NYC Opportunity ("Poverty Measure").

TABLE 7. Characteristics of study boroughs, 2000

	Bronx	Brooklyn	Manhattan	Queens
Population	1,332,650	2,465,326	1,537,195	2,229,379
Percentage white	14.5	34.7	45.8	32.9
Percentage Black	31.2	34.4	15.3	19
Percentage Hispanic	48.4	19.8	27.2	25
Percentage Asian	2.9	7.5	9.5	17.5
Median household income[a]	$27,611	$32,135	$47,030	$42,439
Median home value[b]	$190,400	$224,100	$1,000,000+	$212,600
As percentage of city median[b]	90%	106%	472%	100%
Percentage of units, owner-occupied, of occupied units	19.5	27.1	20.1	42.8
Percentage of units, renter occupied, of occupied units	80.5	72.9	79.9	57.2

a. Reported in constant 1999 dollars.
b. Reported in constant 2000 dollars.

TABLE 8. Characteristics of study boroughs, 2016

	Bronx	Brooklyn	Manhattan	Queens
Population	1,471,160	2,648,771	1,664,727	2,358,582
Percentage white	22.3	43.2	55.6	37.5
Change in white population, 2000–2017	7.8	8.5	9.8	4.6
Change in Black population, 2000–2017	4	−2.3	−0.5	−0.9
Change in Hispanic population, 2000–2017	7.8	−0.7	−1.1	3
Change in Asian population, 2000–2017	1	4.8	3	8.7
Median household income (2017 inflation-adjusted dollars)	37,397	56,942	85,071	64,509
Percentage change in median household income, 1990–2016	15.1	27.8	28.8	20.6
Median home value	400,300	701,800	976,100	545,800
As percentage of city median	65.7	115.1	161.8	89.5
Percentage change in median home value, 1990–2016	35.5	51.6	−1.2	43.9
Percentage of units owner-occupied, of occupied units	19.1	30.4	24.7	44.3
Change in owner-occupied units, 1990–2016	−0.4	3.3	4.6	1.5
Change in renter-occupied units, 1990–2016	0.4	−3.3	−4.6	−1.5

neighborhood schools have served as central pillars for social interaction and community engagement. When families opt for schools outside of the neighborhood, this significantly weakens these localized social networks. Parents and children interact less frequently with those who live nearby, reducing opportunities for forming strong, supportive relationships within their own communities.

Parents' decisions to exit the neighborhood for school can have an unintentional impact on their ability to engage in the neighborhood and their children's sense of community in the neighborhood. The school choice literature has long focused on the factors that shape how parents view school quality and the characteristics that drive parents to search for schools outside of their catchment area. However, fewer studies address the community consequences of school choice expansion. In search of improved educational opportunities elsewhere, parents may be less able to engage in local events and activities. Diminished local engagement can lead to a sense of isolation and a weaker connection to the immediate neighborhood.

While school choice policy significantly expands the options available to families, it further complicates and constrains the relationships parents and their children have with their local communities. Limited connections with neighbors in residential areas can significantly impact children's social outcomes and well-being and reduce trust among families.[38] As students are increasingly scattered across distant schools, families may find that their neighborhoods are no longer close-knit or cohesive. Even as the range of options has increased, schools continue to vary in quality, placing the burden on families to search distant geographic areas to find quality schools for their children and further complicating their neighborhood relationships. Although school options have expanded, neighborhoods remain persistently segregated, shaping how parents navigate relationships in and outside of schools. Addressing these challenges requires intentional efforts to create equitable educational opportunities and foster local engagement to rebuild and maintain strong community connections.

An Uncertain Future

SCHOOL DECISION-MAKING AT A CROSSROADS

WHEN I TEACH urban sociology and sociology of education to undergraduate students, one of my favorite class activities is adopted from the American Sociological Association's Teaching Resources and Innovations Library for Sociology (TRAILS) website. I frequently use the class activity, developed by Professor Alanna Gillis, designed to help students understand the vast inequalities families experience when selecting schools for their children.[1]

Each student is given a unique family profile with key demographic variations. Some families are Black, some families make $30,000 while others make $500,000. Some families live close to a high-performing zoned school, and others do not. Students are provided with a map of school locations and a chart that outlines the racial makeup, admission policy, graduation rate, and, if applicable, tuition requirements of each school. The very real structural limitations families experience are clearest in the moments when students speak aloud with frustration, "But this just isn't possible!" "There are options, but there really aren't options!" "How is this fair when that family makes so much more than me?" "But my family has *no* choice!"

Though this class activity is designed to help students understand how school choice contributes to growing inequality, it is also a useful concluding point for this book. We can learn quite a lot from students' reactions to the process of selecting schools. Their bewilderment and frustration are reflective of the growing uncertainty parents in my study experience. Just as the activity demonstrates to students how residential segregation and school zoning practices reproduce racial and class disparities, the parents I interviewed experienced the same glaring inequalities.

As research has demonstrated, not all families have equal access to school choice options. Low-income families and families of color face substantial barriers, including the limited availability of quality choices. School choice policies can lead to greater segregation along racial, socioeconomic, and academic lines. I have argued that school choice policies have created additional labor for parents. By significantly expanding the available school choices, school districts have introduced new responsibilities and challenges for parents. The proliferation of choices has now made the process of selecting a school complex, demanding a substantial investment of time and effort, and for many parents the process may lead to feelings of concern and anxiety.

As a result of the increased number of options, parents are now required to engage in time-consuming efforts to evaluate and compare various school alternatives. This situation has created an unprecedented demand for parents to make school-related decisions. Parents engage in decision-making labor to search for schools, to determine their school preferences, and to monitor their children's experience in school.

Persistent inequalities in the education system lead to significant variations in how families take on this additional decision-making labor. Consequently, these differences further perpetuate educational inequities within New York City's high-stakes school choice environment. The disparities in resources, information access, and decision-making power contribute to uneven outcomes and opportunities for students from different backgrounds, ultimately shaping the landscape of education in the city.

I use the concept of school decision-making labor to describe how parents manage these ongoing moments of uncertainty. I argue that parents engage in decision-making labor to handle the increased uncertainty of the school choice process. Parents' decision-making labor and perceptions of the risks of school decision-making vary across socioeconomic background and place of residence. Today, nearly 20 percent of families do not send their child to their regularly assigned school.[2] The options they have include district transfers, magnet schools, and charter schools. These school options offer more choices but also place more responsibility on parents to make decisions.

During the school choice activity with my students, I ask a pointed question that I believe is relevant here: So why should we care about the decisions parents make for their children? Students pause for a moment and after a short time generally explain how they felt attempting to make school decisions. They reason together as a class that while school choice provides some with opportunities, it can reproduce structural inequality by race and class. They explain that school choice affects people at the individual level and on a broader structural level. The college students' explanations are the same reasoning that I use here. We must care about the decisions parents are making because they have long-term social consequences and are reflective of important inequalities.

The decisions parents make in elementary school can shape how students are tracked in middle school, high school, and college.[3] Beyond education, these findings shed light on decision-making as an important area of inequality.

We tend to think of wealth and income as the most intuitive measures of inequality. But through the concept of decision-making labor, I demonstrate how inequality is experienced in the everyday decisions people make.

When low-income parents must invest more energy in everyday decisions like choosing a public school, this can perpetuate disparities between the rich and the poor. When high-income mothers can "wheedle" their way in to coveted schools through their zip codes, network resources, and persistent contact, this reproduces class-based disparities and reinforces residential inequality. When families of color engage in additional labor to find academically rigorous *and* racially inclusive schools for their children, this significantly amplifies inequalities across race and ethnicity. And when intensive mothering expectations and increasingly complex school enrollment procedures expand the school search responsibilities mothers take on compared to fathers, this broadens and intensifies household gender inequalities. We cannot ignore the unintended consequences of school choice for families raising young children.

Decision-Making Labor and School Choice Policy

In the context of school choice, parents engage in a decision-making process that involves evaluating the benefits and perceived risks associated with different schools. I have argued that the increase in school options, variations in school quality, and the increased responsibility parents now take on to search for schools contribute to heightened feelings of decision-making uncertainty.

My research contributes new insights into how advantage and disadvantage manifest in the context of school decision-making, particularly considering the intensification of relational risks in contemporary times.[4] By analyzing how parents grapple with uncertainty and employ labor strategies, we can better understand the complex dynamics at play when families make school choices. The expansion of school choice options has significantly curtailed the government's authority in school assignments, transferring decision-making power to parents. However, this shift in responsibility has made the task of choosing a school more complex and unpredictable than ever before. School choice policies prioritize individual decision-making, necessitating intense relational efforts by parents to gather and assess information effectively. Over the years, legislative changes and recent open enrollment policies have shifted the burden onto parents to navigate the multitude of school options. This shift in legislation has occurred in tandem with the state's reduced responsibility toward its citizens. Consequently, parents are now tasked with seeking and selecting suitable schools for their children, making school decision-making an unpredictable endeavor.

I argue that substantial economic and social disparities influence how parents construct their decision-making strategies and perceive of the risks inherent in school decision-making. All the parents interviewed recognized the critical role of school quality in shaping their child's prospects. Consequently, they managed the uncertainties of school choice with careful consideration of its implications for their child's future. Nonetheless, parents' capacity to make school decisions, their perceptions of risks, and their ability to navigate these risks through labor strategies were intrinsically linked to their relative social positions and access to resources. Throughout this book, I have examined the persistent inequalities that shape parents' conceptualization and management of school decision-making within today's high-stakes school choice environment. A decision-making labor framework is essential for recognizing the new responsibility parents take on to search for schools.

Conceptualizing school decision-making labor foregrounds the experiences of parents selecting schools for their young children and demonstrates how the decision-making labor strategies parents develop are deeply influenced by the intersecting factors of race, class, and gender. The decision-making labor framework also provides crucial insights into the challenges parents face in choosing schools. Parents' steps to minimize uncertainties during the school search are entwined with existing inequalities in schools and may inadvertently perpetuate and exacerbate these disparities. Here, I draw attention to the book's major takeaways regarding school choice and the persistence of inequality.

Gender and School Decision-Making Labor

Educational policies that increase the burden of decision-making for families disproportionately affect mothers due to prevailing gendered expectations. Consequently, the risks and uncertainties associated with school enrollment also predominantly fall on mothers. Regardless of partnership status or socioeconomic background, mothers predominantly engage in intensive labor to research school options and assess preferences.

For mothers, school decision-making labor is closely tied to their conceptions of "good parenting" and significantly shapes their sense of identity. Across different class and racial backgrounds, mothers adhere to the principles of intensive mothering, involving time-consuming and self-sacrificing efforts in searching for schools and evaluating options. The advent of new school choice systems has permanently transformed the work of mothering.

Class, Identity, and School Decision-Making Labor

Parents also engage in class-based decision-making labor to form school preferences. Their strategies for minimizing the risks and uncertainties associated with school decisions are shaped by their relative class backgrounds. Likewise, parents' class backgrounds are instrumental in determining the types of school uncertainties they perceive. Working-class parents described varying concerns;

some are apprehensive about unfamiliar schools, while others worry about school underperformance and the potential for downward social mobility. Similarly, middle-class parents' perceptions of risks are multifaceted. Some are anxious about status reproduction and prioritize access to advanced curriculum offerings, while others express concerns about standardized testing and their child's individuality within the school environment.

Despite their different backgrounds and concerns, all the parents interviewed shared the belief that school quality significantly impacts their children's prospects. However, their decision-making strategies and the school preferences they developed varied considerably. These persistent disparities in how parents conceptualize and manage the school decision-making process contribute to unequal educational outcomes. The clear distinctions in parents' decision-making logics and school preferences are tied to the increased responsibility parents now have in searching for schools. School choice policies inadvertently perpetuate inequality as parents face new requirements to actively search for schools. School districts must make concerted efforts to provide equitable access to high-quality public education for all families. Doing so will promote greater equity for parents in their school decision-making process and, ultimately, ensure better educational opportunities for their children.

Race and School Decision-Making Labor

Black, Latina/o, and immigrant parents undertake additional decision-making labor to ensure that schools provide a sense of racial comfort and safety for their children. Despite the increase in school options, significant disparities in school quality and racial and ethnic composition persist. Neighborhood and school segregation pose obstacles for parents attempting to find racially balanced and high-quality schools. Racial biases among teachers and other parents also influence how parents of color are treated during school engagements and shape their children's daily experiences in schools.

Racial and ethnic disparities manifest in how parents experience the risk of school decision-making. White parents do not approach the school search with concerns about their children's racial identity, viewing a school's racial diversity as an enrichment opportunity or a stance for racial justice. The implications are significant; if parents of color are increasingly burdened with searching for schools in a high-stakes environment, we must address how school choice policies perpetuate inequality. Black, Latina/o, and immigrant parents experience discrimination during their school search and encounter uncertainty when they struggle to find racially inclusive and rigorous schools. Addressing these disparities becomes crucial in crafting equitable educational policies and providing inclusive and supportive learning environments for all students and families.

Neighborhood Interaction and School Decision-Making Labor

Parents employ various strategies to cope with potential community loss due to their school choice decisions. Some parents embraced their children's school community, distancing from the neighborhood in favor of strong school support. Other parents selectively engaged with their neighborhood while also maintaining connections with their child's school community, aiming to strike a balance between the two. Cultivating and maintaining these dual relationships demanded considerable time and effort. A third group of parents drew intentionally closer to their neighborhood, cultivating strong community bonds. The diversity in parents' neighborhood interaction strategies has significant implications for their school decisions and how they perceive urban neighborhoods. Opting for schools outside the neighborhood may inadvertently impact parents' comfort in engaging with the local community and their children's sense of community within the neighborhood. Increased school options complicate and restrict the relationships parents and their children have with their local communities. With students attending distant schools, families may discover that their neighborhoods are no longer as closely knit or cohesive.

Social class, neighborhood quality, and racial background together shape how parents establish a sense of community amid neighborhood demographic changes and the expansion of school choice. Parents grapple with the sense of community loss they encounter when their children attend schools outside their home neighborhoods. I shed light on how parents interpret their school decision-making within the framework of their children's neighborhood experiences. By understanding these processes, we gain valuable insights into how parents navigate the changing dynamics of their communities and the impact of school choice on neighborhood connections.

Pivoting toward the Future

Parents' school decision-making labor highlights the increased emotional costs of searching for a school—costs that are differentially experienced depending on parents' social class background, race and ethnicity, and place of residence. As we think about the rapid expansion of school choice in recent years and in the future, we must contend with the substantial inequality parents experience as they engage in school decision-making. Policymakers, district leaders, and researchers must think carefully about the relative costs and benefits of school choice especially for parents and determine avenues for softening the disparate outcomes parents experience.

Making school choice more equitable and reducing inequalities requires a comprehensive approach that centers on parents' experiences engaging in school decision-making. I outline strategies aimed to improve access and equity in New York City that are also in line with inequalities parents are likely to experience in similar urban school choice systems. By foregrounding the experiences of parents, educational policymakers and stakeholders can work toward creating a more equitable school choice system, where all families have access to high-quality education regardless of their background or neighborhood.

Support for Parents and Periodic Review

Parents have an important role to play in today's school choice landscape. While research often focuses on how school districts adapt to increasing school options or how students preform across different types of schools, parents make decisions that shape where students enroll. My interviews with parents provided an important framework for understanding parent involvement and behaviors during the school search process. Parents' frustrations, anxieties, and uncertainties demonstrate the importance of involving families in the decision-making process to address specific needs and preferences of different communities.

School districts must also provide support and guidance to parents during the school choice process, especially those who may face language barriers or lack familiarity with the system. Throughout the interviews working-class and immigrant parents struggled to find information, interpret policies, and make decisions simply because they needed more support. As school choice policies expand the options available and make choosing a school more complex, resources must also be invested in demystifying the school search process.

Parents also struggled to interpret new and changing school enrollment policies, which in turn increased their decision-making labor. Parents explained that they constantly found out about new information and were not always able to rely on parents with older children for correct information. Due to the constantly changing school choice environment, policymakers and education decision-makers must ensure that inadequacies in the system are addressed. For example, in their study on late registration and school choice, Fong and Faude suggest that improving outreach efforts, enhancing informational materials, and streamlining social and educational services may help families manage a complex school choice system.[5] Regularly evaluating and refining school choice policies will help address emerging challenges and ensure regular improvement. School choice continues to expand across New York City, and aligning reviews and changes with this expansion may reduce the additional labor parents must invest in making school decisions.

Improving Information Access and Eliminating Structural Barriers

Throughout the book I have demonstrated the various ways parents engage in decision-making labor across socioeconomic background. Many of the reasons parents take on this additional labor is because they have unequal access to school information. Some working-class parents remained in traditional neighborhood schools simply because school alternatives were new and unfamiliar. If we ensure that all parents have access to comprehensive and transparent information about school options, then this may lessen the intensive work parents invest in the school search process.

A host of barriers shaped how working-class parents engaged in decision-making labor during the school search. Removing obstacles that may deter families, particularly those from low-income backgrounds, from applying to certain schools will substantially improve outcomes. New York City's Family Welcome Centers currently provide enrollment assistance. Increasing the number of centers especially in low-income neighborhoods and conducting outreach to the most disadvantaged students can help make the school search more equitable for all families. Urban and rural school districts across the United States must also prioritize broadening support and assistance to disadvantaged families. Targeted efforts such as one-on-on and group support to reach families who may struggle the most to search for and access school options may improve outcomes and enrollment patterns.

In chapter 1, I demonstrated how middle-class mothers found different ways to wheedle into schools and how working-class mothers were often unaware of these strategies. Broadening access and reducing barriers to enrollment will ensure that parents do not have to engage in decision-making labor in such disparate ways. If school choice plans are to benefit the children they are designed to help, they must be implemented under a more equitable framework. Simplifying the enrollment process, reducing the number of schools that can be selected and ranked, and streamlining school transitions from prekindergarten through elementary school may lessen burdens for mothers and for low-income families. Carolyn Sattin-Bajaj and Allison Roda explain how specific policy features like priority enrollment and geography-based enrollment encourage parents to engage in opportunity hoarding behaviors.[6]

In the context of elementary school choice in New York City, the design of school choice admissions processes must be shifted with the goal of equalizing access and opportunity for all families. School districts could consider updating current admissions methods to provide easier access for low-income families. Reducing the administrative complexity, providing specific resources geared toward less advantaged parents, and expanding the number of high-quality schools in low-income neighborhoods will significantly reduce working-class parents' decision-making labor.

Expanding Diverse School Options and Promoting Integration

In chapter 3, I discussed how families of color engaged in additional school decision-making labor as they struggled to find high-performing and diverse schools for their children. They worried considerably about how their children would fare in underperforming schools and schools with few other children of color. To reduce the decision-making labor parents of color experience, school choice programs must be intentionally designed to increase socioeconomic integration. New York City's District 1 offers a system of "controlled choice" by using a combination of parental preferences, income background, and other demographic preferences to balance enrollment across schools in the district. Future school choice policies would benefit from using similar methods to integrate schools. To provide more diverse, high-quality options, districts must promote diversity within schools by implementing policies that encourage a mix of students from different socioeconomic and cultural backgrounds. By implementing preference policies that prioritize students from disadvantaged backgrounds or those living in underserved neighborhoods, districts can ensure more socioeconomic diversity within schools. School districts can consider overhauling traditional admissions procedures and using a weighted lottery process that increases access for students meeting a specified criterion. The weighted lottery alternative can prioritize enrollment opportunities for disadvantaged students and those living in low-income zip codes.

School choice policies also inherently reinforce competition and perceptions of school scarcity that push parents to invest in school decision-making labor at all costs. Competitive test-based forms of school choice like G&T programs then benefit more advantaged families who can invest more resources and decision-making labor. This also means families of color may be unable to find high-quality and racially diverse school options. Overhauling the current design of G&T programming and eliminating the bureaucratic barriers families face may in turn broaden access for students from diverse backgrounds.

All the parents I interviewed wanted to find high-quality schools for their children and wanted to ensure that their children had strong prospects. Even as school options have expanded, many schools were underperforming. As, I discuss in chapter 2, low-income parents were more likely to send their children to zoned schools and schools that were lower performing relative to middle-class parents. As options expand, the most disadvantaged students are more greatly concentrated in zoned schools, and zoned schools may lose students and be forced to close.[7] In New York City, expanding options for families has resulted in shrinking enrollments and budgets at zoned schools.[8]

School districts must work to ensure that schools in disadvantaged areas receive adequate funding to provide high-quality education and necessary resources for students. Likewise, school districts must also invest in improving the quality of all schools, ensuring that every school provides a supportive and conducive learning environment. To this end, the most disadvantaged students should not be concentrated in a single school. Districts should work to identify schools that serve overwhelming numbers of the neediest children so that these students have easier access to a range of schools. For schools with large numbers of unhoused children and students from low-income housing developments, school districts could consider broadening out-of-zone school access and rezoning the schools in low-income neighborhoods. By equalizing school options and creating more diverse school options, parents will be more satisfied with available options and less uncertain about their child's future at a particular school.

Expanding Residential Access and Prioritizing School Performance Improvement

My findings in chapter 4 revealed parents' experiences of community loss as they travel great distances to send their children to school. Many parents living in low-income neighborhoods increasingly feel that they must exit their neighborhood to access higher-quality schools for their children. Current school choice policies place the onus on parents to travel great distances to find school options because school quality is still driven by residential segregation. A limited number of high-quality school options will inevitably create scarcity and leave some families with few viable school options. School choice often contributes to socioeconomic inequality across schools because neighborhoods remain segregated and unequal. School choice programs alone cannot decouple residential address and school location. Proximity to schooling can limit families' choices and alter the school decisions they make for their children.

When reforming school choice policies, district leaders should carefully assess geographic preferences and the location of choice-based schools to ensure greater access to high-quality schools regardless of residential location. Pursuing a more socioeconomically and racially integrated school choice system will require intentional policies that take residential segregation and geographic limitations seriously. School choice policy cannot ignore practical realities parents may experience, for instance, the trek to schools rated more highly that are well outside their neighborhood. Across the United States, policies must provide viable transportation options for families to make school choice options more accessible. Additional commute times and transportation challenges can discourage disadvantaged families in urban and rural areas from seeking out-of-neighborhood options. Leaders must increase the supply of high-quality schools across a diverse range of neighborhoods. State governments must also prioritize equity-focused school location policies. Recognizing the geographic constraints parents experience can reduce parents' decision-making labor and ensure schools are more equitable.

Parents and the Future of School Choice

Parents play a fundamental role in the development of current and future school choice policy. Parents are the primary decision-makers when it comes to choosing schools for their children. They are the ones who actively explore various educational options, evaluate schools based on their preferences and needs, and ultimately make the decision about where their child will receive an education. Parents' direct experiences should carry significant weight in shaping education policy and creating more equitable school choice options.

Parental feedback is crucial for school improvement. By actively participating in the school choice process, parents can provide valuable insights to educators and administrators, helping them identify areas for improvement. School districts will benefit from intentionally incorporating parents' perspectives and providing parents with access to plans for improving school quality, enhancing educational instruction, and increasing high-quality school options. Involving parents in school choice policy is essential to ensure that educational decisions are well-informed, are responsive to the needs of families, and promote equity.

School choice policy increasingly puts the burden on individual parents to search and find schools for their young children. Just as we cannot expect widespread changes when the burden lies on an individual parent, we also cannot expect fundamental change to school disparities without implementing systemwide change and relying only on school choice policies. District leaders and policymakers across urban areas with school choice must promote large-scale district and statewide reform to create a pathway toward greater equity for families. My hope is that by sharing parents' experiences engaging in intensive school decision-making labor we can reevaluate the costs and consequences of school choice policy to reduce educational inequalities.

To conclude, I turn back to one of the parents I interviewed. Marian's story illustrates clearly the burdens parents take on to make school decisions. Marian, a working-class single mother who stays at home to take care of her infant, described her growing disappointment with her children's school and the sacrifice required to find better options. When her son and daughter first started at the school, Marian was living in a homeless shelter in the Bronx. With limited support, Marian felt she had no choice but to put her kids in the school nearby: "I felt defeated because I couldn't actually pick a school and get them in." Marian's concerns deepened as she learned more about her kids' day-to-day experiences at the school. "I asked them what they did, how was school. And they said, 'We did absolutely nothing. We sat there while the teacher read the newspaper.' I was so appalled."

Later, after the New York City Housing Authority placed Marian in an apartment, she called the DOE to request that her kids be moved to a different school. Reflecting on her experiences, Marian noted with exasperation,

> It's not a challenge to find a school, it's a challenge to find a good school. To find one that you feel comfortable with, that has the best benefits for your child, now that's the hard part. . . . I have to make sure the school has every-thing I need for my child. And I have to know that my child is safe and that they're going to give my child a high education.

Marian's explanation of what it takes to find a "good school" details the great difficulty parents, especially working-class families and mothers, experience trying to find quality schools for their children. Ultimately, Marian needed to be sure the school she selected would keep her kids safe and encourage high academic achievement. To make this possible, Marian travels to and from school thirty minutes by train. She is sometimes worried about the great distance her kids travel to school each day but feels that the time is a sacrifice she must make to ensure a quality education for her children. As school choice policy has shifted the burden on individual parents to find schools for their children, the sacrifices parents like Marian must make are ever increas-ing. The challenges also loom large for middle-class parents like Tamar, who explained, "Just having easy access to a high-quality zoned school wasn't a reality in the places that we could afford. . . . I really believed that the choice option was more real than clearly it is." For parents across socioeconomic background, the commitments required and challenges experienced contrib-ute to the very inequalities school choice policies were meant to reduce. If parents are increasingly tasked with finding schools for their young children, we must urgently address how school choice policy perpetuates inequality. We must also invest in ensuring that all families have broad access to equi-table schools.

Research Overview

This study centers on school choice and parent decision-making in New York City. New York City provides a key area of study with its long-standing tradition of public and nonpublic school choice, its population of socioeconomically diverse families, and its recent demographic shifts across neighborhoods. New York City's urban context and widespread availability of school options allow me to address parents' school decision-making labor and neighborhood engagement strategies. The parents included in the study live in a range of neighborhoods across New York City, which allows me to account for heterogenous neighborhood and school experiences within a single urban locale.

The rise in school options in New York City has led to a turn away from the traditional neighborhood school and has greatly contributed to how parents envision the landscape of school options. The New York school choice process is unique due to the high levels of competition to enroll in the highest-performing preschools early on in a child's education and the reliance on testing and applications for enrollment into top high schools.[1] New York City is also an ideal setting for investigating elementary school choice. While features of the city's system are distinct, the early development of charter and other specialized schools at the elementary level is a growing pattern throughout the United States. New York City's competitive school choice model and constrained residential choices for low-income families reflect trends in educational reform that are occurring in urban districts on a national scale. This study considers the way national and local policies have informed the school choice landscape for families.

I focus exclusively on the elementary school enrollment process in New York City for several reasons. School choice at the elementary level expanded substantially at the start of the study in New York City, allowing me to learn from parents of young children first experiencing this recent policy shift. Additionally, parents of elementary-aged children often limit the distance their young children travel to school.[2] At the high school level, school choices are less constrained by neighborhood and older students have significantly more autonomy to travel to and from school on their own. Unlike in high school, parents also take over much of the school decision-making in elementary school with little assistance from their young children. Furthermore, the educational decisions made during the early childhood years influence later school enrollment patterns. I focus on the elementary years to best capture parents' residential constraints, family decision-making, and parents' first experiences with new enrollment procedures.

Data Collection and Recruitment

I began data collection in New York City during June 2014 and concluded data collection in November 2018. I conducted three pilot interviews in 2014 to provide insight for interview questions and the interview strategy. Following the pilot interviews, I revised the interview questions and clarified my focus on parents with children who were at least five years of age.[3] I resumed data collection in January 2015.

As I arranged interviews with parents, I simultaneously conducted field observations at school district meetings—referred to as Community Education Councils (CECs) in New York City. I attended the semimonthly meetings, spoke with school leaders and representatives, took notes, and gathered meeting materials. Most CEC districts in New York City offer a mixture of zoned, nonzoned, and charter schools. I attended CEC meetings across New York City in which at least 50 percent of kindergartners did not attend their assigned school. Because districts in Manhattan offer more school options relative to Brooklyn, the Bronx, Queens, and Staten Island, I primarily observed three school districts in Manhattan.

Parents were recruited to allow for some variation in school enrollment, socioeconomic background, and place of residence across New York City. While observing CEC meetings, I met teachers, school leaders, and parent leaders who reached out to parents on my behalf. I also connected with parent coordinators at these meetings. Parent coordinators serve as each school's administrator for handling students' families. Parent coordinators helped to introduce me to parents at the schools and often invited me to attend schoolwide events.

Outside of official CEC meetings, I also observed school events and admissions seminars to fully embed myself in the school enrollment process. As part of these observations, I also examined district websites, district meeting minutes, and school websites and collected documents related to the school enrollment process. I evaluated blogs, books, and tutorials that were advertised to parents enrolling their children in New York City elementary schools. Through these events, I learned about online parent communities and joined parent online groups.

I also recruited parents outside of CEC meetings and school-related events and groups to allow for more variation in my sample. I build on Mario Small's seminal works by relying on neighborhood-based community organizations and parent networks for a portion of my data collection and observations.[4] Because I was focused on decision-making patterns, I wanted to ensure that I accounted for a range of potential strategies. For instance, parents who attended school district meetings and who were connected to school leaders were likely more engaged in the school decision-making process. To expand my sample of parents, I also recruited about half of all the parents I interviewed from neighborhood establishments like community service organizations, food banks, and after-school programs. I also connected with parents by distributing fliers at public libraries, grocery stores, laundromats, and playgrounds.

Opting to recruit parents exclusively from the same neighborhoods and districts might have enhanced sample uniformity. However, my goal was to capture a diverse range of parents' experiences with school choice across New York City. Likewise, while conducting interviews with both parents could have offered a more comprehensive understanding of the school choice process, potential social class differences in household compositions may have led to a skewed representation, favoring middle-class families over working-class two-parent households. To be inclusive of various household structures and considering logistical constraints associated with interviewing both parents, I chose to recruit only one parent (either the mother or father) per household.[5]

Following the recruitment phase, interviews were conducted in a variety of settings, including public and private locations such as coffee shops, homes, libraries, parks, and workplaces. The interviews, which ranged from sixty to ninety minutes, were recorded for accuracy. As a token of appreciation, each participating parent received a twenty-dollar gift card. Additionally, at the conclusion of each interview, parents were asked to complete a brief survey regarding demographic information.

In accordance with IRB protocol, at the start of each interview applicants received a consent form to review and sign and provided their verbal and written consent for the interview. I dedicated five to ten minutes to answering questions and describing my project in further detail. To maintain confidentiality, I use pseudonyms for each parent and altered school names and identifying school and residential information, such as street names. All participants agreed to the interview and agreed for their responses to be recorded and later transcribed.

Sample Characteristics

The sample consists of 102 parents of elementary-aged children who lived in New York City. I limited the investigation to the experiences of parents of elementary-aged children to examine how recent exposure to a new choice system shaped decision-making experiences. To gain analytic leverage, I focused exclusively on parents who either were currently in the process of finding a kindergarten or had done so within the past three years.

While the study predominantly included mothers as respondents, twelve fathers actively participated. The underrepresentation of fathers aligns with the anticipated expectations outlined in existing literature, considering both methodological constraints associated with interviewing fathers and the prevalent societal expectation of mothers playing the primary caregiving role for young children.[6]

To evaluate the parents' class background and relative disadvantage, I asked interview questions and had parents complete a demographic survey that addressed factors such as educational attainment, income history, occupation type, receipt of government assistance, and experiences with unemployment or economic challenges. Among the participants, 12 identified as Asian, 41 as Black, 32 as Latina/o, and 17 as white. In terms of income, 41 percent reported earnings above $50,000, while 52 percent had attained a college degree or higher. Social class categorization was determined through a combination of educational background, household income, and employment details. Building on established classifications from prior research,[7] parents were classified as middle class if they or their partners held positions requiring educationally certified skills or positions with managerial authority, possessed a college degree or higher, and reported household incomes exceeding $50,000. The $50,000 income threshold was chosen as a marker given that most parents in the sample earning less than $50,000 lacked a college degree and did not occupy managerial roles. Consequently, parents were classified as working class if their employment involved minimal to no managerial authority, their household incomes were below $50,000, and their educational attainment was less than a college degree.

Interview Strategy and Positionality

I employed qualitative methodological approaches using a case study design.[8] The qualitative components of the study build on previous approaches used by Lareau and by Edin and Kefalas.[9] I combined participant observations at school district meetings and semistructured qualitative interviews. Semistructured interviews provided a useful approach for developing and modifying interview questions as important findings emerged.[10] I designed interview questions to be flexible and conversational and to allow parents to share their experiences of school decision-making alongside other aspects of their daily lives and their biographical narratives.[11]

I developed my interview questions to examine the mechanisms shaping how parents made school decisions for elementary school and how they perceived of their neighborhoods. In the first part of the interview, I focused on parents' educational background and life histories. I used a targeted life history approach to investigate how parents depicted their past experiences at schools and in their homes and neighborhoods.[12] This section provided specific information about parents' housing and larger community experiences as children, which I then used to inform and evaluate their later decision-making.

The next section of the interview centered on how parents viewed their neighborhood. These questions focused on their overall perception of their neighborhood and their experiences associated with their block, their home, their neighborhood schools, and other community resources. I also had parents walk me through how they ended up living in their home and neighborhood and any previous homes or neighborhoods they had lived in prior to the interview. Parents described how they connected to other individuals, their number of friends, close community members, and relatives who live in the area.

The following section of the interview focused on how parents first began searching for schools. I asked about the search processes in an open-ended format to allow parents to identify their most salient experiences when making school decisions and to outline their general search strategies, which I then explored in more detail with secondary questions. Overall, parents provided detailed information about their experiences through the new school choice system in New York City. They were generally very forthcoming about their search experiences, expressing frustrations, challenges, and relief once completing the process.

The study takes a critical race theory stance, and interviews were analyzed using race and class as analytical tools for understanding systemic inequity in education.[13] As a young Black woman, I observed that my age and racial and ethnic background, coupled with my status as a former New York City public school student, served to encourage participants to delve into the intricacies of their decision-making. While my racial background and experience as a student in New York City schools helped build rapport, I was also not a mother and had not gone through the school search process as a parent. During the study, I was in a phase of life without children, making me notably younger than many of the parents I interviewed. This age and experiential difference often positioned me as a perceived less knowledgeable outsider, fostering an environment in which parents openly shared their experiences.[14] Parents often presumed that I knew very little about the search process and went into extensive detail to describe what the process was like. I found this level of detail to be helpful in identifying parents' labor and substantial differences in how parents engaged in the school search process.

As a Black woman, I also noted that parents from diverse backgrounds were willing to engage in discussions about their concerns related to racial marginalization in schools. I perceived that Black and Latina/o families felt at ease explaining their experiences in schools and their fears for their child's well-being. At the same time this likely meant that the non-Black parents I interviewed may have felt less comfortable discussing their racial preferences for schools.

My sample is also economically diverse, and I noted key differences in how working-class and middle-class parents approached the interview. Perceptions of my class background, particularly my educational status, may have shaped differences in how comfortable working-class and middle-class parents felt during the interview. My interviews with middle-class parents were often longer and more detailed. The middle-class parents also seemed notably more comfortable and at ease describing their school decision-making. Working-class parents were at times less forthcoming in details about their decision-making verbally. I paid close attention and made note of gestures, changes in their tone of voice, and overall body language when reflecting on the interview.

Overall, I found that very few of the parents I interviewed questioned my research intentions or were weary of my researcher role. Instead, by choosing to reveal that I had attended New York City public schools, I conveyed a personal investment in the subject matter to the parents, making them more at ease in sharing their experiences. As I recruited parents for the study, my institutional affiliation made some local organizations hesitate to connect me with parents. For other organizations, my graduate student status at a well-known school in New York City made them more willing to assist me with recruitment. I found that throughout recruitment, my shared connections to my participants and differences presented strengths and challenges. At each stage of data collection, I reflected on how others interpreted my position and how this in turn shaped the interview and my analysis.

Data Analysis

I transcribed and coded all the interviews using traditional qualitative methods.[15] I used an iterative process to identify repeated patterns and themes across the qualitative data.[16] I developed an initial coding scheme after a preliminary analysis of the data. I then employed pattern analysis techniques to identify and categorize repeated and emerging themes.[17] I compared and identified relationships across the interviews according to the appropriate themes. Using ATLAS.ti, a qualitative coding software package, I reevaluated this coding scheme twice over to ensure consistency and reliability. I then clustered my data by these categories to conduct a final review. I also developed analytical memos that brought together salient themes across the interviews and my ethnographic observations at admissions events and district meetings.

As this was a comparative case study project, interview data were also approached and compared as configurations.[18] Parents' descriptions of the school choice process centered around three stages of the decision-making process—navigating the search for schools, identifying school options, and monitoring school outcomes. In the final round of analysis, I zeroed in on gender, class, and race and compared interviews across parents' intersecting identities. I also rigorously searched for disconfirming evidence as I read through the transcripts and reviewed the results of the coding process.[19]

During all stages of my data analysis, I found that parents' increased anxiety about the school search was clear. Just as past research has indicated, the parents I interviewed did not have equal access to schools. Parents' narratives and observations at a variety of school events and meetings demonstrated that school choice policies had created additional work for parents to manage. The interviews also detailed the complexities of parents' experiences and provided key narratives of parents' perceptions of the process of school decision-making. The school search process required an intensive investment of time and effort. The parents I interviewed described spending countless hours researching school options and comparing and evaluating school alternatives. I also found that significant economic and social disparities shaped how parents took on the new responsibility of searching for schools. My goal in presenting these findings has been to show the realities of school decision-making and the significance of parents' uneven labor through this process.

NOTES

Introduction

1. Schneider, Teske, and Marschall, *Choosing Schools*; Berends, "Sociology and School Choice"; Archbald, "School Choice, Magnet Schools, and the Liberation Model."

2. National Center for Education Statistics, "School Choice in the United States."

3. Mader, Hemphill, and Abbas, "Paradox of Choice."

4. Mader, Hemphill, and Abbas; New York City Independent Budget Office, "Student Demographics and Enrollment Trends."

5. O'Day, Bitter, and Gomez, *Education Reform in New York City*.

6. Randles, "'Willing to Do Anything for My Kids'"; Daminger, "Cognitive Dimension of Household Labor"; Hochschild and Machung, *Second Shift*; Hays, *Cultural Contradictions of Motherhood*; Brown, "Intensive Mothering and the Unequal School-Search Burden."

7. Billingham et al., "In Search of a Safe School"; Small, "Neighborhood Institutions as Resource Brokers"; Ceballo and McLoyd, "Social Support and Parenting"; Dahl, Ceballo, and Huerta, "In the Eye of the Beholder"; Newman, *No Shame in My Game*.

8. Posey-Maddox, "Race in Place"; Posey-Maddox et al., "No Choice Is the 'Right' Choice"; Lareau and Horvat, "Moments of Social Inclusion and Exclusion"; Dow, *Mothering while Black*.

9. All eligible children whose family submits a pre-K application are guaranteed a pre-K offer. Pre-K children may have priority to attend schools in the district where they live, including their zoned school, however not all elementary schools offer pre-K.

10. Throughout the book, I use Latina/o when referring to the parents I interviewed to reflect how they self-identified. However, I retain the terminology used by other respondents and other authors and sources to maintain accuracy and consistency with original source material.

11. Schneider, Teske, and Marschall, *Choosing Schools*; Bell, "All Choices Created Equal?"; Bader, Lareau, and Evans, "Talk on the Playground"; Ball and Vincent, "'I Heard It on the Grapevine.'"

12. Lareau and Horvat, "Moments of Social Inclusion and Exclusion"; Chen and Moskop, "School Choice's Idealized Premises and Unfulfilled Promises"; Sattin-Bajaj and Roda, "Opportunity Hoarding in School Choice Contexts"; Orfield and Frankenberg, *Educational Delusions?*; Beal and Hendry, "Ironies of School Choice."

13. Chen and Moskop, "School Choice's Idealized Premises and Unfulfilled Promises"; Garn and Cobb, "Framework for Understanding Charter School Accountability"; Harvey, *Brief History of Neoliberalism*; Henig, *Rethinking School Choice*.

14. Cooper, *Cut Adrift*; Nelson, *Parenting Out of Control*; Griesbach, "Dioquis."

15. Schwartz, *Paradox of Choice*.

16. Cooper, *Cut Adrift*.

17. Ben-Porath and Johanek, *Making Up Our Mind*; Chen and Moskop, "School Choice's Idealized Premises and Unfulfilled Promises"; No Child Left Behind Act of 2001.

18. Berends, "Sociology and School Choice."

19. Walberg and Bast, *Education and Capitalism*; Chen and Moskop, "School Choice's Idealized Premises and Unfulfilled Promises."

20. Jennings, "School Choice or Schools' Choice?"; Beal and Hendry, "Ironies of School Choice"; Sattin-Bajaj, "Two Roads Diverged"; Sattin-Bajaj and Roda, "Opportunity Hoarding in School Choice Contexts."

21. Archbald, Hurwitz, and Hurwitz, "Charter Schools, Parent Choice, and Segregation"; Bifulco and Ladd, "School Choice, Racial Segregation, and Test-score Gaps"; Cohodes and Parham, "Charter schools' effectiveness, mechanisms, and competitive influence"; Chubb and Moe, *Politics, Markets, and America's Schools*; Henig, *Rethinking School Choice*; Schneider, Teske, and Marschall, *Choosing Schools*.

22. André-Bechely, *Could It Be Otherwise?*; Bell, "All Choices Created Equal?";Cucchiara and Horvat, "Choosing Selves"; Cooper, "School Choice as 'Motherwork.'"

23. O'Day, Bitter, and Gomez, *Education Reform in New York City*; Mader, Hemphill, and Abbas, "Paradox of Choice."

24. Cucchiara, "'Are We Doing Damage?'"; Grady, Bielick, and Aud, "Trends in the Use of School Choice"; National Center for Education Statistics, "Public Charter School Enrollment."

25. Race to the Top Act of 2011; No Child Left Behind Act of 2001.

26. Wenning et al., "No Child Left Behind."

27. Cookson and Lucks, "School Choice in New York City."

28. For more information about Children First, see *Center for American Progress,* "New York City's Children First."

29. Whitehurst and Whitfield, "School Choice and School Performance."

30. District priority admission at the elementary level means one's chances of receiving acceptance to some schools is still restricted by the location of one's residence.

31. Whitehurst and Whitfield, "School Choice and School Performance."

32. Mader, Hemphill, and Abbas, "Paradox of Choice."

33. Posey-Maddox, *When Middle-Class Parents Choose Urban Schools*.

34. Friedman, "Role of Government in Education."

35. Jabbar et al., "Competitive Effects of School Choice."

36. Chubb and Moe, *Politics, Markets, and America's Schools*; Orfield and Frankenberg, *Educational Delusions?*

37. Bergman and McFarlin, "Education for All?"; Hamilton and Guin, "Understanding How Families Choose Schools"; Bell, "All Choices Created Equal?"

38. Farrie, *School Choice and Segregation*; Garcia, "Charter Schools Challenging Traditional Notions of Segregation"; Rich, Candipan, and Owens, "Segregated Neighborhoods, Segregated Schools"; Scott and Holme, "Political Economy of Market-Based Educational Policies."

39. Denice and Gross, "Choice, Preferences, and Constraints"; Garcia, "Impact of School Choice on Racial Segregation in Charter Schools."

40. West, Ingram, and Hind, "'Skimming the Cream'"; Lacireno-Paquet et al., "Creaming versus Cropping"; Kho, Zimmer, and McEachin, "Descriptive Analysis of Cream Skimming and Pushout."

41. Bader, Lareau, and Evans, "Talk on the Playground"; Lareau, Evans, and Yee, "Rules of the Game"; Renzulli and Evans, "School Choice, Charter Schools, and White Flight"; Sattin-Bajaj and Roda, "Opportunity Hoarding in School Choice Contexts."

42. Chen and Moskop, "School Choice's Idealized Premises and Unfulfilled Promises."

43. Kimelberg, "Middle-Class Parents, Risk, and Urban Public Schools."

44. Shedd, *Unequal City.*

45. André-Bechely, *Could It Be Otherwise?*

46. National Center for Education Statistics, "Digest of Education Statistics, 2022."

47. Snyder, de Brey, and Dillow, "Digest of Education Statistics 2017."

48. Bell, "All Choices Created Equal?"; Bell, "Geography in Parental Choice."

49. O'Day, Bitter, and Gomez, *Education Reform in New York City*; Corcoran et al., "Leveling the Playing Field for High School Choice."

50. While many of the parents I interviewed were currently searching for kindergarten options, others had children who were attending first, second, or third grade.

51. I interviewed parents at different stages in their school choice process. Just fewer than half of the parents I interviewed had a child under the age of six and were just starting their school search journey, and just over half had children older than six and reflected on their experiences searching for schools during prior academic years.

52. A few districts in New York City are considered "choice districts." In District 1 (Lower East Side), District 7 (South Bronx), and District 23 (East New York in Brooklyn), parents can apply to any school within their district and are given the same priority as any other student living in the district. All the schools in these particular districts are unzoned.

53. Yee, "Kindergarten Applications Going Digital"; New York City Department of Education, "Kindergarten Application Process."

54. See table 1 and figure 1 for New York City elementary school admission data.

55. In 2021, New York City mayor Bill de Blasio introduced Brilliant NYC, an initiative that would eliminate gifted and talented testing, instead offering an accelerated curriculum to all kindergarteners.

56. Whitehurst, "2016 Education Choice and Competition Index."

57. Sattin-Bajaj and Roda, "Opportunity Hoarding in School Choice Contexts"; Lareau, Evans, and Yee, "Rules of the Game."

58. Mader, Hemphill, and Abbas, "Paradox of Choice."

59. Mader, Hemphill, and Abbas.

60. Bifulco, Ladd, and Ross, "Effects of Public School Choice on Those Left Behind"; Roda and Wells, "School Choice Policies and Racial Segregation."

Chapter 1

1. Palkovitz, Trask, and Adamsons, "Essential Differences in the Meaning and Processes of Mothering and Fathering"; Randles, "Role Modeling Responsibility"; Randles, "'Manning Up' to Be a Good Father."

2. Hays, *Cultural Contradictions of Motherhood*; Nelson, *Parenting Out of Control.*

3. Collins, "It's All in the Family"; Collins, "Shifting the Center."

4. Christopher, "Extensive Mothering"; Coltrane, "Research on Household Labor"; Daminger, "Cognitive Dimension of Household Labor"; Gerson, "Moral Dilemmas, Moral Strategies, and the Transformation of Gender."

5. Brown, "Intensive Mothering and the Unequal School-Search Burden"; Parcel, Hendrix, and Taylor, "'How Far Is Too Far?'"; Reay, "Useful Extension of Bourdieu's Conceptual Framework?"

6. For information on the mothers and fathers I interviewed, see table 3.

7. Collins, *Making Motherhood Work*; Calarco, *Holding It Together*; Gerson, "Moral Dilemmas, Moral Strategies, and the Transformation of Gender"; Hays, *Cultural Contradictions of Motherhood*; Hochschild and Machung, *Second Shift*.

8. From the 2012–13 academic year through the 2017–18 academic year, citywide K–3 class sizes averaged around 24 students, an increase from the 20.9 average in the 2007–8 academic year. Average class sizes in New York City are 15 to 30 percent higher on average than class sizes across the rest of the state. For more information, see New York City Public Schools, "Class Size Reports."

9. Early intervention services in New York City help children from age birth to age 3 who are "not learning, playing, growing, talking or walking like other children their age." The program works with families to set goals for their children and create a service plan in partnership with the family. See NYC Health, "Early Intervention."

10. New York State law requires that each student with a disability have an IEP (individualized education program) in effect for each academic year. In New York City, the IEP team includes IEP professionals and the parents, who work together to determine eligibility for disability services. In order for children to be evaluated for disability services, a parent or Department of Education official submits a referral letter. The parent provides consent for an initial evaluation. Preschool-age students are evaluated at approved evaluation sites, elementary-age students at their current school.

11. Calarco, *Holding It Together*; Collins, *Making Motherhood Work*; Elliott, Powell, and Brenton, "Being a Good Mom."

12. Christopher, "Extensive Mothering"; Sattin-Bajaj and Roda, "Opportunity Hoarding in School Choice Contexts."

13. Ball and Vincent, "'I Heard It on the Grapevine'"; Horvat, Weininger, and Lareau, "From Social Ties to Social Capital"; Lareau, Evans, and Yee, "Rules of the Game."

14. Ball and Vincent, "'I Heard It on the Grapevine'"; Sattin-Bajaj and Roda, "Opportunity Hoarding in School Choice Contexts"; Calarco, *Negotiating Opportunities*; Lareau, *Unequal Childhoods*; Posey-Maddox, *When Middle-Class Parents Choose Urban Schools*.

15. Fong, "Subject to Evaluation"; Lareau and Horvat, "Moments of Social Inclusion and Exclusion"; Cucchiara and Horvat, "Perils and Promises"; Horvat, Weininger, and Lareau, "From Social Ties to Social Capital"; Lareau, Evans, and Yee, "Rules of the Game."

16. Schneider et al., "Networks to Nowhere"; Schneider, Teske, and Marschall, *Choosing Schools*.

17. Sattin-Bajaj and Roda, "Opportunity Hoarding in School Choice Contexts"; Cucchiara and Horvat, "Perils and Promises"; Kimelberg, "Middle-Class Parents, Risk, and Urban Public Schools."

18. Elliott and Aseltine, "Raising Teenagers in Hostile Environments"; Elliott and Reid, "Low-Income Black Mothers Parenting Adolescents in the Mass Incarceration Era";

Elliott, Powell, and Brenton, "Being a Good Mom"; Randles, "'Willing to Do Anything for My Kids'"; Daminger, "Cognitive Dimension of Household Labor."

19. Villalobos, *Motherload*; McCormack, "Stratified Reproduction and Poor Women's Resistance"; Edin and Kefalas, *Promises I Can Keep*.

20. Dow, "Deadly Challenges of Raising African American Boys"; Fox-Williams, "Rules of (Dis)Engagement"; Jarrett, "African American Family and Parenting Strategies in Impoverished Neighborhoods"; Jarrett and Jefferson, "'A Good Mother Got to Fight for Her Kids'"; Verduzco-Baker, "'I Don't Want Them to Be a Statistic.'"

21. Research finds that frequent school changes can negatively impact student performance. For more information, see Rumberger, "Causes and Consequences of Student Mobility"; Mehana and Reynolds, "School Mobility and Achievement"; Grigg, "School Enrollment Changes and Student Achievement Growth."

22. Bell, "Geography in Parental Choice"; Bell, "All Choices Created Equal?"; Bell, "Space and Place."

23. Burdick-Will, "Neighborhood Violence, Peer Effects, and Academic Achievement in Chicago"; Shedd, *Unequal City*.

24. Families can apply for a child transfer at a Family Welcome Center for one or more of the following reasons: (1) school safety, (2) accessibility needs, (3) academic or social concerns, (4) new residence, (5) sibling at a different school, (6) childcare hardship, (7) travel hardship. For more information, see New York City Department of Education, "Transfers."

25. Goldweber, Waasdorp, and Bradshaw, "Examining Associations between Race, Urbanicity, and Patterns of Bullying Involvement."

26. For more information about neighborhood poverty levels for the sample participants, see table 3.

27. Hays, *Cultural Contradictions of Motherhood*.

28. Milkie, Raley, and Bianchi, "Taking on the Second Shift"; Daminger, "Cognitive Dimension of Household Labor."

29. Bianchi, Robinson, and Milke, *Changing Rhythms of American Family Life*; Craig, "Does Father Care Mean Fathers Share?"; Doucet, "'It's Just Not Good for a Man to Be Interested in Other People's Children.'"

30. Christiansen and Palkovitz, "Why the 'Good Provider' Role Still Matters"; Connell and Messerschmidt, "Hegemonic Masculinity"; Wall and Arnold, "How Involved Is Involved Fathering?"; Randles, "'Manning Up' to Be a Good Father."

31. Townsend, *Package Deal*; Posey-Maddox, "Schooling in Suburbia."

32. Allen, "'They Think Minority Means Lesser Than'"; Allen, "'Tell Your Own Story.'"

33. Daminger, "Cognitive Dimension of Household Labor."

34. Cooper, "School Choice as 'Motherwork.'"

35. Shows and Gerstel, "Fathering, Class, and Gender."

36. Daminger, "Cognitive Dimension of Household Labor."

37. Doucet, "'It's Just Not Good for a Man to Be Interested in Other People's Children.'"

38. Parcel, Hendrix, and Taylor, "'How Far Is Too Far?'"; Randles, "'Willing to Do Anything for My Kids'"; Reay and Ball, "'Making Their Minds Up'"; Townsend, *Package Deal*.

39. Lareau, "My Wife Can Tell Me Who I Know."

40. Daminger, "Cognitive Dimension of Household Labor"; Milkie, Raley, and Bianchi, "Taking on the Second Shift."

Chapter 2

1. Gandini, "Fundamentals of the Reggio Emilia Approach to Early Childhood Education."

2. The Common Core Standards Initiative is a multi-state initiative aimed at increasing k-12 educational consistency across the United States. The New York Board of Regents adopted the Common Core State Standards (CCSS) in 2010 and later revised them in 2017.

3. Cucchiara, "'Are We Doing Damage?'"; Cucchiara and Horvat, "Choosing Selves"; Lareau, Evans, and Yee, "Rules of the Game"; Nelson, *Parenting Out of Control*.

4. Ben-Porath and Johanek, *Making Up Our Mind*; Chen and Moskop, "School Choice's Idealized Premises and Unfulfilled Promises."

5. Cucchiara, "'Are We Doing Damage?'"; Cucchiara and Horvat, "Choosing Selves."

6. Bader, Lareau, and Evans, "Talk on the Playground"; Rhodes, Szabo, and Warkentien, "'I Went There'"; Hamlin and Cheng, "Parental Empowerment, Involvement, and Satisfaction"; Sattin-Bajaj, "Two Roads Diverged"; Sattin-Bajaj and Roda, "Opportunity Hoarding in School Choice Contexts"; Fong, "Subject to Evaluation"; Lareau, Evans, and Yee, "Rules of the Game"; Schneider, Teske, and Marschall, *Choosing Schools*.

7. For more information about the distribution of the decision-making logics and the school performance data, see table 4.

8. For more information about school characteristics, see table 4.

9. Nickson, "Embracing the City"; Bell, "Space and Place"; Ewing, *Ghosts in the Schoolyard*.

10. Burdick-Will, "School Location, Social Ties, and Perceived Neighborhood Boundaries."

11. Bell, "Space and Place"; Rhodes, Szabo, and Warkentien, "'I Went There.'"

12. Raudenbush, "'I Stay by Myself.'"

13. Burdick-Will, "School Location, Social Ties, and Perceived Neighborhood Boundaries"; Small, *Unanticipated Gains*; Small, *Villa Victoria*; Montgomery, "'Living in Each Other's Pockets.'"

14. Hailey, "Racialized Perceptions of Anticipated School Belonging."

15. Ewing, *Ghosts in the Schoolyard*.

16. Burdick-Will, "School Location, Social Ties, and Perceived Neighborhood Boundaries."

17. Morris, "Pillar of Strength."

18. Hunter, *Black Citymakers*; Hunter and Robinson, *Chocolate Cities*.

19. Ewing, *Ghosts in the Schoolyard*; Fullilove, *Root Shock*; Bailey-Fakhoury, Perhamus, and Ma, "Feeling Displaced, Enacting Resistance"; Green, "'We Felt They Took the Heart out of the Community.'"

20. Bulman, "School-Choice Stories."

21. Rhodes, Szabo, and Warkentien, "'I Went There'"; Sikkink and Schwarz, "Apple Doesn't Fall Far from the Parent's School."

22. Rhodes, Szabo, and Warkentien, "'I Went There'"; Szabo, "'I Just Didn't Want to Risk It'"; Pattillo, "Everyday Politics of School Choice in the Black Community"; Hamlin, "Flight to Safety in Deindustrialized Cities."

23. Pattillo, "Everyday Politics of School Choice in the Black Community"; Ellison and Aloe, "Strategic Thinkers and Positioned Choices"; Szabo, "'I Just Didn't Want to Risk It.'"

24. Rhodes, Szabo, and Warkentien, "'I Went There.'"

25. Rhodes, Szabo, and Warkentien.

26. Ramirez, "Dismay and Disappointment"; Taylor Haynes, Phillips, and Goldring, "Latino Parents' Choice of Magnet School."

27. Coleman, "Social Capital in the Creation of Human Capital"; Portes and Rivas, "Adaptation of Migrant Children"; Portes, "Social Capital."

28. Szalacha et al., "Academic Pathways and Children of Immigrant Families"; Kao and Tienda, "Optimism and Achievement"; Portes and Rivas, "Adaptation of Migrant Children."

29. Perreira, Harris, and Lee, "Making It in America"; Feliciano, "Beyond the Family."

30. Roubeni et al., "'If We Can't Do It, Our Children Will Do It One Day.'"

31. Alba, Sloan, and Sperling, "Integration Imperative"; Feliciano and Lanuza, "An Immigrant Paradox?"; Feliciano, "Educational Selectivity in U.S. Immigration."

32. Feliciano, "Beyond the Family"; Fuligni, "Academic Achievement of Adolescents from Immigrant Families"; Hagelskamp, Suárez-Orozco, and Hughes, "Migrating to Opportunities."

33. Sall, "Selective Acculturation among Low-Income Second-Generation West Africans"; Sall, "Convergent Identifications, Divergent Meanings."

34. Suárez-Orozco, Rhodes, and Milburn, "Unraveling the Immigrant Paradox"; Hollander, "Negotiating Trauma and Loss in the Migration Experience."

35. Debs, *Diverse Families, Desirable Schools*; Kafka, "When Information Is Not Enough"; Kimelberg and Billingham, "Attitudes toward Diversity and the School Choice Process"; Wells, "Process of Racial Resegregation in Housing and Schools"; Holme, "Buying Homes, Buying Schools."

36. Sattin-Bajaj and Roda, "Opportunity Hoarding in School Choice Contexts"; Cooper, *Cut Adrift*; Kimelberg and Billingham, "Attitudes toward Diversity and the School Choice Process"; Wells, "Process of Racial Resegregation in Housing and Schools."

37. Debs et al., "Happiness-Oriented Parents."

38. Acosta and Hutchison, *Happiest Kids in the World*; Payne and Ross, *Simplicity Parenting*.

39. Cucchiara and Horvat, "Perils and Promises"; Cucchiara and Horvat, "Choosing Selves"; Kafka, "When Information Is Not Enough"; Brown, "Intensive Mothering and the Unequal School-Search Burden"; Kimelberg and Billingham, "Attitudes toward Diversity and the School Choice Process"; Roda, "School Choice and the Politics of Parenthood"; Roda and Wells, "School Choice Policies and Racial Segregation."

40. Kimelberg, "Beyond Test Scores."

41. Kimelberg; Debs et al., "Happiness-Oriented Parents"; Underhill, "'Diversity Is Important to Me.'"

42. Cucchiara, "'Are We Doing Damage?'"

Chapter 3

1. Walker, *Their Highest Potential*; Massey and Denton, *American Apartheid*.

2. Allen, "Racial Politics of Elementary School Choice."

3. Posey-Maddox et al., "No Choice Is the 'Right' Choice."

4. Posey-Maddox, "Race in Place"; Lewis-McCoy, *Inequality in the Promised Land*; McCarthy Foubert, "'Damned if You Do, Damned if You Don't.'"

5. Rhodes and DeLuca, "Residential Mobility and School Choice among Poor Families"; Pattillo, "Everyday Politics of School Choice in the Black Community"; Vincent et al., "Intersectional Work and Precarious Positionings"; Diamond and Gomez, "African American Parents' Educational Orientations"; Allen, "Racial Politics of Elementary School Choice."

6. Hailey, "Racialized Perceptions of Anticipated School Belonging"; Hailey, "Racial Preferences for Schools"; Kimelberg and Billingham, "Attitudes toward Diversity and the School Choice Process"; Billingham and Hunt, "School Racial Composition and Parental Choice"; Renzulli and Evans, "School Choice, Charter Schools, and White Flight"; Evans, "'I Wanted Diversity, but Not So Much'"; Sattin-Bajaj and Roda, "Opportunity Hoarding in School Choice Contexts."

7. For more information about the racial composition of the schools parents selected, see table 5.

8. Underhill, "'Diversity Is Important to Me'"; Gillen-O'Neel et al., "From Kindness and Diversity to Justice and Action"; Freeman, Martinez, and Raval, "What Do White Parents Teach Youth about Race?"

9. Based on NYC DOE data from the 2016–17 academic year (see Mader, Hemphill, and Abbas, "Paradox of Choice"), this percentage is similar to rates of enrollment for Black kindergarten students but higher than the average for Latino kindergarteners. Only 40 percent of Latino kindergarteners opted out of their neighborhood school.

10. *Brown v. Board of Education*, 347 U.S. 483 (1954); Lewis and Diamond, *Despite the Best Intentions*; Tyson, *Integration Interrupted*.

11. Scott, "School Choice and the Empowerment Imperative."

12. Dow, *Mothering while Black*.

13. Cooper, "School Choice and the Standpoint of African American Mothers."

14. Posey-Maddox et al., "No Choice Is the 'Right' Choice"; Lewis-McCoy, *Inequality in the Promised Land*; Dumas, "Against the Dark."

15. Hailey, "Racialized Perceptions of Anticipated School Belonging."

16. Beginning in 2014, universal pre-K aimed to provide free full-day care to children turning four (see New York City Office of the Mayor, "Ready to Launch"; Baron, "New York Takes First Step toward Universal Pre-K"; New York City Office of the Mayor, "New York City Launches Historic Expansion of Pre-K to More Than 51,000 Children").

17. Dumas, "Against the Dark"; Lewis and Diamond, *Despite the Best Intentions*.

18. Frankenberg, Siegel-Hawley, and Wang, "Choice without Equity"; Orfield and Frankenberg, *Educational Delusions?*; Orfield and Lee, "Why Segregation Matters"; Reardon and Owens, "60 Years after *Brown*"; Owens, Reardon, and Jencks, "Income Segregation between Schools and School Districts."

19. Cooper, "School Choice as 'Motherwork'"; Lareau and Horvat, "Moments of Social Inclusion and Exclusion."

20. Ladson-Billings, "Toward a Theory of Culturally Relevant Pedagogy."

21. Posey-Maddox, "Race in Place."

22. Powell and Coles, "'We Still Here'"; Reynolds, "'They Think You're Lazy'"; Golann, Debs, and Weiss, "'To Be Strict on Your Own'"; Vincent et al., "Being Strategic, Being Watchful, Being Determined."

23. Dow, *Mothering While Black*; Dow, "Deadly Challenges of Raising African American Boys"; Williams et al., "Black Mothers' Perceptions of the Role of Race in Children's Education."

24. Cooper and Smalls, "Culturally Distinctive and Academic Socialization"; Rowley, Helaire, and Banerjee, "Reflecting on Racism."

25. Chubb and Moe, *Politics, Markets, and America's Schools*; Ellison and Aloe, "Strategic Thinkers and Positioned Choices."

26. Kimelberg and Billingham, "Attitudes toward Diversity and the School Choice Process"; Hailey, "Racial Preferences for Schools"; Scott, *School Choice and Diversity*; Underhill, "'Diversity Is Important to Me'"; Turner, "Marketing Diversity."

27. Vittrup, "Color Blind or Color Conscious?"; Posey-Maddox, *When Middle-Class Parents Choose Urban Schools*; Hagerman, "Reproducing and Reworking Colorblind Racial Ideology"; Hagerman, "White Families and Race."

28. Underhill, "'Diversity Is Important to Me.'"

29. Debs, *Diverse Families, Desirable Schools*.

30. Khan, *Privilege*.

31. Billingham and Hunt, "School Racial Composition and Parental Choice."

32. Horvat, Weininger, and Lareau, "From Social Ties to Social Capital."

33. Scott, "School Choice and the Empowerment Imperative."

Chapter 4

1. New York City Independent Budget Office, "Student Demographics and Enrollment Trends."

2. DeLuca, Darrah-Okike, and Nerenberg, "'I Just Had to Go with It Once I Got There.'"

3. Mader, Hemphill, and Abbas, "Paradox of Choice."

4. See table 6 for information on the relative distances parents travel to their child's school.

5. Mader, Hemphill, and Abbas, "Paradox of Choice."

6. Mader, Hemphill, and Abbas.

7. Aggarwal, *Unsettling Choice*.

8. Cucchiara, *Marketing Schools, Marketing Cities*; Posey-Maddox, *When Middle-Class Parents Choose Urban Schools*.

9. Freidus, "'A Great School Benefits Us All'"; Gordon, "'It's a Little, Tiny Process'"; Makris, "Chimera of Choice"; Pearman and Swain, "School Choice, Gentrification, and the Variable Significance of Racial Stratification in Urban Neighborhoods."

10. Bell, "Geography in Parental Choice"; Bell, "All Choices Created Equal?"; Burdick-Will, "School Location, Social Ties, and Perceived Neighborhood Boundaries"; Foster et al., "Spatial Dimensions of Social Capital"; Henig, "Geo-spatial Analyses and School Choice Research"; Lubienski and Dougherty, "Mapping Educational Opportunity"; Lubienski and Lee, "Geo-spatial Analyses in Education Research."

11. Bell, "Geography in Parental Choice"; Bell, "Space and Place."

12. Bell, "Space and Place"; Small, *Unanticipated Gains*.

13. Crosnoe, "Social Capital and the Interplay of Families and Schools"; Small, "Neighborhood Institutions as Resource Brokers."

14. Sohoni and Saporito, "Mapping School Segregation"; Rhodes and DeLuca, "Residential Mobility and School Choice among Poor Families"; Rhodes and Warkentien, "Unwrapping the Suburban 'Package Deal'"; Grady, Bielick, and Aud, "Trends in the Use of School Choice"; Snyder, de Brey, and Dillow, "Digest of Education Statistics 2017."

15. Burdick-Will, "School Location, Social Ties, and Perceived Neighborhood Boundaries."

16. Pattillo, *Black Picket Fences*; Pattillo, "Black Middle-Class Neighborhoods."

17. Bell, "Geography in Parental Choice"; Bell, "Space and Place."

18. Freeman, *There Goes the Hood*; Zukin et al., "New Retail Capital and Neighborhood Change."

19. Raudenbush, "'I Stay by Myself.'"

20. Bernstein and Isaac, "Gentrification"; Betancur, "Gentrification and Community Fabric in Chicago"; Brown-Saracino, *Neighborhood That Never Changes*.

21. Jarrett and Jefferson, "'A Good Mother Got to Fight for Her Kids'"; Ross and Jang, "Neighborhood Disorder, Fear, and Mistrust."

22. Furstenberg, "Managing to Make It"; Wacquant and Wilson, "Cost of Racial and Class Exclusion in the Inner City"; Tigges, Browne, and Green, "Social Isolation of the Urban Poor."

23. Coulton, Chan, and Mikelbank, "Finding Place in Community Change Initiatives"; Theodos, Coulton, and Budde, "Getting to Better Performing Schools"; Shedd, *Unequal City*.

24. Burdick-Will, "School Location, Social Ties, and Perceived Neighborhood Boundaries"; Bell, "Space and Place."

25. Cahill, "Childhood and Public Life"; Dahl, Ceballo, and Huerta, "In the Eye of the Beholder"; Anderson, *Code of the Street*.

26. For neighborhood information, see table 6.

27. Raudenbush, "'I Stay by Myself.'"

28. Small, "Neighborhood Institutions as Resource Brokers"; Small, *Unanticipated Gains*; Montgomery, "'Living in Each Other's Pockets'"; Jarrett and Jefferson, "'A Good Mother Got to Fight for Her Kids.'"

29. Dahl, Ceballo, and Huerta, "In the Eye of the Beholder"; Montgomery, "'Living in Each Other's Pockets.'"

30. Visser, Bolt, and van Kempen, "A Good Place to Raise Your Children?"; Byrnes and Miller, "Relationship between Neighborhood Characteristics and Effective Parenting Behaviors."

31. Visser, Bolt, and van Kempen, "A Good Place to Raise Your Children?"

32. Betancur, "Gentrification and Community Fabric in Chicago"; Freeman, *There Goes the Hood*.

33. For details about relative poverty levels in Brownsville, see data from the New York City Department of Health, "Community Health Profiles 2015."

34. Montgomery, "'Living in Each Other's Pockets.'"

35. Burdick-Will, "School Location, Social Ties, and Perceived Neighborhood Boundaries"; Thornton et al., "Sociodemographic and Environmental Correlates of Racial Socialization by Black Parents."

36. Briggs, "Brown Kids in White Suburbs"; Coleman, "Social Capital in the Creation of Human Capital"; De Silva et al., "Social Capital and Mental Illness"; Small, *Unanticipated Gains*; DiPrete et al., "Segregation in Social Networks Based on Acquaintanceship and Trust."

37. See table 6 for specific neighborhood information.

38. Sharkey and Faber, "Where, When, Why, and for Whom Do Residential Contexts Matter?"; Byrnes and Miller, "Relationship between Neighborhood Characteristics and Effective Parenting Behaviors"; Ceballo and McLoyd, "Social Support and Parenting"; Dahl, Ceballo, and Huerta, "In the Eye of the Beholder"; Tigges, Browne, and Green, "Social Isolation of the Urban Poor"; Burdick-Will, "School Location, Social Ties, and Perceived Neighborhood

Boundaries"; Tran et al., "Participation in Context"; Carpiano and Kimbro, "Neighborhood Social Capital, Parenting Strain, and Personal Mastery"; Silva et al., "Social Capital and Mental Illness"; Browning and Cagney, "Neighborhood Structural Disadvantage, Collective Efficacy, and Self-Rated Physical Health in an Urban Setting"; McMahon, Felix, and Nagarajan, "Social Support and Neighborhood Stressors among African American Youth."

Conclusion

1. Gillis, "School Choice and Inequality"; Gillis, "Teaching Sociology of Education."

2. National Center for Education Statistics, "School Choice in the United States."

3. Jennings, "School Choice or Schools' Choice?"; Rich and Jennings, "Choice, Information, and Constrained Options"; Oakes, *Keeping Track.*

4. Urena, "Relational Risk."

5. Fong and Faude, "Timing Is Everything."

6. Sattin-Bajaj and Roda, "Opportunity Hoarding in School Choice Contexts."

7. Nuamah, *Closed for Democracy*; Ewing, *Ghosts in the Schoolyard*; Caven, "Quantification, Inequality, and the Contestation of School Closures in Philadelphia"; Lee and Lubienski, "Impact of School Closures on Equity of Access in Chicago"; Green, "'We Felt They Took the Heart out of the Community.'"

8. Mader, Hemphill, and Abbas, "Paradox of Choice."

Methodological Appendix

1. Jennings, "School Choice or Schools' Choice?"; O'Day, Bitter, and Gomez, *Education Reform in New York City.*

2. Bell, "Geography in Parental Choice"; Bell, "Space and Place"; Bell, "All Choices Created Equal?"

3. I decided to focus on parents with children who were at least five years of age because universal pre-K policies were just developing and 3K programs had yet to be established. Interviewing parents with children five and older would also allow parents to reflect on school decision-making for potentially two or more enrollment cycles.

4. Small, *Unanticipated Gains*; Small, *Villa Victoria.*

5. While I asked about parents' partnership status and gender identity, I did not explicitly ask about their sexual orientation. The absence of this information reflects a limitation to the scope of the study and highlights the need for future studies to examine school decision-making labor from the perspective of LGBTQ+ families.

6. Hays, *Cultural Contradictions of Motherhood*; Lareau, "My Wife Can Tell Me Who I Know"; Randles, "'Willing to Do Anything for My Kids'"; Daminger, "Cognitive Dimension of Household Labor."

7. Lareau, *Home Advantage*; Lareau, Evans, and Yee, "Rules of the Game."

8. Small, "'How Many Cases Do I Need?'"; Yin, *Case Study Research and Applications.*

9. Lareau, *Unequal Childhoods*; Edin and Kefalas, *Promises I Can Keep.*

10. Weiss, *Learning from Strangers.*

11. Cooper, "School Choice as 'Motherwork'"; Merriam, *Qualitative Research and Case Study Applications in Education.*

12. Weiss, *Learning from Strangers*.

13. Ladson-Billings and Tate, "Toward a Critical Race Theory of Education."

14. Weiss, *Learning from Strangers*.

15. Strauss and Glaser, *Discovery of Grounded Theory*.

16. Miles, Huberman, and Saldana, *Qualitative Data Analysis*.

17. Miles, Huberman, and Saldana.

18. Ragin, *Comparative Method*.

19. My interviews captured parents' experiences within a few years of making an elementary school decision for their children. Interviewing parents a few academic years after enrollment may result in retrospective bias. I carefully compared interviews with parents who had just completed the process and those with parents who had done so earlier during my data analysis.

BIBLIOGRAPHY

Acosta, Rina Mae, and Michele Hutchison. *The Happiest Kids in the World: How Dutch Parents Help Their Kids (and Themselves) by Doing Less*. The Experiment, 2017.

Aggarwal, Ujju. *Unsettling Choice: Race, Rights, and the Partitioning of Public Education*. University of Minnesota Press, 2024.

Alba, Richard, Jennifer Sloan, and Jessica Sperling. "The Integration Imperative: The Children of Low-Status Immigrants in the Schools of Wealthy Societies." *Annual Review of Sociology* 37, no. 1 (2011): 395–415. https://doi.org/10.1146/annurev-soc-081309-150219.

Allen, Quaylan. "'Tell Your Own Story': Manhood, Masculinity and Racial Socialization among Black Fathers and Their Sons." *Ethnic and Racial Studies* 39, no. 10 (August 8, 2016): 1831–48. https://doi.org/10.1080/01419870.2015.1110608.

———. "'They Think Minority Means Lesser Than': Black Middle-Class Sons and Fathers Resisting Microaggressions in the School." *Urban Education* 48, no. 2 (March 1, 2013): 171–97. https://doi.org/10.1177/0042085912450575.

Allen, Shannon N. "The Racial Politics of Elementary School Choice for Black Parents Living in Brooklyn, NY." PhD dissertation, City University of New York, 2017.

Anderson, Elijah. *Code of the Street*. Norton, 1999.

André-Bechely, Lois. *Could It Be Otherwise? Parents and the Inequalities of Public School Choice*. Routledge, 2013.

Archbald, Douglas A. "School Choice, Magnet Schools, and the Liberation Model: An Empirical Study." *Sociology of Education* 77, no. 4 (October 1, 2004): 283–310. https://doi.org/10.1177/003804070407700402.

Archbald, Doug, Andrew Hurwitz, and Felicia Hurwitz. "Charter Schools, Parent Choice, and Segregation: A Longitudinal Study of the Growth of Charters and Changing Enrollment Patterns in Five School Districts over 26 Years." *Education Policy Analysis Archives* 26 (February 19, 2017): 22.

Bader, Michael D. M., Annette Lareau, and Shani A. Evans. "Talk on the Playground: The Neighborhood Context of School Choice." *City & Community* 18, no. 2 (June 1, 2019): 483–508. https://doi.org/10.1111/cico.12410.

Bailey-Fakhoury, Chasity, Lisa M. Perhamus, and Kin M. Ma. "Feeling Displaced, Enacting Resistance: Race, Place, and Schooling in the Face of Gentrifying Forces." *Urban Review* 54, no. 1 (March 1, 2022): 1–40. https://doi.org/10.1007/s11256-021-00608-z.

Ball, Stephen J., and Carol Vincent. "'I Heard It on the Grapevine': 'Hot' Knowledge and School Choice." *British Journal of Sociology of Education* 19, no. 3 (1998): 377–400.

Baron, Kathryn. "New York Takes First Step toward Universal Pre-K." *Education Week*, August 27, 2014. www.edweek.org/leadership/new-york-takes-first-step-toward-universal-pre-k/2014/08.

Beal, Heather K. Olson, and Petra Munro Hendry. "The Ironies of School Choice: Empowering Parents and Reconceptualizing Public Education." *American Journal of Education* 118, no. 4 (2012): 521–50.

Bell, Courtney A. "All Choices Created Equal? The Role of Choice Sets in the Selection of Schools." *Peabody Journal of Education* 84, no. 2 (2009): 191–208.

———. "Geography in Parental Choice." *American Journal of Education* 115, no. 4 (2009): 493–521.

———. "Space and Place: Urban Parents' Geographical Preferences for Schools." *Urban Review* 39, no. 4 (2007): 375–404.

Ben-Porath, Sigal R., and Michael C. Johanek. *Making Up Our Mind: What School Choice Is Really About.* University of Chicago Press, 2019.

Berends, Mark. "Sociology and School Choice: What We Know after Two Decades of Charter Schools." *Annual Review of Sociology* 41 (2015): 159–80.

Bergman, Peter, and Isaac McFarlin Jr. "Education for All? A Nationwide Audit Study of School Choice." National Bureau of Economic Research, December 2018. https://doi.org/10.3386/w25396.

Bernstein, Arla G., and Carol A. Isaac. "Gentrification: The Role of Dialogue in Community Engagement and Social Cohesion." *Journal of Urban Affairs* 45, no. 4 (April 21, 2023): 753–70. https://doi.org/10.1080/07352166.2021.1877550.

Betancur, John. "Gentrification and Community Fabric in Chicago." *Urban Studies* 48, no. 2 (February 1, 2011): 383–406. https://doi.org/10.1177/0042098009360680.

Bianchi, Suzanne M., John P. Robinson, and Melissa A. Milke. *The Changing Rhythms of American Family Life.* Russell Sage Foundation, 2006.

Bifulco, Robert, and Helen F. Ladd. "School Choice, Racial Segregation, and Test-Score Gaps: Evidence from North Carolina's Charter School Program." *Journal of Policy Analysis and Management* 26, no. 1 (2007): 31–56. https://doi.org/10.1002/pam.20226.

Bifulco, Robert, Helen F. Ladd, and Stephen L. Ross. "The Effects of Public School Choice on Those Left Behind: Evidence from Durham, North Carolina." *Peabody Journal of Education* 84, no. 2 (April 10, 2009): 130–49. https://doi.org/10.1080/01619560902810104.

Billingham, Chase M., and Matthew O. Hunt. "School Racial Composition and Parental Choice: New Evidence on the Preferences of White Parents in the United States." *Sociology of Education* 89, no. 2 (2016): 99–117.

Billingham, Chase M., Shelley M. Kimelberg, Sarah Faude, and Matthew O. Hunt. "In Search of a Safe School: Racialized Perceptions of Security and the School Choice Process." *Sociological Quarterly* 61, no. 3 (July 2, 2020): 474–99. https://doi.org/10.1080/00380253.2019.1711257.

Briggs, Xavier de Souza. "Brown Kids in White Suburbs: Housing Mobility and the Many Faces of Social Capital." *Housing Policy Debate* 9, no. 1 (January 1, 1998): 177–221. https://doi.org/10.1080/10511482.1998.9521290.

Brown, Bailey A. "Intensive Mothering and the Unequal School-Search Burden." *Sociology of Education* 95, no. 1 (January 1, 2022): 3–22. https://doi.org/10.1177/00380407211048453.

Browning, Christopher R., and Kathleen A. Cagney. "Neighborhood Structural Disadvantage, Collective Efficacy, and Self-Rated Physical Health in an Urban Setting." *Journal of Health and Social Behavior* 43, no. 4 (2002): 383–99. https://doi.org/10.2307/3090233.

Brown-Saracino, Japonica. *A Neighborhood That Never Changes: Gentrification, Social Preservation, and the Search for Authenticity.* University of Chicago Press, 2009.

Bulman, Robert C. "School-Choice Stories: The Role of Culture." *Sociological Inquiry* 74, no. 4 (2004): 492–519. https://doi.org/10.1111/j.1475-682X.2004.00102.x.

Burdick-Will, Julia. "Neighborhood Violence, Peer Effects, and Academic Achievement in Chicago." *Sociology of Education* 91, no. 3 (July 1, 2018): 205–23. https://doi.org/10.1177/00380 40718779063.

———. "School Location, Social Ties, and Perceived Neighborhood Boundaries." *City & Community* 17, no. 2 (2018): 418–37. https://doi.org/10.1111/cico.12295.

Byrnes, Hilary F., and Brenda A. Miller. "The Relationship between Neighborhood Characteristics and Effective Parenting Behaviors: The Role of Social Support." *Journal of Family Issues* 33, no. 12 (December 1, 2012): 1658–87. https://doi.org/10.1177/0192513X12437693.

Cahill, Spencer E. "Childhood and Public Life: Reaffirming Biographical Divisions." *Social Problems* 37, no. 3 (1990): 390–402.

Calarco, Jessica. *Holding It Together: How Women Became America's Safety Net.* Penguin, 2024.

———. *Negotiating Opportunities: How the Middle Class Secures Advantages in School.* Oxford University Press, 2018.

Carpiano, Richard M., and Rachel T. Kimbro. "Neighborhood Social Capital, Parenting Strain, and Personal Mastery among Female Primary Caregivers of Children." *Journal of Health and Social Behavior* 53, no. 2 (2012): 232–47.

Caven, Meg. "Quantification, Inequality, and the Contestation of School Closures in Philadelphia." *Sociology of Education* 92, no. 1 (January 2019): 21–40. https://doi.org/10.1177/0038040718815167.

Ceballo, Rosario, and Vonnie C. McLoyd. "Social Support and Parenting in Poor, Dangerous Neighborhoods." *Child Development* 73, no. 4 (2002): 1310–21.

Center for American Progress. "New York City's Children First." March 21, 2014. https://www.americanprogress.org/article/new-york-citys-children-first/.

Chen, Katherine K., and Megan Moskop. "School Choice's Idealized Premises and Unfulfilled Promises: How School Markets Simulate Options, Encourage Decoupling and Deception, and Deepen Disadvantages." *Sociology Compass* 14, no. 3 (2020): e12766.

Christiansen, Shawn L., and Rob Palkovitz. "Why the 'Good Provider' Role Still Matters: Providing as a Form of Paternal Involvement." *Journal of Family Issues* 22, no. 1 (2001): 84–106.

Christopher, Karen. "Extensive Mothering: Employed Mothers' Constructions of the Good Mother." *Gender & Society* 26, no. 1 (2012): 73–96.

Chubb, John E., and Terry M. Moe. *Politics, Markets, and America's Schools.* Brookings Institution Press, 1990.

Cohodes, Sarah R., and Katharine S. Parham. "Charter Schools' Effectiveness, Mechanisms, and Competitive Influence." National Bureau of Economic Research, February 2021. https://doi.org/10.3386/w28477.

Coleman, James S. "Social Capital in the Creation of Human Capital." *American Journal of Sociology* 94 (1988): S95–120.

Collins, Caitlyn. *Making Motherhood Work: How Women Manage Careers and Caregiving*. Princeton University Press, 2019.

Collins, Patricia Hill. "It's All in the Family: Intersections of Gender, Race, and Nation." *Hypatia* 13, no. 3 (1998): 62–82.

———. "Shifting the Center: Race, Class, and Feminist Theorizing about Motherhood." In *Mothering: Ideology, Experience, and Agency*, edited by Evelyn Nakano Glenn, Grace Chang, and Linda Rennie Forcey, 45–65. Routledge, 2016.

Coltrane, Scott. "Research on Household Labor: Modeling and Measuring the Social Embeddedness of Routine Family Work." *Journal of Marriage and Family* 62, no. 4 (2000): 1208–33.

Connell, Robert W., and James W. Messerschmidt. "Hegemonic Masculinity: Rethinking the Concept." *Gender & Society* 19, no. 6 (2005): 829–59.

Cookson, Peter W., Jr., and Charlotte S. Lucks. "School Choice in New York City: Preliminary Observations." In *Restructuring Schools: Promising Practices and Policies*, edited by Maureen T. Hallinan, 99–110. Springer, 1995.

Cooper, Camille Wilson. "School Choice and the Standpoint of African American Mothers: Considering the Power of Positionality." *Journal of Negro Education* 74, no. 2 (2005): 174–89.

———. "School Choice as 'Motherwork': Valuing African-American Women's Educational Advocacy and Resistance." *International Journal of Qualitative Studies in Education* 20, no. 5 (2007): 491–512.

Cooper, Marianne. *Cut Adrift: Families in Insecure Times*. University of California Press, 2014.

Cooper, Shauna M., and Ciara Smalls. "Culturally Distinctive and Academic Socialization: Direct and Interactive Relationships with African American Adolescents' Academic Adjustment." *Journal of Youth and Adolescence* 39 (2010): 199–212.

Corcoran, Sean, Jennifer Jennings, Sarah Cohodes, and Carolyn Sattin-Bajaj. "Leveling the Playing Field for High School Choice: Results from a Field Experiment of Informational Interventions." National Bureau of Economic Research, March 2018. https://doi.org/10.3386/w24471.

Coulton, Claudia, Tsui Chan, and Kristen Mikelbank. "Finding Place in Community Change Initiatives: Using GIS to Uncover Resident Perceptions of Their Neighborhoods." *Journal of Community Practice* 19, no. 1 (2011): 10–28.

Craig, Lyn. "Does Father Care Mean Fathers Share? A Comparison of How Mothers and Fathers in Intact Families Spend Time with Children." *Gender & Society* 20, no. 2 (2006): 259–81.

Crosnoe, Robert. "Social Capital and the Interplay of Families and Schools." *Journal of Marriage and Family* 66, no. 2 (2004): 267–80.

Cucchiara, Maia. "'Are We Doing Damage?' Choosing an Urban Public School in an Era of Parental Anxiety." *Anthropology & Education Quarterly* 44, no. 1 (March 1, 2013): 75–93. https://doi.org/10.1111/aeq.12004.

———. *Marketing Schools, Marketing Cities: Who Wins and Who Loses When Schools Become Urban Amenities*. University of Chicago Press, 2013.

Cucchiara, Maia, and Erin McNamara Horvat. "Choosing Selves: The Salience of Parental Identity in the School Choice Process." *Journal of Education Policy* 29, no. 4 (2014): 486–509.

———. "Perils and Promises: Middle-Class Parental Involvement in Urban Schools." *American Educational Research Journal* 46, no. 4 (2009): 974–1004.

Dahl, Trayci, Rosario Ceballo, and Marisela Huerta. "In the Eye of the Beholder: Mothers' Perceptions of Poor Neighborhoods as Places to Raise Children." *Journal of Community Psychology* 38, no. 4 (2010): 419–34. https://doi.org/10.1002/jcop.20372.

Daminger, Allison. "The Cognitive Dimension of Household Labor." *American Sociological Review* 84, no. 4 (August 1, 2019): 609–33. https://doi.org/10.1177/0003122419859007.

Debs, Mira. *Diverse Families, Desirable Schools: Public Montessori in the Era of School Choice.* Harvard Education Press, 2021.

Debs, Mira, Judith Kafka, Molly Vollman Makris, and Allison Roda. "Happiness-Oriented Parents: An Alternative Perspective on Privilege and Choosing Schools." *American Journal of Education* 129, no. 2 (February 1, 2023): 145–76. https://doi.org/10.1086/723066.

DeLuca, Stefanie, Jennifer Darrah-Okike, and Kiara Millay Nerenberg. "'I Just Had to Go with It Once I Got There': Inequality, Housing, and School Re-optimization." *City & Community* 23, no. 3 (2024): 187–215. https://doi.org/10.1177/15356841241240685.

Denice, Patrick, and Betheny Gross. "Choice, Preferences, and Constraints: Evidence from Public School Applications in Denver." *Sociology of Education* 89, no. 4 (October 2016): 300–320. https://doi.org/10.1177/0038040716664395.

De Silva, Mary J., Kwame McKenzie, Trudy Harpham, and Sharon R. A. Huttly. "Social Capital and Mental Illness: A Systematic Review." *Journal of Epidemiology & Community Health* 59, no. 8 (August 1, 2005): 619–27. https://doi.org/10.1136/jech.2004.029678.

Diamond, John B., and Kimberley Gomez. "African American Parents' Educational Orientations: The Importance of Social Class and Parents' Perceptions of Schools." *Education and Urban Society* 36, no. 4 (August 1, 2004): 383–427. https://doi.org/10.1177/0013124504266827.

DiPrete, Thomas A., Andrew Gelman, Tyler McCormick, Julien Teitler, and Tian Zheng. "Segregation in Social Networks Based on Acquaintanceship and Trust." *American Journal of Sociology* 116, no. 4 (2011): 1234–83.

Doucet, Andrea. "'It's Just Not Good for a Man to Be Interested in Other People's Children': Fathers, Public Displays of Care and 'Relevant Others.'" In *Displaying Families: A New Concept for the Sociology of Family Life*, edited by Esther Dermott and Julie Seymour, 81–101. Springer, 2011.

Dow, Dawn Marie. "The Deadly Challenges of Raising African American Boys: Navigating the Controlling Image of the 'Thug.'" *Gender & Society* 30, no. 2 (April 1, 2016): 161–88. https://doi.org/10.1177/0891243216629928.

———. *Mothering while Black: Boundaries and Burdens of Middle-Class Parenthood.* University of California Press, 2019.

Dumas, Michael J. "Against the Dark: Antiblackness in Education Policy and Discourse." *Theory Into Practice* 55, no. 1 (January 2, 2016): 11–19. https://doi.org/10.1080/00405841.2016.1116852.

Edin, Kathryn, and Maria Kefalas. *Promises I Can Keep: Why Poor Women Put Motherhood before Marriage.* University of California Press, 2011.

Elliott, Sinikka, and Elyshia Aseltine. "Raising Teenagers in Hostile Environments: How Race, Class, and Gender Matter for Mothers' Protective Carework." *Journal of Family Issues* 34, no. 6 (2013): 719–44.

Elliott, Sinikka, Rachel Powell, and Joslyn Brenton. "Being a Good Mom: Low-Income, Black Single Mothers Negotiate Intensive Mothering." *Journal of Family Issues* 36, no. 3 (February 1, 2015): 351–70. https://doi.org/10.1177/0192513X13490279.

Elliott, Sinikka, and Megan Reid. "Low-Income Black Mothers Parenting Adolescents in the Mass Incarceration Era: The Long Reach of Criminalization." *American Sociological Review* 84, no. 2 (2019): 197–219.

Ellison, Scott, and Ariel M. Aloe. "Strategic Thinkers and Positioned Choices: Parental Decision Making in Urban School Choice." *Educational Policy* 33, no. 7 (2019): 1135–70.

Evans, Shani Adia. "'I Wanted Diversity, but Not So Much': Middle-Class White Parents, School Choice, and the Persistence of Anti-Black Stereotypes." *Urban Education* 59, no. 3 (2024): 911–40. https://doi.org/10.1177/00420859211031952.

Ewing, Eve L. *Ghosts in the Schoolyard: Racism and School Closings on Chicago's South Side.* University of Chicago Press, 2018.

Farrie, Danielle C. *School Choice and Segregation: How Race Influences Choices and the Consequences for Neighborhood Public Schools.* ProQuest, 2008.

Feliciano, Cynthia. "Beyond the Family: The Influence of Premigration Group Status on the Educational Expectations of Immigrants' Children." *Sociology of Education* 79, no. 4 (October 1, 2006): 281–303. https://doi.org/10.1177/003804070607900401.

———. "Educational Selectivity in U.S. Immigration: How Do Immigrants Compare to Those Left Behind?" *Demography* 42, no. 1 (February 1, 2005): 131–52. https://doi.org/10.1353/dem.2005.0001.

Feliciano, Cynthia, and Yader R. Lanuza. "An Immigrant Paradox? Contextual Attainment and Intergenerational Educational Mobility." *American Sociological Review* 82, no. 1 (February 2017): 211–41. https://doi.org/10.1177/0003122416684777.

Fong, Kelley. "Subject to Evaluation: How Parents Assess and Mobilize Information from Social Networks in School Choice." *Sociological Forum* 34, no. 1 (2019): 158–80. https://doi.org/10.1111/socf.12483.

Fong, Kelley, and Sarah Faude. "Timing Is Everything: Late Registration and Stratified Access to School Choice." *Sociology of Education* 91, no. 3 (2018): 242–62. https://doi.org/10.1177/0038040718785201.

Foster, Kirk A., Ronald Pitner, Darcy A. Freedman, Bethany A. Bell, and Todd C. Shaw. "Spatial Dimensions of Social Capital." *City & Community* 14, no. 4 (2015): 392–409.

Fox-Williams, Brittany N. "The Rules of (Dis)Engagement: Black Youth and Their Strategies for Navigating Police Contact." *Sociological Forum* 34, no. 1 (2019): 115–37. https://doi.org/10.1111/socf.12484.

Frankenberg, Erica, Genevieve Siegel-Hawley, and Jia Wang. "Choice without Equity: Charter School Segregation and the Need for Civil Rights Standards." UCLA, Civil Rights Project / Proyecto Derechos Civiles, 2010. https://www.civilrightsproject.ucla.edu.

Freeman, Lance. *There Goes the Hood: Views of Gentrification from the Ground Up.* Temple University Press, 2011.

Freeman, McKenna, Andrew Martinez, and Vaishali V. Raval. "What Do White Parents Teach Youth about Race? Qualitative Examination of White Racial Socialization." *Journal of Research on Adolescence* 32, no. 3 (2022): 847–62. https://doi.org/10.1111/jora.12782.

Freidus, Alexandra. "'A Great School Benefits Us All': Advantaged Parents and the Gentrification of an Urban Public School." *Urban Education* 54, no. 8 (October 1, 2019): 1121–48. https://doi.org/10.1177/0042085916636656.

Friedman, Milton. "The Role of Government in Education." In *Economics and the Public Interest*, edited by Robert A. Solo, 123–44. Rutgers University Press, 1955.

Fuligni, Andrew J. "The Academic Achievement of Adolescents from Immigrant Families: The Role of Family Background, Attitudes, and Behavior." *Child Development* 68, no. 2 (1997): 351–63. https://doi.org/10.1111/j.1467-8624.1997.tb01944.x.

Fullilove, Mindy Thompson. *Root Shock: How Tearing Up City Neighborhoods Hurts America, and What We Can Do about It.* New Village Press, 2016.

Furstenberg, Frank F. "Managing to Make It: Afterthoughts." *Journal of Family Issues* 22, no. 2 (2001): 150–62.

Gandini, Lella. "Fundamentals of the Reggio Emilia Approach to Early Childhood Education." *Young Children* 49, no. 1 (1993): 4–8.

Garcia, David R. "Charter Schools Challenging Traditional Notions of Segregation." In *The Charter School Experiment: Expectations, Evidence, and Implications*, edited by Christopher Lubienski and Peter C. Weitzel, 33–50. Harvard Education Press, 2010.

———. "The Impact of School Choice on Racial Segregation in Charter Schools." *Educational Policy* 22, no. 6 (November 1, 2008): 805–29. https://doi.org/10.1177/0895904807310043.

Garn, Gregg, and Casey D. Cobb. "A Framework for Understanding Charter School Accountability." *Education and Urban Society* 33, no. 2 (2001): 113–28.

Gerson, Kathleen. "Moral Dilemmas, Moral Strategies, and the Transformation of Gender: Lessons from Two Generations of Work and Family Change." *Gender & Society* 16, no. 1 (2002): 8–28.

Gillen-O'Neel, Cari, Virginia W. Huynh, Taylor Hazelbaker, and Asya Harrison. "From Kindness and Diversity to Justice and Action: White Parents' Ethnic-Racial Socialization Goals." *Journal of Family Issues* 43, no. 4 (April 1, 2022): 944–73. https://doi.org/10.1177/0192513X21996392.

Gillis, Alanna. "School Choice and Inequality: Choosing Schools Activity." TRAILS: Teaching Resources and Innovations Library for Sociologists, American Sociological Association, 2018. http://trails.asanet.org.

———. "Teaching Sociology of Education: Recommendations for Mini-Units and Full Courses." In *Handbook of Teaching and Learning in Sociology*, edited by Sergio A. Cabrera and Stephen Sweet, 231–43. Edward Elgar, 2023.

Golann, Joanne W., Mira Debs, and Anna Lisa Weiss. "'To Be Strict on Your Own': Black and Latinx Parents Evaluate Discipline in Urban Choice Schools." *American Educational Research Journal* 56, no. 5 (October 1, 2019): 1896–1929. https://doi.org/10.3102/0002831219831972.

Goldweber, Asha, Tracy Evian Waasdorp, and Catherine P. Bradshaw. "Examining Associations between Race, Urbanicity, and Patterns of Bullying Involvement." *Journal of Youth and Adolescence* 42, no. 2 (February 1, 2013): 206–19. https://doi.org/10.1007/s10964-012-9843-y.

Gordon, Hava Rachel. "'It's a Little, Tiny Process': Gentrification, Inequality, and Fragmented Resistance to School Choice." *Urban Education* 59, no. 6 (2024): 1994–2022. https://doi.org/10.1177/00420859221086508.

Grady, Sarah, Stacey Bielick, and Susan Aud. "Trends in the Use of School Choice: 1993 to 2007. Statistical Analysis Report. NCES 2010-004." National Center for Education Statistics, 2010.

Green, Terrance L. "'We Felt They Took the Heart out of the Community': Examining a Community-Based Response to Urban School Closure." *Education Policy Analysis Archives / Archivos Analíticos de Políticas Educativas* 25 (2017): 1–30.

Griesbach, Kathleen. "Dioquis: Being without Doing in the Migrant Agricultural Labor Process." *Ethnography* 21, no. 4 (December 1, 2020): 481–505. https://doi.org/10.1177/1466138118805772.

Grigg, Jeffrey. "School Enrollment Changes and Student Achievement Growth: A Case Study in Educational Disruption and Continuity." *Sociology of Education* 85, no. 4 (2012): 388–404.

Hagelskamp, Carolin, Carola Suárez-Orozco, and Diane Hughes. "Migrating to Opportunities: How Family Migration Motivations Shape Academic Trajectories among Newcomer Immigrant Youth." *Journal of Social Issues* 66, no. 4 (2010): 717–39. https://doi.org/10.1111/j.1540-4560.2010.01672.x.

Hagerman, Margaret Ann. "Reproducing and Reworking Colorblind Racial Ideology: Acknowledging Children's Agency in the White Habitus." *Sociology of Race and Ethnicity* 2, no. 1 (January 1, 2016): 58–71. https://doi.org/10.1177/2332649215594817.

———. "White Families and Race: Colour-Blind and Colour-Conscious Approaches to White Racial Socialization." *Ethnic and Racial Studies* 37, no. 14 (December 6, 2014): 2598–614. https://doi.org/10.1080/01419870.2013.848289.

Hailey, Chantal A. "Racial Preferences for Schools: Evidence from an Experiment with White, Black, Latinx, and Asian Parents and Students." *Sociology of Education* 95, no. 2 (April 1, 2022): 110–32. https://doi.org/10.1177/00380407211065179.

———. "Racialized Perceptions of Anticipated School Belonging." *Educational Policy* 36, no. 4 (June 1, 2022): 879–910. https://doi.org/10.1177/08959048221087211.

Hamilton, Laura S., and Kacey Guin. "Understanding How Families Choose Schools." *Getting Choice Right: Ensuring Equity and Efficiency in Education Policy*, edited by Julian R. Betts and Tom Loveless, 40–60. Brookings Institution Press, 2005.

Hamlin, Daniel. "Flight to Safety in Deindustrialized Cities: Perceptions of School Safety in Charter and Public Schools in Detroit, Michigan." *Education and Urban Society* 52, no. 3 (March 1, 2020): 394–414. https://doi.org/10.1177/0013124519846288.

Hamlin, Daniel, and Albert Cheng. "Parental Empowerment, Involvement, and Satisfaction: A Comparison of Choosers of Charter, Catholic, Christian, and District-Run Public Schools." *Educational Administration Quarterly* 56, no. 4 (October 1, 2020): 641–70. https://doi.org/10.1177/0013161X19888013.

Harvey, David. *A Brief History of Neoliberalism*. Oxford University Press, 2007.

Hays, Sharon. *The Cultural Contradictions of Motherhood*. Yale University Press, 1998.

Henig, Jeffrey R. "Geo-spatial Analyses and School Choice Research." *American Journal of Education* 115, no. 4 (2009): 649–57.

———. *Rethinking School Choice: Limits of the Market Metaphor*. Princeton University Press, 1995.

Hochschild, Arlie, and Anne Machung. *The Second Shift: Working Families and the Revolution at Home*. Penguin, 1989.

Hollander, Nancy Caro. "Negotiating Trauma and Loss in the Migration Experience: Round-table on Global Woman." *Studies in Gender and Sexuality* 7, no. 1 (January 1, 2006): 61–70. https://doi.org/10.2513/s15240657sgs0701_6.

Holme, Jennifer Jellison. "Buying Homes, Buying Schools: School Choice and the Social Construction of School Quality." *Harvard Educational Review* 72, no. 2 (2002): 177–206.

Horvat, Erin McNamara, Elliot B. Weininger, and Annette Lareau. "From Social Ties to Social Capital: Class Differences in the Relations between Schools and Parent Networks." *American Educational Research Journal* 40, no. 2 (2003): 319–51.

Hunter, Marcus Anthony. *Black Citymakers: How The Philadelphia Negro Changed Urban America*. Oxford University Press, 2013.

Hunter, Marcus Anthony, and Zandria F. Robinson. *Chocolate Cities: The Black Map of American Life*. University of California Press, 2018.

Jabbar, Huriya, Carlton J. Fong, Emily Germain, Dongmei Li, Joanna Sanchez, Wei-Ling Sun, and Michelle Devall. "The Competitive Effects of School Choice on Student Achievement: A Systematic Review." *Educational Policy* 36, no. 2 (March 1, 2022): 247–81. https://doi.org/10.1177/0895904819874756.

Jarrett, Robin L. "African American Family and Parenting Strategies in Impoverished Neighborhoods." *Qualitative Sociology* 20, no. 2 (June 1, 1997): 275–88. https://doi.org/10.1023/A:1024717803273.

Jarrett, Robin L., and Stephanie R. Jefferson. "'A Good Mother Got to Fight for Her Kids': Maternal Management Strategies in a High-Risk, African-American Neighborhood." *Journal of Children and Poverty* 9, no. 1 (March 1, 2003): 21–39. https://doi.org/10.1080/1079612002000052706.

Jennings, Jennifer L. "School Choice or Schools' Choice? Managing in an Era of Accountability." *Sociology of Education* 83, no. 3 (July 1, 2010): 227–47. https://doi.org/10.1177/0038040710375688.

Kafka, Judith. "When Information Is Not Enough: School Choice, Segregation, and the Elusive Notion of Fit." *Teachers College Record* 124, no. 4 (2022): 95–123.

Kao, Grace, and Marta Tienda. "Optimism and Achievement: The Educational Performance of Immigrant Youth." *Social Science Quarterly* 76, no. 1 (1995): 1–19.

Khan, Shamus Rahman. *Privilege: The Making of an Adolescent Elite at St. Paul's School*. Princeton University Press, 2012.

Kho, Adam, Ron Zimmer, and Andrew McEachin. "A Descriptive Analysis of Cream Skimming and Pushout in Choice versus Traditional Public Schools." *Education Finance and Policy* 17, no. 1 (2022): 160–187. https://doi.org/10.1162/edfp_a_00333.

Kimelberg, Shelley McDonough. "Beyond Test Scores: Middle-Class Mothers, Cultural Capital, and the Evaluation of Urban Public School." *Sociological Perspectives* 57, no. 2 (2014): 208–28.

———. "Middle-Class Parents, Risk, and Urban Public Schools." In *Choosing Homes, Choosing Schools*, edited by Annette Lareau and Kimberly Goyette, 207–36. Russell Sage Foundation, 2014.

Kimelberg, Shelley McDonough, and Chase M. Billingham. "Attitudes toward Diversity and the School Choice Process: Middle-Class Parents in a Segregated Urban Public School District." *Urban Education* 48, no. 2 (2013): 198–231.

Lacireno-Paquet, Natalie, Thomas T. Holyoke, Michele Moser, and Jeffrey R. Henig. "Creaming versus Cropping: Charter School Enrollment Practices in Response to Market Incentives." *Educational Evaluation and Policy Analysis* 24, no. 2 (June 1, 2002): 145–58. https://doi.org /10.3102/01623737024002145.

Ladson-Billings, Gloria. "Toward a Theory of Culturally Relevant Pedagogy." *American Educational Research Journal* 32, no. 3 (1995): 465–91.

Ladson-Billings, Gloria, and William F. Tate. "Toward a Critical Race Theory of Education." In *Critical Race Theory in Education: All God's Children Got a Song*, edited by Adrienne D. Dixson and Celia K. Rousseau, 11–30. Routledge, 2006.

Lareau, Annette. *Home Advantage: Social Class and Parental Intervention in Elementary Education.* Rowman & Littlefield, 2000.

———. "My Wife Can Tell Me Who I Know: Methodological and Conceptual Problems in Studying Fathers." *Qualitative Sociology* 23, no. 4 (2000): 407–33.

———. *Unequal Childhoods: Class, Race, and Family Life.* University of California Press, 2011.

Lareau, Annette, Shani Adia Evans, and April Yee. "The Rules of the Game and the Uncertain Transmission of Advantage: Middle-Class Parents' Search for an Urban Kindergarten." *Sociology of Education* 89, no. 4 (2016): 279–99.

Lareau, Annette, and Erin McNamara Horvat. "Moments of Social Inclusion and Exclusion: Race, Class, and Cultural Capital in Family-School Relationships." *Sociology of Education* 72, no. 1 (1999): 37–53. https://doi.org/10.2307/2673185.

Lee, Jin, and Christopher Lubienski. "The Impact of School Closures on Equity of Access in Chicago." *Education and Urban Society* 49, no. 1 (2017): 53–80.

Lewis, Amanda E., and John B. Diamond. *Despite the Best Intentions: How Racial Inequality Thrives in Good Schools.* Oxford University Press, 2015.

Lewis-McCoy, R. L'Heureux. *Inequality in the Promised Land: Race, Resources, and Suburban Schooling.* Stanford University Press, 2014.

Lubienski, Christopher, and Jack Dougherty. "Mapping Educational Opportunity: Spatial Analysis and School Choices." *American Journal of Education* 115, no. 4 (2009): 485–91.

Lubienski, Christopher, and Jin Lee. "Geo-spatial Analyses in Education Research: The Critical Challenge and Methodological Possibilities." *Geographical Research* 55, no. 1 (2017): 89–99.

Mader, Nicole, Clara Hemphill, and Qasim Abbas. "The Paradox of Choice: How School Choice Divides New York City Elementary Schools." Center for New York City Affairs, May 2018. http://www.centernyc.org/the-paradox-of-choice.

Makris, Molly Vollman. "The Chimera of Choice: Gentrification, School Choice, and Community." *Peabody Journal of Education* 93, no. 4 (August 8, 2018): 411–29. https://doi.org/10 .1080/0161956X.2018.1488394.

Massey, Douglas S., and Nancy A. Denton. *American Apartheid: Segregation and the Making of the Underclass.* Harvard University Press, 1993.

McCarthy Foubert, Jennifer L. "'Damned if You Do, Damned if You Don't': Black Parents' Racial Realist School Engagement." *Race Ethnicity and Education* 25, no. 5 (July 29, 2022): 647–64. https://doi.org/10.1080/13613324.2019.1631782.

McCormack, Karen. "Stratified Reproduction and Poor Women's Resistance." *Gender & Society* 19, no. 5 (2005): 660–79.

McMahon, Susan D., Erika D. Felix, and Thara Nagarajan. "Social Support and Neighborhood Stressors among African American Youth: Networks and Relations to Self-Worth." *Journal of Child and Family Studies* 20, no. 3 (June 1, 2011): 255–62. https://doi.org/10.1007/s10826-010-9386-3.

Mehana, Majida, and Arthur J. Reynolds. "School Mobility and Achievement: A Meta-Analysis." *Children and Youth Services Review* 26, no. 1 (2004): 93–119.

Merriam, Sharan B. *Qualitative Research and Case Study Applications in Education.* Jossey-Bass, 1998.

Miles, Matthew B., A. Michael Huberman, and Johnny Saldana. *Qualitative Data Analysis: A Methods Sourcebook.* 3rd ed. Sage, 2014.

Milkie, Melissa A., Sara B. Raley, and Suzanne M. Bianchi. "Taking on the Second Shift: Time Allocations and Time Pressures of U.S. Parents with Preschoolers." *Social Forces* 88, no. 2 (December 1, 2009): 487–517. https://doi.org/10.1353/sof.0.0268.

Montgomery, Alesia F. "'Living in Each Other's Pockets': The Navigation of Social Distances by Middle Class Families in Los Angeles." *City & Community* 5, no. 4 (December 1, 2006): 425–50. https://doi.org/10.1111/j.1540-6040.2006.00192.x.

Morris, Jerome E. "A Pillar of Strength: An African American School's Communal Bonds with Families and Community since *Brown.*" *Urban Education* 33, no. 5 (January 1, 1999): 584–605. https://doi.org/10.1177/0042085999335003.

National Center for Education Statistics. "Digest of Education Statistics, 2022." Accessed January 16, 2025. https://nces.ed.gov/programs/digest/d22/tables/dt22_215.30.asp.

———. "Public Charter School Enrollment." May 2023. https://nces.ed.gov/programs/coe/indicator/cgb/public-charter-enrollment.

———. "Public School Enrollment." May 2024. https://nces.ed.gov/programs/coe/indicator/cga/public-school-enrollment.

———. "School Choice in the United States: 2019." Accessed December 13, 2023. https://nces.ed.gov/programs/schoolchoice/intro.asp.

Nelson, Margaret K. *Parenting Out of Control: Anxious Parents in Uncertain Times.* New York University Press, 2010.

Newman, Katherine S. *No Shame in My Game: The Working Poor in the Inner City.* Vintage, 2009.

New York City Department of Health. "Community Health Profiles 2015: Brooklyn Community District 16: Brownsville." 2015. www.nyc.gov/assets/doh/downloads/pdf/data/2015chp-bk16.pdf

———. "Kindergarten Application Process." 2018. www.schools.nyc.gov/enrollment/enroll-grade-by-grade/kindergarten.

———. "Transfers." 2024. www.schools.nyc.gov/enrollment/enrollment-help/transfers.

New York City Independent Budget Office. "Student Demographics and Enrollment Trends: Traditional Public Schools." Accessed July 20, 2023. www.ibo.nyc.ny.us/iboreports/school-enrollment-trends-2021.html.

New York City Office of the Mayor. "New York City Launches Historic Expansion of Pre-K to More Than 51,000 Children." September 4, 2014. http://www.nyc.gov/office-of-the-mayor/news/425-14/new-york-city-launches-historic-expansion-pre-k-more-51-000-children.

———. "Ready to Launch: New York City's Implementation Plan for Free, High-Quality, Full-Day Universal Pre-kindergarten." January 2014. www.nyc.gov/assets/home/downloads/pdf

/reports/2014/Ready-to-Launch-NYCs-Implementation-Plan-for-Free-High-Quality-Full
-Day-Universal-Pre-Kindergarten.pdf.

New York City Public Schools. "Class Size Reports." Accessed January 27, 2025. https://infohub
.nyced.org/reports/government-reports/class-size-reports.

Nickson, Dana. "Embracing the City: Black Families' Place Attachments and (Re)Imaginings
of the City and Suburb in Search of Educational Opportunity." *AERA Open* 8 (January 1,
2022): 23328584221126479. https://doi.org/10.1177/23328584221126479.

No Child Left Behind Act of 2001, 20 U.S.C. § 6319 (2002).

Nuamah, Sally A. *Closed for Democracy: How Mass School Closure Undermines the Citizenship of
Black Americans*. Cambridge University Press, 2022.

NYC Health. "Early Intervention." Accessed December 19, 2023. www.nyc.gov/site/doh/health
/health-topics/early-intervention.page.

Oakes, Jeannie. *Keeping Track*. Yale University Press, 1985.

O'Day, Jennifer A., Catherine S. Bitter, and Louis M. Gomez. *Education Reform in New York
City: Ambitious Change in the Nation's Most Complex School System*. Harvard Education Press,
2011.

Orfield, Gary, and Erica Frankenberg. *Educational Delusions? Why Choice Can Deepen Inequality
and How to Make Schools Fair*. University of California Press, 2013.

Orfield, Gary, and Chungmei Lee. "Why Segregation Matters: Poverty and Educational
Inequality." Harvard University, Civil Rights Project, 2005.

Owens, Ann, Sean F. Reardon, and Christopher Jencks. "Income Segregation between Schools
and School Districts." *American Educational Research Journal* 53, no. 4 (2016): 1159–97.

Palkovitz, Rob, Bahira Sherif Trask, and Kari Adamsons. "Essential Differences in the Meaning
and Processes of Mothering and Fathering: Family Systems, Feminist and Qualitative Perspectives." *Journal of Family Theory & Review* 6, no. 4 (2014): 406–20. https://doi.org/10
.1111/jftr.12048.

Parcel, Toby L., Joshua A. Hendrix, and Andrew J. Taylor. "'How Far Is Too Far?' Gender,
Emotional Capital, and Children's Public School Assignments." *Socius* 2 (January 1, 2016):
2378023116669955. https://doi.org/10.1177/2378023116669955.

Pattillo, Mary. "Black Middle-Class Neighborhoods." *Annual Review of Sociology* 31 (2005):
305–29.

———. *Black Picket Fences: Privilege and Peril among the Black Middle Class*. University of Chicago Press, 2013.

———. "Everyday Politics of School Choice in the Black Community." *Du Bois Review* 12, no. 1
(2015): 41–71.

Payne, Kim John, and Lisa M. Ross. *Simplicity Parenting: Using the Extraordinary Power of Less
to Raise Calmer, Happier, and More Secure Kids*. Random House, 2010.

Pearman, Francis A., and Walker A. Swain. "School Choice, Gentrification, and the Variable
Significance of Racial Stratification in Urban Neighborhoods." *Sociology of Education* 90,
no. 3 (2017): 213–35.

Perreira, Krista M., Kathleen Mullan Harris, and Dohoon Lee. "Making It in America: High
School Completion by Immigrant and Native Youth." *Demography* 43, no. 3 (August 1,
2006): 511–36. https://doi.org/10.1353/dem.2006.0026.

Portes, Alejandro. "Social Capital: Its Origins and Applications in Modern Sociology." *Annual
Review of Sociology* 24 (1998): 1–24.

Portes, Alejandro, and Alejandro Rivas. "The Adaptation of Migrant Children." *Future of Children* 21, no. 1 (2011): 219–46.

Posey-Maddox, Linn. "Race in Place: Black Parents, Family–School Relations, and Multispatial Microaggressions in a Predominantly White Suburb." *Teachers College Record* 119, no. 11 (November 1, 2017): 1–42. https://doi.org/10.1177/016146811711901107.

———. "Schooling in Suburbia: The Intersections of Race, Class, Gender, and Place in Black Fathers' Engagement and Family–School Relationships." *Gender and Education* 29, no. 5 (July 29, 2017): 577–93. https://doi.org/10.1080/09540253.2016.1274389.

———. *When Middle-Class Parents Choose Urban Schools: Class, Race, and the Challenge of Equity in Public Education.* University of Chicago Press, 2014.

Posey-Maddox, Linn, Maxine McKinney de Royston, Alea R. Holman, Raquel M. Rall, and Rachel A. Johnson. "No Choice Is the 'Right' Choice: Black Parents' Educational Decision-Making in Their Search for a 'Good' School." *Harvard Educational Review* 91, no. 1 (2021): 38–61.

Powell, Tunette, and Justin A. Coles. "'We Still Here': Black Mothers' Personal Narratives of Sense Making and Resisting Antiblackness and the Suspensions of Their Black Children." *Race Ethnicity and Education* 24, no. 1 (January 2, 2021): 76–95. https://doi.org/10.1080/13613324.2020.1718076.

Race to the Top Act of 2011, Pub. L. No. H.R. 1532, § Committee on Education and the Workforce, 15 U.S.C. 3601 (2011). https://www.govinfo.gov/app/details/BILLS-112hr1532ih.

Ragin, Charles C. *The Comparative Method: Moving beyond Qualitative and Quantitative Strategies.* University of California Press, 1987.

Ramirez, A. Y. Fred. "Dismay and Disappointment: Parental Involvement of Latino Immigrant Parents." *Urban Review* 35, no. 2 (June 1, 2003): 93–110. https://doi.org/10.1023/A:1023705511946.

Randles, Jennifer. "'Manning Up' to Be a Good Father: Hybrid Fatherhood, Masculinity, and US Responsible Fatherhood Policy." *Gender & Society* 32, no. 4 (2018): 516–39.

———. "Role Modeling Responsibility: The Essential Father Discourse in Responsible Fatherhood Programming and Policy." *Social Problems* 67, no. 1 (February 1, 2020): 96–112. https://doi.org/10.1093/socpro/spy027.

———. "'Willing to Do Anything for My Kids': Inventive Mothering, Diapers, and the Inequalities of Carework." *American Sociological Review* 86, no. 1 (2021): 35–59. https://doi.org/10.1177/0003122420977480.

Raudenbush, Danielle. "'I Stay by Myself': Social Support, Distrust, and Selective Solidarity Among the Urban Poor." *Sociological Forum* 31, no. 4 (2016): 1018–39.

Reardon, Sean F., and Ann Owens. "60 Years after *Brown*: Trends and Consequences of School Segregation." *Annual Review of Sociology* 40 (2014): 199–218.

Reay, Diane. "A Useful Extension of Bourdieu's Conceptual Framework? Emotional Capital as a Way of Understanding Mothers' Involvement in Their Children's Education?" *Sociological Review* 48, no. 4 (November 1, 2000): 568–85. https://doi.org/10.1111/1467-954X.00233.

Reay, Diane, and Stephen J. Ball. "'Making Their Minds Up': Family Dynamics of School Choice." *British Educational Research Journal* 24, no. 4 (September 1, 1998): 431–48. https://doi.org/10.1080/0141192980240405.

Renzulli, Linda A., and Lorraine Evans. "School Choice, Charter Schools, and White Flight." *Social Problems* 52, no. 3 (2005): 398–418.

Reynolds, Rema. "'They Think You're Lazy' and Other Messages Black Parents Send Their Black Sons: An Exploration of Critical Race Theory in the Examination of Educational Outcomes for Black Males." *Journal of African American Males in Education* 1, no. 2 (2010): 144–63.

Rhodes, Anna, and Stefanie DeLuca. "Residential Mobility and School Choice among Poor Families." In *Choosing Homes, Choosing Schools*, edited by Annette Lareau and Kimberly Goyette, 137–66. Russell Sage Foundation, 2014.

Rhodes, Anna, Julia Szabo, and Siri Warkentien. "'I Went There': How Parent Experience Shapes School Decisions." *Social Currents* 10, no. 6 (March 1, 2023): 512–33. https://doi.org/10.1177/23294965231159306.

Rhodes, Anna, and Siri Warkentien. "Unwrapping the Suburban 'Package Deal': Race, Class, and School Access." *American Educational Research Journal* 54, no. 1 (2017): 168S–189S.

Rich, Peter, Jennifer Candipan, and Ann Owens. "Segregated Neighborhoods, Segregated Schools: Do Charters Break a Stubborn Link?" *Demography* 58, no. 2 (April 1, 2021): 471–98. https://doi.org/10.1215/00703370-9000820.

Rich, Peter M., and Jennifer L. Jennings. "Choice, Information, and Constrained Options: School Transfers in a Stratified Educational System." *American Sociological Review* 80, no. 5 (2015): 1069–98.

Roda, Allison. "School Choice and the Politics of Parenthood: Exploring Parent Mobilization as a Catalyst for the Common Good." *Peabody Journal of Education* 93, no. 4 (August 8, 2018): 430–49. https://doi.org/10.1080/0161956X.2018.1488400.

Roda, Allison, and Amy Stuart Wells. "School Choice Policies and Racial Segregation: Where White Parents' Good Intentions, Anxiety, and Privilege Collide." *American Journal of Education* 119, no. 2 (2013): 261–93.

Ross, Catherine E., and Sung Joon Jang. "Neighborhood Disorder, Fear, and Mistrust: The Buffering Role of Social Ties with Neighbors." *American Journal of Community Psychology* 28, no. 4 (2000): 401–20.

Roubeni, Sonia, Lucia De Haene, Eva Keatley, Nira Shah, and Andrew Rasmussen. "'If We Can't Do It, Our Children Will Do It One Day': A Qualitative Study of West African Immigrant Parents' Losses and Educational Aspirations for Their Children." *American Educational Research Journal* 52, no. 2 (April 1, 2015): 275–305. https://doi.org/10.3102/0002831215574576.

Rowley, Stephanie J., Lumas J. Helaire, and Meeta Banerjee. "Reflecting on Racism: School Involvement and Perceived Teacher Discrimination in African American Mothers." *Journal of Applied Developmental Psychology* 31, no. 1 (January 1, 2010): 83–92. https://doi.org/10.1016/j.appdev.2009.08.001.

Rumberger, Russell W. "The Causes and Consequences of Student Mobility." *Journal of Negro Education* 72, no. 1 (2003): 6–21.

Sall, Dialika. "Convergent Identifications, Divergent Meanings: The Racial and Ethnic Identities of Second-Generation West African Youth." *African and Black Diaspora* 12, no. 2. (2019): 137–55. https://doi.org/10.1080/17528631.2018.1559785.

———. "Selective Acculturation among Low-Income Second-Generation West Africans." *Journal of Ethnic and Migration Studies* 46, no. 11 (August 17, 2020): 2199–2217. https://doi.org/10.1080/1369183X.2019.1610367.

Sattin-Bajaj, Carolyn. "Two Roads Diverged: Exploring Variation in Students' School Choice Experiences by Socioeconomic Status, Parental Nativity, and Ethnicity." *Journal of School Choice* 8, no. 3 (2014): 410–45.

Sattin-Bajaj, Carolyn, and Allison Roda. "Opportunity Hoarding in School Choice Contexts: The Role of Policy Design in Promoting Middle-Class Parents' Exclusionary Behaviors." *Educational Policy* 34, no. 7 (2020): 992–1035. https://doi.org/10.1177/0895904818802106.

Schneider, Mark, Paul Teske, and Melissa Marschall. *Choosing Schools: Consumer Choice and the Quality of American Schools.* Princeton University Press, 2000.

Schneider, Mark, Paul Teske, Christine Roch, and Melissa Marschall. "Networks to Nowhere: Segregation and Stratification in Networks of Information about Schools." *American Journal of Political Science* 41, no. 4 (1997): 1201–23.

Schwartz, Barry. *The Paradox of Choice: Why More Is Less.* Rev. ed. HarperCollins, 2009.

Scott, Janelle T. *School Choice and Diversity: What the Evidence Says.* Teachers College Press, 2005.

———. "School Choice and the Empowerment Imperative." *Peabody Journal of Education* 88, no. 1 (January 1, 2013): 60–73. https://doi.org/10.1080/0161956X.2013.752635.

Scott, Janelle, and Jennifer Jellison Holme. "The Political Economy of Market-Based Educational Policies: Race and Reform in Urban School Districts, 1915 to 2016." *Review of Research in Education* 40, no. 1 (March 1, 2016): 250–97. https://doi.org/10.3102/0091732X16681001.

Sharkey, Patrick, and Jacob W. Faber. "Where, When, Why, and for Whom Do Residential Contexts Matter? Moving Away from the Dichotomous Understanding of Neighborhood Effects." *Annual Review of Sociology* 40 (2014): 559–79.

Shedd, Carla. *Unequal City: Race, Schools, and Perceptions of Injustice.* Russell Sage Foundation, 2015.

Shows, Carla, and Naomi Gerstel. "Fathering, Class, and Gender: A Comparison of Physicians and Emergency Medical Technicians." *Gender & Society* 23, no. 2 (2009): 161–87.

Sikkink, David, and Jonathan D. Schwarz. "The Apple Doesn't Fall Far from the Parent's School: Intergenerational Continuity in School Sector Enrollment." *Journal of School Choice* 12, no. 3 (2018): 318–53.

Small, Mario Luis. "'How Many Cases Do I Need?' On Science and the Logic of Case Selection in Field-Based Research." *Ethnography* 10, no. 1 (2009): 5–38.

———. "Neighborhood Institutions as Resource Brokers: Childcare Centers, Interorganizational Ties, and Resource Access among the Poor." *Social Problems* 53, no. 2 (2006): 274–92.

———. *Unanticipated Gains: Origins of Network Inequality in Everyday Life.* Oxford University Press, 2009.

———. *Villa Victoria: The Transformation of Social Capital in a Boston Barrio.* University of Chicago Press, 2004.

Snyder, Thomas D., Cristobal de Brey, and Sally A. Dillow. "Digest of Education Statistics 2017, 53rd Edition. NCES 2018–070." National Center for Education Statistics, January 2019. https://eric.ed.gov/?id=ED592104.

Sohoni, Deenesh, and Salvatore Saporito. "Mapping School Segregation: Using GIS to Explore Racial Segregation between Schools and Their Corresponding Attendance Areas." *American Journal of Education* 115, no. 4 (2009): 569–600.

Strauss, Anselm L., and Barney Glaser. *Discovery of Grounded Theory: Strategies for Qualitative Research.* Routledge, 2017. https://doi.org/10.4324/9780203793206.

Suárez-Orozco, Carola, Jean Rhodes, and Michael Milburn. "Unraveling the Immigrant Paradox: Academic Engagement and Disengagement among Recently Arrived Immigrant

Youth." *Youth & Society* 41, no. 2 (December 1, 2009): 151–85. https://doi.org/10.1177/0044118X09333647.

Szabo, Julia. "'I Just Didn't Want to Risk It': How Perceptions of Risk Motivate Charter School Choice among Latinx Parents." *American Educational Research Journal* 59, no. 4 (August 1, 2022): 651–86. https://doi.org/10.3102/00028312221078579.

Szalacha, Laura A., Amy Kerivan Marks, Meaghan Lamarre, and Cynthia Garcia Coll. "Academic Pathways and Children of Immigrant Families." *Research in Human Development* 2, no. 4 (September 1, 2005): 179–211. https://doi.org/10.1207/s15427617rhd0204_2.

Taylor Haynes, Katherine, Kristie J. R. Phillips, and Ellen B. Goldring. "Latino Parents' Choice of Magnet School: How School Choice Differs across Racial and Ethnic Boundaries." *Education and Urban Society* 42, no. 6 (September 1, 2010): 758–89. https://doi.org/10.1177/0013124510370943.

Theodos, Brett, Claudia Coulton, and Amos Budde. "Getting to Better Performing Schools: The Role of Residential Mobility in School Attainment in Low-Income Neighborhoods." *Cityscape* 16, no. 1 (2014): 61–84.

Thornton, Michael C., Linda M. Chatters, Robert Joseph Taylor, and Walter R. Allen. "Sociodemographic and Environmental Correlates of Racial Socialization by Black Parents." *Child Development* 61, no. 2 (1990): 401–9.

Tigges, Leann M., Irene Browne, and Gary P. Green. "Social Isolation of the Urban Poor: Race, Class, and Neighborhood Effects on Social Resources." *Sociological Quarterly* 39, no. 1 (January 1, 1998): 53–77. https://doi.org/10.1111/j.1533-8525.1998.tb02349.x.

Townsend, Nicholas. *Package Deal: Marriage, Work and Fatherhood in Men's Lives.* Temple University Press, 2010.

Tran, Van C., Corina Graif, Alison D. Jones, Mario L. Small, and Christopher Winship. "Participation in Context: Neighborhood Diversity and Organizational Involvement in Boston." *City & Community* 12, no. 3 (2013): 187–210.

Turner, Erica O. "Marketing Diversity: Selling School Districts in a Racialized Marketplace." *Journal of Education Policy* 33, no. 6 (November 2, 2018): 793–817. https://doi.org/10.1080/02680939.2017.1386327.

Tyson, Karolyn. *Integration Interrupted: Tracking, Black Students, and Acting White after Brown.* Oxford University Press, 2011.

Underhill, Megan R. "'Diversity Is Important to Me': White Parents and Exposure-to-Diversity Parenting Practices." *Sociology of Race and Ethnicity* 5, no. 4 (2019): 486–99.

Urena, Anthony. "Relational Risk: How Relationships Shape Personal Assessments of Risk and Mitigation." *American Sociological Review* 87, no. 5 (2022): 723–49.

Verduzco-Baker, Lynn. "'I Don't Want Them to Be a Statistic': Mothering Practices of Low-Income Mothers." *Journal of Family Issues* 38, no. 7 (2017): 1010–38.

Villalobos, Ana. *Motherload: Making It All Better in Insecure Times.* University of California Press, 2014.

Vincent, Carol, Nicola Rollock, Stephen Ball, and David Gillborn. "Being Strategic, Being Watchful, Being Determined: Black Middle-Class Parents and Schooling." *British Journal of Sociology of Education* 33, no. 3 (May 1, 2012): 337–54. https://doi.org/10.1080/01425692.2012.668833.

———. "Intersectional Work and Precarious Positionings: Black Middle-Class Parents and Their Encounters with Schools in England." *International Studies in Sociology of Education* 22, no. 3 (September 1, 2012): 259–76. https://doi.org/10.1080/09620214.2012.744214.

Visser, Kirsten, Gideon Bolt, and Ronald van Kempen. "A Good Place to Raise Your Children? The Diversity of Parents' Neighbourhood Perceptions and Parenting Practices in a Low-Income, Multi-ethnic Neighbourhood: A Case Study in Rotterdam." *Geoforum* 64 (August 1, 2015): 112–20. https://doi.org/10.1016/j.geoforum.2015.06.011.

Vittrup, Brigitte. "Color Blind or Color Conscious? White American Mothers' Approaches to Racial Socialization." *Journal of Family Issues* 39, no. 3 (February 1, 2018): 668–92. https://doi.org/10.1177/0192513X16676858.

Wacquant, Loïc J. D., and William Julius Wilson. "The Cost of Racial and Class Exclusion in the Inner City." *Annals of the American Academy of Political and Social Science* 501, no. 1 (1989): 8–25.

Walberg, Herbert J., and Joseph Lee Bast. *Education and Capitalism: How Overcoming Our Fear of Markets and Economics Can Improve America's Schools.* Vol. 521. Hoover Institution Press, 2003.

Walker, Vanessa Siddle. *Their Highest Potential: An African American School Community in the Segregated South.* University of North Carolina Press, 1996.

Wall, Glenda, and Stephanie Arnold. "How Involved Is Involved Fathering? An Exploration of the Contemporary Culture of Fatherhood." *Gender & Society* 21, no. 4 (2007): 508–27.

Weiss, Robert S. *Learning from Strangers: The Art and Method of Qualitative Interview Studies.* Simon & Schuster, 1995.

Wells, Amy Stuart. "The Process of Racial Resegregation in Housing and Schools: The Sociology of Reputation." In *Emerging Trends in the Social and Behavioral Sciences*, edited by Robert A. Scott and Marlis C. Buchmann, 1–14. Wiley, 2018.

Wenning, Richard, Paul A. Herdman, Nelson Smith, Neal McMahon, and Kadesha Washington. "No Child Left Behind: Testing, Reporting, and Accountability. ERIC Digest, 2003. https://eric.ed.gov/?id=ED480994.

West, Anne, Dabney Ingram, and Audrey Hind. "'Skimming the Cream': Admissions to Charter Schools in the United States and to Autonomous Schools in England." *Educational Policy* 20, no. 4 (September 1, 2006): 615–39. https://doi.org/10.1177/0895904805284054.

Whitehurst, Grover J. "Russ." "The 2016 Education Choice and Competition Index." *Brookings* (blog), March 29, 2017. www.brookings.edu/interactives/the-2016-education-choice-and-competition-index/.

Whitehurst, Grover J. "Russ," and Sarah Whitfield. "School Choice and School Performance in the New York City Public Schools—Will the Past Be Prologue?" Brown Center on Education Policy at the Brookings Institution, October 8, 2013. www.brookings.edu/articles/school-choice-and-school-performance-in-the-new-york-city-public-schools-will-the-past-be-prologue/

Williams, Amber D., Meeta Banerjee, Fantasy Lozada-Smith, Danny Lambouths III, and Stephanie J. Rowley. "Black Mothers' Perceptions of the Role of Race in Children's Education." *Journal of Marriage and Family* 79, no. 4 (2017): 932–46. https://doi.org/10.1111/jomf.12410.

Yee, Vivian. "Kindergarten Applications Going Digital." *New York Times*, September 12, 2013. www.nytimes.com/2013/09/13/nyregion/kindergarten-applications-going-digital.html.

Yin, Robert K. *Case Study Research and Applications: Design and Methods.* Sage, 2017.

Zukin, Sharon, Valerie Trujillo, Peter Frase, Danielle Jackson, Tim Recuber, and Abraham Walker. "New Retail Capital and Neighborhood Change: Boutiques and Gentrification in New York City." *City & Community* 8, no. 1 (2009): 47–64.

INDEX

Page numbers in *italics* refer to figures and tables.

GPSR Authorized Representative: Easy Access System Europe - Mustamäe tee
50, 10621 Tallinn, Estonia, gpsr.requests@easproject.com